European Union Port Policy

TRANSPORT ECONOMICS, MANAGEMENT AND POLICY

Series Editor: Kenneth Button, *Professor of Public Policy, School of Public Policy, George Mason University, USA*

Transport is a critical input for economic development and for optimizing social and political interaction. Recent years have seen significant new developments in the way that transport is perceived by private industry and governments, and in the way academics look at it.

The aim of this series is to provide original material and up-to-date synthesis of the state of modern transport analysis. The coverage embraces all conventional modes of transport but also includes contributions from important related fields such as urban and regional planning and telecommunications where they interface with transport. The books draw from many disciplines and some cross disciplinary boundaries. They are concerned with economics, planning, sociology, geography, management science, psychology and public policy. They are intended to help improve the understanding of transport, the policy needs of the most economically advanced countries and the problems of resource-poor developing economies. The authors come from around the world and will represent some of the outstanding young scholars as well as established names.

Titles in the series include:

Transport and Environment
In Search of Sustainable Solutions
Edited by Eran Feitelson and Erik T. Verhoef

Environmental Costs and Liberalization in European Air Transport
A Welfare Economic Analysis
Youdi Schipper

Reforming Transport Pricing in the European Union
A Modelling Approach
Edited by Bruno De Borger and Stef Proost

Travel Behaviour
Spatial Patterns, Congestion and Modelling
Edited by Eliahu Stern, Ilan Salomon and Piet H.L. Bovy

Financing Transportation Networks
David Levinson

Transportation Networks and the Optimal Location of Human Activities
A Numerical Geography Approach
Isabelle Thomas

European Union Port Policy
The Movement Towards a Long-Term Strategy
Constantinos I. Chlomoudis and Athanasios A. Pallis

European Union Port Policy

The Movement Towards a Long-Term Strategy

Constantinos I. Chlomoudis
Department of Maritime Studies,
University of Piraeus, Greece

and

Athanasios A. Pallis
Department of Shipping, Trade and Transport,
University of the Aegean, Greece

TRANSPORT ECONOMICS, MANAGEMENT AND POLICY

Edward Elgar
Cheltenham, UK • Northampton, MA, USA

Published by
Edward Elgar Publishing Limited
Glensanda House
Montpellier Parade
Cheltenham
Glos GL50 1UA
UK

Edward Elgar Publishing, Inc.
136 West Street
Suite 202
Northampton
Massachusetts 01060
USA

A catalogue record for this book
is available from the British Library

Library of Congress Cataloguing in Publication Data
Chlomoudis, Constantinos.
 European Union Port Policy : the movement towards a long-term strategy /
Constantinos I. Chlomoudis and Athanasios A. Pallis.
  p.cm — (Transport economics, management, and policy series)
 Includes bibliographical references and index.
 1. Harbors—Government policy—European Union countries. I. Pallis,
Athanasios A. II. Title. III. Transport economics, management, and policy.

HE557.A.3 C48 2002
341.7'5667'094—dc21   2002024587

ISBN 1 84376 093 2
Printed and bound in Great Britain by MPG Books Ltd, Bodmin, Cornwall

This book was made possible, in part, by the support of
the Piraeus Port Authority, Greece.

(

Contents

List of Figures

List of Tables

Abbreviations

AMRIE	Alliance of Maritime Regions in Europe
CEU	Commission of the European Union
CMTP	Common Maritime Transport Policy
CoR	Committee of the Regions
CTP	Common Transport Policy
DG	Directorate General
ECJ	European Court of Justice
Ecosoc	Economic Social Committee
ECSA	European Community Shipowners Association
ECSC	European Coal and Steel Community
EDI	Electronic Data Interchange
EIB	European Investment Bank
EP	European Parliament
ERDF	European Regional Development Fund
ESC	European Shippers Council
ESPO	European Sea Ports Organisation
EU	European Union
FEPORT	Federation of Private Port Operators
GDP	Gross Domestic Product
ILO	International Labour Organisation
IMO	International Maritime Organisation
IT	Information Technology
ITI	Investments in Transport Infrastructure
MARPOL	IMO Convention for the prevention of Maritime Pollution from ships
MIF	Maritime Industries Forum
OECD	Organisation for Economic Cooperation and Development
PSC	Port State Control
SEM	Single European Market
TEN-T	Trans-European Transport Network
TEU	Twenty-foot Equivalent Unit
UNCTAD	United Nations Conference on Trade and Development

Foreword

I am very honoured to have been asked to write a foreword to this book.

It appears at a very important time for the port sector. Its main theme is whether or not the European institutions will develop a common ports policy. Whether your view is that such a policy represents a straitjacket, or whether your view is that this represents a welcome freeing up of a well-established sector, this book sheds new light on how policy and ports have changed over the last few decades.

Unlike other parts of the transport sector, ports have tended to develop in their own diverse ways, reflecting their markets and national characteristics. It was during the 1990s in particular that increases in traffic volumes brought to the fore a number of delicate competition issues. The setting up of the Single Market in the early 1990s was a major catalyst for change and the past decade has seen both the Commission and the port sector wrestling with two major issues – how can ports compete effectively and how can they best serve the needs of their users?

The answers have been as diverse as the sector itself. I compliment the writers of this book who have summarised admirably the background to these problems, the 'solutions' that have been offered and what the future might bring. Not only are there some excellent sections on the 1997 Green Paper and the 2001 Ports Package, there is equally valuable material on a range of topics, including Trans-European Networks, short sea shipping, MARPOL and the Environment.

The book represents a very valuable reference point not only for students of port and transport policy but also for ESPO, the organisation which has the primary task of representing port opinion to the legislators.

David Whitehead

Chairman, ESPO

Brussels January 2002

Preface

The book sets out to examine the progress towards a European Union (EU) Port Policy in the 1990s. It presents and analyses the implications of a wide range of EU policy developments aiming to promote the competitiveness of the European port industry within the context of a long-term sustainable mobility strategy.

Since the early 1990s, the development of a European port policy has been at the centre of attention. Policy makers involved in national and supranational policy making recognised the strategic importance of integrating efficient and competitive ports into the multimodal European transport system. Consequently, the relevant EU institutions have contributed to the formulation of policy proposals and the definition of a long-term European strategy regarding the port industry. Additionally, the port industry itself has opted for the representation of its interests at a EU-level, in an attempt to obtain collective European responses to the industry's needs for adjustment to the new economic reality. The recently published (2001) policy proposals (the so-called 'port package') comprise a EU framework aiming to improve the quality of port services, highlight the progress that has been made in certain issues, and provide the general outline of the future policy developments in this specific area. Though there is still no comprehensive policy framework, the development of a European Port Policy is a critical part of the Common EU Transport Policy. The latter aims, among others, to single-out and highlight the comparative advantages of each transport method and each transport mode; and to create/facilitate the necessary conditions that will allow their optimal utilisation in the context of the EU sustainable mobility strategy.

All these policy initiatives reflect the undergoing reorganisation of the port industry. New organisational structures and operational logic, the supply of new services, an increase of the private sector participation in the provision of port services, and the application of innovations and new technologies, are parameters of the structural developments that have taken place in European ports. The EU-level policy developments also reflect the interconnection of European port adjustment with the achievement of several socio-economic targets, such as the social cohesion of the Union, the existence of the essential framework of infrastructures to develop competitive economic activities, and the achievement of environmentally friendly economic growth and sustainable mobility.

Several intrinsic peculiarities endow the port industry with a unique character. Firstly, the port product essentially does not have any substitutes. Secondly, it is difficult to adjust the production process to short-term demand fluctuations. Thirdly, the port product, which is extremely complex, exhibits characteristics of a both private and public good. Finally, the operation of a port is closely intertwined with issues such as regional development, quality of life, the environment and other issues of general societal and political significance. Some or all of these features prevail in the markets of other products as well. However, in the case of the port industry the frequency and intensity of these characteristics magnify their importance and potential impact on various aspects of the social and economic life (at least as far as their surrounding area is concerned and even beyond). Perhaps because of them, there are few attempts to examine policy issues related to the port industry. The volume of international literature on transport policy has increased in recent years; however, the absence of studies examining the formulation and development of explicit port policies is still remarkable.

The ambitious aim of the present book is to fill some of the gaps in the literature. Hence, this book attempts to examine the progress that has been made towards the creation of a European port policy, the expected developments, and the problems that remain since the launching of the first Community initiatives. The development of a EU port policy constitutes a critical parameter of European integration whose significance will continuously increase for two reasons. The first reason is that the EU has adopted a strategy to develop a multimodal European transport system. Second, such a policy would certainly contribute to the reinforcement of the four freedoms stipulated by the Single European Market: the free movement of goods, persons, and capital, and the freedom of establishment.

The introductory *Chapter 1* presents the importance of the port system to Europe. It also introduces the European Union as an additional supranational policy-making level in the field of transport. *Chapter 2* analyses the ongoing transformation, the characteristics, and the diversity of the European port industry. *Chapter 3* proceeds to an examination of the historical evolution of the EU port policy.

Chapter 4 presents the implications of the contemporary EU transport strategy to the port production and industry. The two main themes explored in this chapter are: (a) ports and their potential contribution to socio-economic cohesion and sustainable mobility in the EU, and (b) the financing and charging of transport infrastructure. *Chapter 5* examines the attempts of the EU to advance the interoperability and interconnection of transport modes and networks, as well as the eventual integration of ports in Trans-European Transport Networks (TEN-T). Then, *Chapter 6* analyses the elements of port policy incorporated into the progress of the common maritime transport policy.

Chapter 7 analyses the thoughts, the policy proposals, and the decisions of the policy actors (national and supranational institutions, interest groups) dealing explicitly, and exclusively, with the adjustment of the European port system in the new economic reality. *Chapter 8* presents the institutional debate between the EU institutions (as expressed by the various policy and strategy documents) and the representatives of the port industry, as well as the various stakeholders after the publication of the Commission's *Green Paper on sea ports and maritime infrastructure.*

Concluding, *Chapter 9* attempts to approach the 'next day', it discusses the contents of and the initial reactions to the so-called 'port package' published by the European Commission in 2001, by describing the prospects and the expected further developments towards a European Port Policy.

Hereby, a stylistic note is essential. As many scholars have repeatedly observed, anyone studying the process of European integration faces a possibly unique in the social sciences problem, namely the uncertainty regarding the institutional point of reference. In legal terms, any decision taken in the framework of Common Transport Policy is based on the founding Treaty of the European Economic Community (EEC), which was signed in Rome in 1957. By the ratification of the Treaty of Maastricht on the 1st of November 1993, the EEC was transformed into the European Community. The European Community was incorporated into the new institutional form of integration and comprises the first pillar *(Pillar I)* of the European Union (EU). For this reason, in this book the term European Union is used even when reference is made to facts taking place before 1993.

The authors would like to thank all those who by kindly providing data, information, and feedback have decisively contributed to the completion of the present study. Especially Dr. Panayiotis Kanellopoulos, Ass. Professor in European Union Law at the University of Piraeus, and Mr. Stavros Hatzakos, Representative of the Piraeus Port Authority in the European Sea Port Organisation, for their invaluable comments.

A special note of gratitude goes to Apostolos Karalis who translated the Greek manuscript and provided detailed editorial suggestions for improving the text and ironing out inconsistencies.

The authors are indebted to the Piraeus Port Authority for contributing financially to the translation of this book, originally written in Greek, to English.

This study is the product of the common effort of the two writers, who are jointly and exclusively responsible for any mistakes or omissions.

1. Introduction

1.1 SETTING THE SCENE

Europe is undergoing significant change. With the completion of the Single European Market (SEM), the ratification of the Maastricht Treaty on the European Union (EU), the Amsterdam Treaty and the intergovernmental agreement of Nice in December 2000, the process of European integration has entered a new economic and political period. Part of the integration process comprises the common sectoral European policies developed to address issues concerning important aspects of the European economy. These policies also include initiatives aiming at the development of a Common Transport Policy (CTP).

The Treaty of Rome, which was signed in 1957 and established the European Economic Community, contained provisions on the principles of a Common Transport Policy. Since 1974, the EU is an additional level of international discussion and decision making in the field of maritime transport. Over the last years, particularly throughout the 1990s, in the context of the previously mentioned policies many proposals and decisions have been adopted, which involved EU actions aiming to improve the efficiency and competitiveness of European ports. Those efforts were oriented towards the achievement of sustainable mobility, the integration of the local transport networks, the improvement of the overall transport system and the development of Trans-European Transport Networks (TEN-T).

The interest of the EU institutions in the port industry was a result of the will to speed up economic development, to improve the efficiency of the overall transport system and of combined transport in particular. Seaports have always been regarded as a vital element of the development of intermodal transport networks and an important means of achieving sustainable mobility.

Transport exhibits characteristics of a systemic economic sector where several interdependent industries operate. Ports undoubtedly constitute a distinctive component of this system. Whenever sea transport is a part of the transportation process, ports provide the main means of access for shipping to land transport networks and *vice versa*. By facilitating the continuous flow of cargo and passengers, ports have become an indispensable link of the transport chain. The operation of efficient ports equipped with modern infrastructure and providing reliable services that are used by competitive and complementary means of transport, increases the benefits accruing to the users, the providers of transport services and to society as a whole. Fundamental changes in the production and distribution of goods, which are leading to the formation of a continuous chain of door-to-door services, intensify the significance of ports as a determining element of the price, the quality and the speed of transport services. The increasing use of containerised cargo and the augmented demand for higher-quality transport services (involving criteria such as speed, strict scheduling and transportation according to the needs of the just-in-time delivery system) necessitate the operational co-ordination of road, rail and inland-waterway transport systems in a coherent transport framework.

As a result, it should not be surprising that policy initiatives, aiming at the development of a common European transport policy, are gradually incorporating policies concerning the improvement of the competitiveness of the European port industry. Attempts to enhance port efficiency, the provision of funds for the modernisation of port infrastructure, the inclusion of ports in trans-European transport networks have become part of the recent policy agenda. Policy measures to increase the transparency of financial and accounting figures of ports, to upgrade port competition, improve the quality and the organisation of port services, and actions to achieve higher levels of safety, as well as the concern for environmental issues, are also under consideration. An intensive and systematic effort with reference to a mixture of policies concerning various policy areas   (such as the environment, transport and mobility) incorporates elements that may eventually result in the creation and development of a European Port Policy.

The study at hand refers to the measures, adopted by the EU, which concern, directly or indirectly, the productive activity of the port industry. Specifically, the writers attempt to present and analyse all the above-mentioned proposals and decisions, including the implications of other European policies to the port industry. At the same time, they are aiming to critically examine the process leading to the formation of a European Port Policy and the implications of this process to the competitiveness of European ports. All these are preceded by an analysis of the conditions prevailing in European ports along with a comparison of the various perceptions regarding port organisation and management in Europe.

The competitiveness of European ports and the measures adopted at a supranational level concern not only the European institutions but several other policy actors as well. These include port industry, port users, and policy makers acting at the national level. How do port users, producers and those responsible for ports and port planning perceive the recent developments?

Their policy proposals comprise very important ideas on the prospective of a European Port Policy and may influence decisively the course and the progress of the latter. Taking into consideration the view of the representatives of the port industry and all those involved in the activities of the port economy, an analysis of the policy formation process is undertaken along with a presentation of the views of the stakeholders on the potential of the competitiveness of European ports.

1.2   DEFINING 'PORT'

Over the course of time, the definition of the term *port* has changed significantly. Many factors have contributed to this: the technological development of maritime transport, the importance of maritime transport to the national economies as well as to the entire European economy, and the increasing importance of combined transport. Initially ports were synonymous with natural ports (harbours). They encompassed the area of the sea where depth and morphology of the coastline provided adequate shelter for ships. In that context the maximum draught of vessels depended on the harbours' depth; thus ports were a function of shipyard technology.

The need to upgrade the physical characteristics of harbours and to create ports, even in locations where morphology did not provide natural shelter, necessitated the construction of infrastructure in order to define the part of the sea that would be used for the provision of shelter and various other services to ships. Hence, the natural port was transformed to a locus of infrastructures with the aim of providing shelter and services to ships, thus becoming a vital component of maritime transport. In the past, such ports were unquestionably of paramount importance to a nation's economy and to its external communications. On many occasions, the creation of ports characterised and significantly influenced the development of seaside regions. Consequently, it should not be surprising that ports were regarded as very important 'tools' for the promotion of regional development.

Nowadays, ports constitute an important link in an integrated combined transport chain that includes maritime transport. Ports were performing this task long before the contemporary notion of combined transport was even conceived and before their infrastructure was extended to cater for new port activities. The role of the port industries in the transport chains, as well as the various forms of contemporary port activity, require that ports be defined as:

Terrestrial and seaside areas consisting of specific constructions and equipment so as to enable the deployment of commercial activities with the main functions being ships' reception, loading, transloading, unloading, warehousing, reception and delivery of goods via inland transport modes and the boarding and transportation of passengers. Within the confines of those areas, several enterprises operate and utilise the available port infrastructure and superstructure, as well as conventional road and railway infrastructures. Additionally, the port market is regulated or administered by a port authority.

The aforementioned definition demonstrates the economic significance of a port. An issue that should not be underestimated, though, is that the specific (basic) functions of a port remain the same (as stated in previous definitions of a port), namely the provision of shelter, revictualling services for ships and connection with other modes of transport. On that basis, it is only fair to acknowledge the approach of the EU institutions according to which sea ports:

> shall permit the development of sea transport and shall constitute shipping links for islands and the points of interconnection between sea transport and other modes of transport. They shall provide equipment and services to transport operators. Their infrastructure shall provide a range of services for passenger and goods transport, including ferry facilities and short- and long-distance shipping services, including coastal shipping, within the Community and between the latter and third countries.[1]

The emphasis above is on the economic functions of the ports without underestimating the importance of their integration in and contribution to the economic system. The latter depend on the volume of trade activity that a port attracts and on the importance of this activity to a region's economy.

The financial situation and the development prospects of the port industry depend largely on the development of the volume of transport. The development of transport, in turn, depends on the progress of the world economy. The demand for port services is essentially a derived demand. There is a strong correlation between economic growth and total volume of seagoing transport. At the same time, there is a correlation between the activities of ports and the development of transportation of specific types of tradable goods (such as the increasing use of containers). Finally, vital are the economic aspects of various technologies and of the utilisation of capital equipment, along with the introduction of environmental safety rules which require the use of more expensive technology per unit of transported product.

1.3   THE IMPERATIVE OF THE PORT INDUSTRY

The Importance and Prospects of the Maritime Sector

The port sector is important to the European economy primarily since it comprises a vital link in the transport chain. In 1999, 1,215 million tonnes or

70.8% of total trade between the EU Member States with third countries (extra-EU trade), and 295 million tonnes or 28.2% of intra-EU trade were transported by the sea.[2] In the case of some Member States, the flow of maritime transport accounts for practically all of their international trade. According to the latest data available (1996), international short-sea shipping accounts for 13% of the total combined transport traffic in Europe (in terms of tonne-kilometres), with an average short sea distance of 800 kilometres per tonne. The addition of the national coastal traffic (cabotage) and the value of goods transported from one European port to another (feeder traffic) or from a port to the hinterland (inland traffic), lead to the conclusion that the EU indisputably constitutes a mass user of port services. Maritime cabotage trade in the EU reached 1,625 billion tonnes with national maritime flows being particularly important for some Member States: 42% of the entire cargo volume shipped from Danish ports, 39% of Italian, and 32% of Spanish maritime traffic has national destinations.

The overall transport sector is strategically significant to the EU. In 1999, this sector accounted for 5% of the EU GDP (400 billion Euro) and 5.5% of employment (8.3 million employees in the production of transport services and equipment plus more than 6 million employees in industries related to transport). Investments in transport infrastructure by the Member States exceed 1% of GDP and the energy consumption of transport amounts to 30% of total EU energy consumption. During the last two decades an, almost uninterrupted, increase in the demand for transport services took place, especially in the case of intra-EU transport.

It is remarkable that the growth rates of transporting exceeded the economic growth rate of the EU (Table 1.1). Intra-EU transport of goods increased by 114% during the period 1970–1999 and, in 1999, it amounted to 2,970 billion tonne-miles (12,700 tonne-miles per capita), an increase of 122% compared to the data of 1970. The same period, passenger transport increased by 123%, reaching 4,790 billion persons per kilometre (pkm).

Table 1.1 Annual Growth of EU Member States (% change)

	1980–1990	1990–1997	1998	1999
GDP	2.4	1.6	2.6	2.1
Industrial Production	1.8	0.7	3.4	2.0
Passenger Transport	3.1	2.0	2.1	2.0
Freight Transport (tkm)	1.9	2.7	3.5	3.0

Source: CEU – DGVII. Transport in Figures, 2001.

Table 1.2 presents the most important providers of port services in Europe and the development of transport activity served by each port. Projections of the present trends suggest an increase exceeding 20% of the current transport activity in European ports by the year 2010. Containerised traffic of goods is expected to account for the largest part of this increase. The total cargo that will be transported by European ports in 2010 is expected to amount to 3,385 million tonnes. This figure in 1980 amounted to 1,836 million tonnes, while in 1990 it exceeded 2,000 million tonnes of cargo (ESPO, 1995).

Table 1.2 Transport Activity: The Major European Ports (million tonnes)

Port	Country	1970	1980	1990	1997	1998	1999
Rotterdam	NL	226.0	276.0	288.0	303.3	306.6	299.1
Antwerp	B	78.0	82.0	102.0	111.9	119.8	115.7
Marseille	F	74.0	103.0	90.0	94.3	93.4	90.3
Hamburg	D	47.0	63.0	61.0	76.5	76.3	81.0
Le Havre	F	58.0	77.0	54.0	59.7	66.4	63.9
Amsterdam	NL	21.0	34.0	47.0	56.5	55.7	55.7
London	UK	64.0	48.0	58.0	55.7	56.4	52.4
Tees & Hartlep.	UK	23.0	38.0	40.0	51.2	51.5	49.3
Genoa	I	53.0	51.0	44.0	45.9	45.9	45.9
Forth ports	UK	25.0	29.0	25.4	43.1	44.4	45.4
Trieste	I	27.0	38.0	34.0	46.4	47.2	44.8
Algeciras	E	8.0	22.0	25.0	37.3	42.1	41.9
Wilhelmshaven	D	22.0	32.0	16.0	36.4	43.8	39.8
Dunkerque	F	25.0	41.0	37.0	36.5	39.2	38.3
Bremen/B'haven	D	23.0	25.0	28.0	34.0	34.5	36.0
Zeebrugge	B	8.0	12.0	30.0	32.4	33.3	35.4
Southampton	UK	28.0	25.0	29.0	33.1	34.3	33.3
Milford Haven	UK	41.0	39.0	32.0	34.5	28.8	32.2
Gothenburg	S	20.0	22.0	26.0	30.3	30.7	30.4
Liverpool	UK	31.0	13.0	23.0	30.8	30.3	28.9
Bilbao	E	11.0	21.0	25.0	22.4	26.4	26.0
Tarragona	E	4.4	19.8	24.2	30.8	25.5	25.1
Dublin	IRL	7.0	7.0	8.0	16.8	18.5	20.0
Pireus	EL	n.a.	n.a.	n.a.	9.9	12,9	13.9
Thessaloniki	EL	8.0	9.0	14.0	13.4	13.7	13.7
Lisbon	P	9.0	14.0	14.0	11.5	11.3	12.0
Helsinki	FIN	4.0	5.0	8.0	11.3	10.7	10.0
København	DK	6.0	7.0	9.0	10.8	11.9	9.7
Sum of above ports		951	1,153	1,192	1,367	1,399	1,376

Source: Institute of Shipping Economics and Logistics, Bremen.

As de Langen (2001) observes, the cargo handling activities that take place in the Member States are clearly geographically concentrated. Eighty three per cent of the total 2,320 million tonnes throughput in European seaports in 1998 was concentrated in the largest 75 ports. The ten largest ports handled 40% of all cargo. That 71% of European ports handle an annual tonagge of less than 5 million tonnes (all comodities), 17% handling between 5 and 20 million tonnes, and only 11% of European ports handling more than 20 million tonnes annualy (ESPO, 2001) is a further indicator of the concentration of cargo handling activities in a limited number of ports. In turn, de Langen (2001) remarks, this concentration advances 'port clustering', that is the presence of a population of geographically concentrated and mutual related business units, associations and public (private) organisations centred around the distinctive economic specialisations developed in the major European port areas.

Apart from cargo handling, European ports are the centres of a great range of activities. There are port-related industrial activities such as oil refining and chemical manufacture, and shipbuilding. The most common land-based commercial activities carried out within the port area are storage and packing (carried out in 79% of European ports), ship repair and engineering (46%), fish market/processing (34%), and general manufacturing (29%) (ESPO, 2001). Apparently European ports attract industrial investment and can often be key local economic generators.

European seaports, from the simple physical sea/land interface they once used to be, have successively turned into commerce and industrial centers, then into logistics and distribution platforms, and are now becoming intermodal nodes in international supply chains networks, the efficiency of which now drives trade competitiveness. This is not least, this is because total logistics costs (packaging, storage, transport, inventories, administration and management) are estimated to reach up to 20% of total production costs in OECD countries. Transport usually accounts for a quarter of total logistics costs, storage for a fifth, and inventories for a sixth.

The prospects of international maritime transport relate closely to the prospects of international trade development. On the other hand, the prospects of intra-EU maritime trade relate significantly to the characteristics of the Member States' transport system and specifically to the cost of transport services offered by alternative modes of transport. Thus, policy choices at EU level may have, among others, an impact on the competition between the alternative modes of transport.

International trade exhibits a dynamically increasing trend, as demonstrated by its annual growth rate (Figure 1.1). The same is the case for maritime transport of liquid and bulk cargo. During the period 1985–1999 this increase was almost uninterruptible, thus the 3,293 million tonnes of maritime trade in 1985 increased to 4,110 million tonnes in 1991 and exceeded 5,000 million tonnes during the period 1997–1999. The increase of maritime trade in tonne-miles during the period 1985–1999 was also remarkable, despite its growth rate being lower than the growth rate of the volume of maritime trade.

According to the data collected by Eurostat,[3] an upward trend in maritime transport was registered throughout the 1990s in all maritime Member States except for Portugal, where the total volume maritime transport stagnates. Whilst the increase in Spain, Finland and Sweden is around 20%, Italy and the UK display growth of around 10%. The 43% growth for Germany is partly explained by the re-unification, with major Baltic ports (i.e. Rostock, Stralsund, or Sassnitz) contributing substantially to this increase. For all Member States, bulk goods constitute an important share. Liquid and dry bulk goods represent more than half of the volume of goods handled in ports of the reporting EU Member States and peak at 86% for Spain.

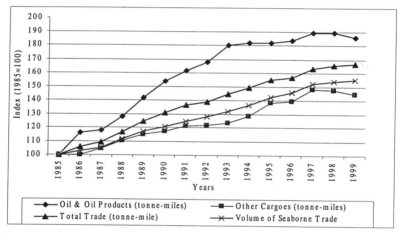

Source: Fearnleys' Review, 2000.

Figure 1.1 Development of World Seaborne Trade

As regards containerised traffic, the most important element of combined transport (to the requirements of which shipbuilding and port technologies are continuously adjusted), in 1999 worldwide reached 184.8 million TEU (twenty-foot-equivalent unit) with an annual growth rate of 7.8%. The 13 maritime Member States accounted for 24.7% of the world market with the transport of 45.8 million TEU in 1999 (12 million TEU in 1983) and an average growth rate of 8.9%. The rest of the world container traffic is

distributed between the Far East (46%), North America (17%), Near and
Middle East (6%), Central and South America (4%), and Africa (3%). Table
1.3 presents the EU ports where the main volume of containerised trade took
place in 1998. The OECD data on world economic development during the
period 1999–2003 (2.3%) reveal that container traffic in Europe could reach
52 million TEU in 2003 and 75 million TEU in 2008 (Containerisation
International, 2000).

Table 1.3 Container Traffic: The Major European Ports (1.000 TEU)

Port	Country	1990	1995	1997	1998	1999	Change 99/98 (%)
Rotterdam	NL	3,667	4,787	5,495	6,011	6,343	+5.5
Hamburg	D	1,969	2,890	3,337	3,547	3,738	+5.4
Antwerp	B	1,549	2,329	2,969	266	3,614	+10.7
Felixstowe	UK	1,436	1,924	2,237	500	2,697	+7.9
Gioia Tauro	I	0	16	1,449	2,126	2,259	+6.3
Bremen/B'haven	D	1,198	1,524	1,538	1,826	2,181	+20.4
Algeciras	E	553	1,155	1,703	1,812	1,833	+0.4
Le Havre	F	858	970	1,185	1,319	1,378	+4.5
Barcelona	E	448	689	972	1,095	1,234	+12.8
Genoa	I	310	615	1,180	1,266	1,235	-2.5
Valencia	E	387	672	832	1,005	1,153	+14.7
Piraeus	EL	426	600	684	933	965	+3.4
Southampton	UK	345	681	806	891	921	+8.9
Zeebrugge	B	342	528	648	776	850	+9.5
La Spezia	I	450	965	616	732	843	+15.2
Marseille	F	482	498	622	660	664	+6.2
Gothenburg	S	352	458	531	520	624	+20.1
Liverpool	UK	239	406	461	487	515	+5.7
Helsinki	FIN	246	296	330	343	321	-7.2
Copenhagen	DK	165	178	160	171	180	+5.3
Sum of 1st 10 ports		11,987	16,899	22,065	24,768	26,512	+7.0
Singapore		5,224	11,846	14,100	15,137	15,945	+5.3
Hong Kong		5,101	12,550	14,385	14,852	16,211	+9.2

Source: Institute of Shipping Economics and Logistics, Bremen.

Notably, the concentration of container handling activities is not a unique
European phenomenon. The top 25 container ports in the United States (US)
handled 98% of the total 14.8 million TEU container traffic in 1997. In total,
the US port industry handles about 95% by weight of all US foreign overseas
trade, that was over 2 billion metric tons of cargo in 1998, and generates
almost $500 billion in personal income (US Department of Transport, 1998),
figures that highlight the importance of the port industry worldwide. The

structural difference, however, when EU ports are compared to those in the US is the widespread role of the public sector in the latter case. Whilst US ports are an industry owned, almost entirely, by the public sector, the institutional framework in Europe is substantially more complex (see: Chapter 2).

On the other hand, similarly to the EU, the US public port industry invests substantial capital resources in port improvement, with the projected expenditures for construction of new facilities and the modernisation and rehabilitation of existing ones throughout the period 1997–2001 being $6.5 billion. Moreover, the major concerns of the US administration (ibid., p.2) do not vary from those expressed by stakeholders and policy makers in Europe, and presented in the forthcoming chapters of this volume. These concerns include port development financing and revenues, environmental regulation, dredging and dredged material disposal, intermodal land transportation access, next generation containerships, and global shipping alliances.

Around the world, there are more than 2,000 ports from single berth locations handling a few hundreds tons a year to multipurpose facilities handling up to 300 million tons a year. The world port traffic is made for 45% of liquid bulks (mainly oil, petroleum products, and chemicals), for 23% of dry bulks (coal, iron ore, grain, and phosphate), and for 32% of general cargo. Port and logistics operations are more and more carried out by a limited number of international operators, specializing in dedicated market segments, and by a few large shipping lines expanding their maritime networks into inland operations to offer integrated transport services. Traffic concentration on large intermodal platforms and shipping alliances translate into fewer ports handling a more important share of world traffic: the first 10 containers ports handled 31% of the world traffic in 1980, and close to 40% today. Simultaneously, the growth of transshipment activities complements the development of hub ports: container transshipment is believed to make 20% of total maritime container traffic today, and is growing.

An Inseparable Part of the EU Transport System

European ports comprise an indispensable part of the European transport system and are of major significance at the micro-, meso-, and macroeconomic levels. At the microeconomic level, economic theory postulates that transport costs comprise a significant parameter of the location decisions of various enterprises (for a review of the theory: see Button, 1993). Within the Single European Market, there is a two-way relation between transport and location of economic activities. Transport serves a given spatial distribution of activities, but differential developments of transport to suit market conditions in different locations affect the future development of these localisations (Vickerman, 1992). The current changes in the structure of productive activities intensify this relation. Transport costs and the existence of a fast, flexible, and high-quality transport system are becoming increasingly important for productive activities that begin to take place in wider geographical areas. Consequently, in these areas, productive and functional systems that are 'transport dependent' (Bayliss & Millington, 1995) are adopted: transporting is thus becoming part of production, through the transport of final or even intermediate products (with the advent of economic integration). Changes in the operation and the cost of transport systems may result in increased demand, thus attracting consumer, trade, and production partners.

At mesoeconomic level, adequate transport systems may constitute a propulsive force for the regional development of an area through the creation of 'axes of development' and 'investment polarisation' (Vanhove & Klaasen, 1987). The cumulative effects of a set of small changes, even a single large piece of infrastructure, improve core–periphery relations and introduce 'corridor' effects (i.e. the development of the necessary links for the spatial and economic development within and between the regions – Vickerman, 1994) and 'shadow' effects ('the diversion of the current traffic away from traditional routes and modes', ibid.). The transport system (along with other factors) facilitates the balanced regional development, but assumes greater importance within the SEM. European Member States have been transformed into open-access economies where the potential of some regions to become losers and others to become winners increases (Rietveld & Nijkamp, 1993).

At macroeconomic level, scholars who concentrate on the economic impact and the productivity effects of transport infrastructure, conclude that the efficiency of the latter favours the growth of an economy as a whole (World Bank, 1994). Controversies may exist but as Button (1993, p. 225) summarises '...sceptical studies accept that an adequate basic transport system is a *sine qua non* for modern economic development, but questioning whether opportunity costs involved in further improving transport are necessarily justified' (see also: Kessides, 1993). Positive linkages between transport provision and economic growth exist, however their precise quantification remains difficult (in the case of the port sector: Chlomoudis & Pallis, 2000).

The economic importance of the port sector relates positively to the progress of economic integration. The Customs Union theory (Viner, 1950; Meadey, 1955), which has been the theoretical basis of European economic integration, has introduced the concepts of trade creation and trade diversion as analytical tools to assess the potential effects of economic integration between two or more countries. Whenever trade creation exceeds trade diversion one could anticipate economic benefits at all stages of integration,[4] due to the separation of demand and supply in space and the consequent increase in transport activities.[5] At the national level, these benefits derive from trade specialisation. At the regional level, they derive from geographical specialisation, and at the micro level, they result from the achievement of economies of scale. Increased trade requires adequate and efficient transport systems. Otherwise, transport costs turn into a 'natural trade barrier' (Nielsen *et al.*, 1992), which acts as an obstacle to further economic growth.

Due to the geographical characteristics of the EU, the increase of maritime trade could potentially strengthen socio-economic cohesion. The existence of some 650 ports, most of them located near centres of industrial activity, comprises the largest port concentration in the world. By providing vital links with islands and distant areas, these ports constitute a propulsive force for the balanced regional development of the European continent. The qualitative importance of these ports has been further intensified by the geopolitical developments in Central and Eastern Europe, which have resulted in a very favourable environment for the development of short sea shipping.

Critical approaches to neo-classical economics do not underestimate the significance of the sector to the process of economic integration (cf. Pelkmans, 1984; Tsoukalis, 1993). What they perceive differently is the potential contribution of public policies to the development of a competitive European transport system. Assuming perfect mobility of capital, as a production factor, economic activities can only be competitive when the framework within which they operate provides the optimal conditions. A high-quality transport infrastructure is clearly an example of such a framework condition. This fact exerts significant pressure on governments to upgrade the productivity of transport industries. Consequently, public policies should promote the effectiveness of the transport industries.

The importance of ports is becoming even higher since maritime transport constitutes an alternative, environmentally friendly and energy saving mode of transport (Chlomoudis *et al.*, 1999). Nowadays, economic growth is more intense than ever. Transport activity has a significant impact on the quality of the environment. Thus, the minimisation of the externalities caused by transport activities – '...the unintended by-products of the transport activity itself that disbenefit third parties outside the customer–carrier relationship, including social and environmental costs' (Whitelegg, 1993, p. 127) – constitutes an additional objective to that of transporting persons and goods at minimum cost. Phenomena that render transport an activity having a negative impact on the environment, such as traffic congestion, the greenhouse effect, and massive energy consumption, cannot be addressed by the current split of the transport modal pie (De Weale, 1993). The achievement of sustainable mobility requires the reinforcement of the environmentally friendly modes of transport, a development that is expected to result in substantial social benefits. Without ignoring that only a part of transport activity can be redirected to sea transport, land traffic congestion can nonetheless be limited as can energy consumption.

Yet, maritime transport may cause negative effects to the ecosystem too. These may be caused by operation pollution in the form of intentional and routine loading/unloading of dangerous or polluting goods, or by accidents at sea and in ports. It is of strategic importance to the citizens of Europe to be served by maritime operations that are effective and competitive in terms of financial costs. However, it is of equal importance that the production and the provision of port services conform to basic safety regulations and bear the lowest costs to the marine environment and to various coastal activities.

In short, either as an autonomous economic sector or as a part of a wider transport system, European ports are an important element of the European economy. An efficient, reliable, and competitive transport system is, in economic and environmental terms, of strategic importance to the European economy and the Single European Market.

1.4 PORT POLICY IN THE PROCESS OF EUROPEAN INTEGRATION

Since 1957, the EU constitutes an additional policy-making jurisdiction in the field of transport.[6] Within the framework of the Treaty of Rome (1957), the Common Transport Policy (CTP) was declared as an indispensable component of the emerging Common Market. The founders of the European Economic Community devoted a whole chapter to it and the common transport policy was one of the policy foundations that gained 'certain autonomy' (Despicht, 1969) through a separate title devoted to it. The six founding members of the European Community had very little interest in maritime (and air) transport. Thus, in the years that followed there was no specific action regarding maritime transport, which was incorporated into the Common Transport Policy after the first enlargement of the Community in 1973, when the inclusion of the United Kingdom, Ireland, and Denmark increased the importance of maritime transport. One year later, after a decision of the European Court of Justice, maritime transport was included in the base of the CTP, along with air transport. During the next seventeen years (1974–1991), progress of the common maritime policy was fragmented and policy mainly focused on possible ways to respond to the crisis caused by the flagging-out of the European fleet towards various flags of convenience.

In 1991, the European Commission introduced the so-called 'horizontal' approach regarding the system of maritime transport within the framework of

CTP. According to the Commission, the new philosophy was 'a policy agenda aiming to give special attention to the maritime economy as a whole' (CEU, 1991a, p. 5). In the context of that approach, the Commission included, for the first time, thoughts and choices regarding the European port industry. After a long period, which was characterised by the absence of any significant interest on the creation of a European Port Policy, the EU initiated a systematic effort to develop an *ad hoc* policy in order to respond to the most important problems concerning port industry. The accession of Greece (1981), of Spain and Portugal (1986), and, not least, of Sweden and Finland (along with Austria in 1998) significantly increased the importance of the port industries to the progress of the European integration process.

Several policy developments signify that a 'mosaic-approach', i.e. an attempt to formulate integrated proposals and a strategy for the European port industry, characterised the 1990s. Those developments included:

- The publication in 1992 of a new strategy document regarding the progress of the CTP (CEU, 1992a), as well as the publication of the White Paper on the incorporation of the objective of sustainable mobility in that strategy (CEU, 1992b).
- The adoption of an EU policy aiming to develop the TEN-T, which was advanced by the provisions of the Maastricht Treaty (signed in 1991; ratified in 1993).
- The reassessment of the EU Maritime Strategy in 1996 (CEU, 1996a; 1996b).
- The provisions of the Green Paper on sea ports and maritime infrastructure in 1997 (CEU, 1997a).
- The reports of the European Parliament on a common policy regarding the European ports (EP, 1993; 1999).

In essence, the above policy strategy also comprised a series of other policy measures, reports, and decisions that concerned, directly or indirectly, the structure and competitive position of European ports. Remarkable examples were the decisions regarding combined transport and the initiatives of the European Commission regarding the importance of transport to the advancement of sustainable mobility (CEU, 1998a) and to the socio-economic cohesion of the EU (CEU, 1998b). Most recent is the political decision of the Council of Transport Ministers, on the incorporation of sea and inland ports into the TEN-T (June 2000).

In early 2001, the Commission completed a proposals package aiming to upgrade the quality of services provided by seaports (CEU, 2001a). The so-called 'port package' includes the results of its research into the public financing and charging practices in the EU sea port sector. It also includes proposals for a Council Directive regarding the transparency of port financial accounts, and the update of the Green Paper on seaports and maritime infrastructure.

As any transport policy (Van der Kamp & Polak, 1980), all these developments towards a European Port Policy consist of a process that takes place in time and are an integral part of the policy developments regarding the total of the transport system. EU policy developments are, explicitly or implicitly, integrated into the strategy on a European Transport Policy for 2010, which the Commission presented in the form of a White Paper in September 2001 (CEU, 2001b).

Overall, the given economic structure of the sector in question, its present condition and its prospects, constitute the foundation of decision making. Three groups of actors, whose choices are important to the content of the final decisions, participate in the process of decision making.

The first group of policy actors comprises the EU institutions responsible for the decision-making process: the Council of Ministers (Council), the European Commission (Commission), the European Parliament (EP), and the European Court of Justice (ECJ). This group also includes two Advisory Committees: the Economic and Social Committee (Ecosoc), and the Committee of the Regions (CoR). The second group of actors comprises the national governments of Member States. Finally, the non-governmental interest groups (port authorities, users, workers, and related to the port industry actors), that are active at the local, national or supranational level (i.e. the two Euro-federations representing port authorities, and private port operators respectively), comprise the third group of actors.

All these policy actors can promote, react to, or favour the adoption of specific measures that promote (or obstruct) the development towards a European Port Policy. Their stance or even the way they express that stance may affect, to a more or less extent, the final form of the common policy. The solutions to the existing problems are neither self-explanatory nor obvious. The rationale of the decision makers shaping the EU policy-making process and the resolutions of market forces may not always coincide. This fact may clearly affect the development prospects of the port policy. Thus, in the following chapters, it is necessary to examine the views, the choices, and the actions of all those actors.

Despite the fact that elements of a European Port Policy did not exist before the 1990s, a presentation referring the development of the CTP during the prior period seems essential. As previously mentioned, the developments regarding ports comprise an inseparable part of the CTP. The latter is a policy aiming to highlight the comparative advantages of various parts of the transport process and to enable the optimal operation of those parts (Erdmenger, 1983). Thus, it is important that the analysis of specific issues, or specific parts of the transport process, or selected transport modes, is taking into account the choices and the developments regarding the overall transport sector.

NOTES

1. Decision No 1692/96/EC of the European Parliament and of the Council of 23 July 1996, in OJ L228 of September 1996, pp 1–103 (extract from Article 12).
2. Unless otherwise stated, the sources of statistical data presented are the statistical databases of Eurostat (i.e. the annual publications: *Basic Statistics, External trade by mode of transport*, and the periodical series *Statistics in Focus – Theme 7 (*Transport*)*), the European Commission's annual publication *Panorama of the EU Industry*, and the periodical statistical collections published by the DG VII entitled *Transport in Figures*.
3. These data are collected in the frame of the EU Maritime Directive (Directive 95/64/EC, Official Journal, L 320 of 30.12.1995 – see: Chapter 6). As in 2001 these data are relatively recent, though not all Member States have reported so far (see: Eurostat (2001), *Statistics in Focus – Theme 7 (Transport), 5/2001*).
4. In a somewhat schematic manner, the Customs Union Theory postulates four distinct stages of integration: Free Trade Area, Customs Union, Common Market, and Economic and Monetary Union, respectively.
5. For an analytical review of this economic doctrine, see among others: Swann, 1999; Molle, 2001.
6. This section aims to introduce the comparatively new policy-making level. An analytic presentation of the policies mentioned in Chapters 3–9.

2. Characteristics and Organisation of European Ports

2.1 THE CHANGING ROLE OF THE PORT INDUSTRY

Structural changes in the world economy that have taken place since 1970 have had a significant impact on international trade. Among others, they have resulted in an unprecedented increase in its volume and a change in the nature of maritime transport. In an era of intense globalisation, the gradually reducing importance of national borders to international trade is a reality. Many economies, originally oriented towards their internal market, are now turning to face the challenges of international markets. Large corporations are undergoing a process of worldwide expansion and integration. The increase of international trade contributed to and coincided with a remarkable progress in maritime technologies, especially those concerning the increase of vessels' capacity, the equipment for cargo handling and the development of IT.

Ports, '...a mixture of industry and services that serve specific production processes' (Suykens, 1986), are undergoing a process of structural transformation. Similarly to other economic sectors, this transformation has been partially the result of the preceding fundamental changes in production processes worldwide and partially the result of endogenous technological developments. Nowadays, ports constitute areas where highly sophisticated logistics activities are concentrated, largely due to fundamental modifications in the production and distribution of goods. The short product lifecycles and the short time-to-market (a trend that, will intensify in the forthcoming years) affect the transport flows, in the sense that the number of products to be shipped and the shipment frequency increase, whereas batch sizes are becoming smaller (cf. Notteboom and Winkelmans, 2001). The creation of functionally comprehensive 'industrial networks' and the implementation of logistics – that is, the management of physical and informational flows into, through, and out of a business – resulted in a new trading context and altered the industry–transport relationship. All types of seagoing trade, even cabotage, are becoming increasingly integrated into the logistics chains. Ports also establish links with inland transport modes along with networks dedicated to multimodal freight transportation (Meersman & Van de Voorde, 1997).

The widespread use of unitised cargo has resulted in the adoption of further criteria, apart from the traditional criteria of price and geographical location, in deciding the route of a cargo as well as in modal choice, a trend that is visible since the late 1980s (Peters, 1989). Since the efficiency of port cargo handling and the links with inland transportation modes are increasingly becoming critical, the geographical monopoly powers of ports have been eroded (Heaver, 1995). Port users, either shippers or ship owners, have assumed the role of multimodal operators and are increasingly demanding 'new' services. Thus, the competitiveness of a port nowadays depends on its ability to provide multiple value-added services (Slack *et al.*, 1996).

The port product becomes complex and may be regarded as a chain of interlinking functions, taking place within the area of a port, aiming to facilitate environmentally friendly and economically efficient transportation. The port, as a whole, is in turn a link in the overall logistics chain. The respective significance of the constituting links is changing over the course of time (Suykens & Van de Voorde, 1998, p. 252). Port productivity partially depends on the improvement of the total transport chain, consequently the competitiveness of a port and of port planning relate to the relevant characteristics of the other parts of the transport network.

In order to respond to the new characteristics of transport demand, the port industry has adopted new technologies and has undertaken large-scale investments over the last few years. The need to recover the respective additional costs has contributed to an increase in port competition. Another significant trend over the last ten years is the emergence of dedicated container terminals in ports, largely attributed to the increasing gap between the objectives of port and shipping lines and the attempts of these stakeholders to be involved in a 'win-win' strategy (Bennacchio *et al.*, 2001). Then, mergers and regional and global expansion, resulting from the port authorities and/or shipping lines willingness to take a financial stake in other ports and to stevedore operations and accept all kind of joint ventures, are structurally changing the industry. Competition and cooperation strategies are being developed by organisations with expertise in container terminal management, in an attempt to enlarge their roles in logistics services by managing terminals in different ports and by participating in the integration of ports with inland transport services (Heaver *et al.*, 2001). These trends create long-term relationships between port users and port services providers, but also generate critical questions regarding the regulatory and institutional framework governing such agreements. Also visible is the increasing level of competition between the various transport modes to attract the most profitable unitised cargo.

All these alterations have had an effect on the nature, the location and the size of a port's hinterland and, as a result, these elements are considered important indicators of a port's success (Hayuth, 1996). In Europe, the North Sea ports serve vast hinterlands. This, in turn, radically alters the relations between a port and the surrounding environment, for which, during the past, ports were the most important development poles. Since the late 1960s, the changes in technology (especially those concerning cargo terminals, containers, and the roll-on/roll-off methods of loading and unloading) have weakened the strong ties between the port and the cities surrounding it (e.g. Rotterdam, Hamburg, Marseilles – Bulck Consultants International, 1996). At the same time, the technological changes have strengthened the relation between a port and its hinterland. Ports have evolved into a service and infrastructure sector that serves national and international transport (Teilet, 1996).

The above-mentioned developments did result in the need to adjust the way those responsible for port planning perceive ports. In the past ports were perceived as a development factor of coastal areas. Today, port policy and port planning need to take into account the existing geography; the standards applying in a territory; the particular characteristics of the population and of local economic activities; the state of port infrastructure and of the connected transport networks. Moreover, there is a need to take into consideration that ports are links that could benefit wider areas that extend beyond the borders of a country.

2.2 THE DIVERSITY OF EUROPEAN PORTS

The European port system is far from being homogeneous. European ports differ significantly with regard to their organisation, their importance on a national or international scale, the level of technical specialisation, the ability to handle all or specific types of cargo. These extensive differences, which affect their efficiency, may be classified as follows:

- *Size*: there are ports of local, national and international interest.
- *Geographical position*: there are coastal and estuarine ports, while the region in which the port is situated also has an influence on its commercial success.
- *Administration*: there are ports with local, public, autonomous, or private administrations.

- *Activities*: some ports follow the comprehensive organisation model; others favour the landlord ports or service ports model.
- *Labour*: port operations may be undertaken by workers on piece rate or wages, and dockers may also be organised in pools or have permanent contracts.

The status and characteristics of ports vary not only between ports located in different EU Member States, but also between ports located within the same Member State. This diversity concerns both the institutional framework and the management policy.

The diverse institutional framework did not always correspond to the different views regarding port management. In fact, typical similarities in several cases were concealing essential differences and vice versa. The institutional points of reference for each port are distinct and depend on the historical, geographical, and political factors and on the diverse economic and social environments of ports. Focusing on the essential elements, a distinction may be made between two frameworks.

Firstly, ports where the prevailing concept of the operational framework of port activities is of public welfare services. This conceptualisation justifies a predominant role of state authorities as regulators and a public sector responsible for the direct management of the activities relating to the transport of goods.

Secondly, ports where the prevailing concept is on the commercial aspects of port activities. According to this institutional concept, state intervention – in the form of local port authorities, port management, or other institutions – is limited to the programming of inland activities and to 'issues of general interest', such as pollution control, safety, pilotage and other services, the supervision of the conditions of fair competition, etc.

It should be noted that the above two categories constitute 'ideal-types' – *idealtypus* in Max Weber's terms – since they are not observed in their entirety. Most ports approach rather than reflect one of the two above models. The first model exists, although tends to be abandoned, in the Mediterranean countries such as Greece, while the second exists in the continental Northern Europe, where private companies undertake the handling of cargo and many other port services.

The type of the port services provided largely affects the size of the port authority, its organisational and financial structure. It also impinges on the determination of port charges. For example, port services may comprise stevedoring, towing, operation of container terminals, maintenance, policing etc. Thus, there is a great variety in the size of port authorities, ranging from a small private company to notably bigger organisations. For instance, the management of ports in Ireland, the United Kingdom and Denmark belongs to wider port authorities. In these countries, there has always been a different ideological approach than the one existing in the Mediterranean countries: i.e. the constant effort to administer ports according to the logic of free market.

During the 1980s, a dominant philosophy of port management arose. Due to competitive pressures, even in ports characterised by the existence of a central port authority, the presence of private companies increased (Haralambides & Veenstra, 1997). Port reform has assumed various forms, from outright sale and transfer of ownership to the sale of particular assets of infrastructure or services, or to long-term lease arrangements, or, in some cases, governments have opted for corporatisation and commercialisation. However there is still neither consensus, nor certainties, regarding the reforms of the port industry. Their effectiveness depends on the existence of certain preconditions and on the process of their introduction itself. Consequently, improved performance has not always been achieved (UNCTAD, 1995) despite the fact that the exact quantification of costs and benefits is difficult, to say the least (Thomas, 1994). Some scholars argue that in the case of the British experience of port privatisation, the benefits outweighed the costs (Johnston, 1995). Others remain critical of the process (Baird, 1995; 2001) or suggest that the involvement of the private sector in the provision of port services is equal to 'private profit, public loss' (Saundry & Turnbull, 1997).

Taking into account the historic and structural factors behind the diversity of European ports and, not least, the lack of any direct correlation between the adopted organisational frameworks and commercial success, there is a wide consensus that an attempt to harmonise the organisation of ports at the European level lacks a logical base.

The European panorama of port organisation and management has changed radically over recent years. Many European countries, especially in the Mediterranean, have introduced laws concerning the reorganisation of ports. In particular, significant changes have taken place in the organisation and management of terminals, in the powers and responsibilities of port authorities, the monopoly powers of labour, their competitiveness targets, the structure of provided services, the role of state aids in their operation, etc. The changing role of ports has significant implications as far as the institutional level is concerned. It requires, on the one hand, the highest possible administrative flexibility in order to face the increasing competition and, on the other hand, the mobilisation of substantial private capital for the financing of infrastructure and superstructure to achieve the necessary technological adjustment for the provided port services.

Processes of institutional restructuring and privatisation are taking place indeed. In the majority of cases, however, a split of port activities and responsibilities among public and private sector organisations for most of the world's significant ports has been observed (Baird, 2001). Despite the variety objectives and methods used to effect privatisation, when several, or all, port activities have been privatised, public port authorities maintain administrative control over the port zone. This mutual interpenetration of the two processes necessitates the presentation of the established models of port management.

According to the above conceptions, two types of operative frameworks have been developed. The *comprehensive* port authority and the *landlord* port authority. Both types involve the existence of a public port authority, while their differences lie in the room for manoeuvring they allow to private companies. On the basis of the different categories of public port authorities (national, regional, or local), in many cases national governments have given the responsibility of port management to an administrative body, accountable to them but enjoying a high degree of autonomy. As presented in Figure 2.1, different practices exist and, as a result, the diversity of the European port system is remarkably wide.

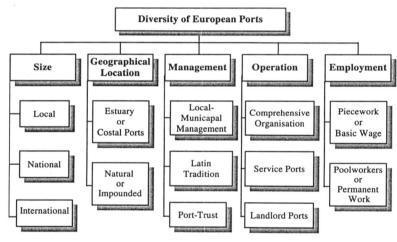

Source: Pallis (1997).

Figure 2.1 Diversity of European Ports

As regards port management practices, three different traditions are observed:

The first one is the tradition of the local or municipal management. This tradition is typical in North-western Europe (Scandinavia, Hamburg, Rotterdam, Antwerp). The ports located in North Europe, except of those situated in the UK and the Baltic countries (that were under the Soviet influence), follow the 'hanseatic' tradition, i.e. of municipal interest with the powerful managerial and economic presence of the local authorities. This is the case for all ports located in the area between Hamburg and Belgium, including the ports situated in Scandinavia.

The second one is the Latin tradition. This tradition involves a varying degree of intervention by central governments and is typical of the Mediterranean countries. In the Mediterranean countries, the responsible managerial body is the state, while in the north the most usually observed managerial body is the municipal or regional authority.

Thirdly, there is the tradition of the port trust. This tradition was observed mainly in Great Britain but tends to be abandoned as the implementation of a privatisation process progresses.

Furthermore, various traditions coexist as far as port operations are concerned. It is possible to distinguish ports according to the intensity of a port authority's participation in the provision of port services, infrastructure, and superstructure (Table 2.1).

Table 2.1 Major Characteristics of the Different Forms of Port Organisation: A Comparison

Organisational model	Functional	Service ports	Providing the tools	Landlord
Infrastructure	Yes	Yes	Yes	Yes (basic)
Superstructure	Yes	Yes	Yes	No
Provision of general services	Yes	Yes	No	Yes
Provision of public welfare services	Yes	Yes	No	Yes
Cargo handling onboard	No	Yes	No	No
Cargo handling at the docks	Yes	Yes	No	No

A first type is that of *comprehensive ports*. In these cases, the port authority owns and maintains the infrastructure and superstructure and, at the same time, provides the port services. These ports are also called 'functional' ports. There are cases of comprehensive ports that do not provide stevedoring; the authorities are responsibility for cargo handling only at the docks but not aboard the ship. Among the main reasons that a port undertakes cargo handling only at the docks is that this practice enables the port to operate as a unit that can guarantee the economic use of docks and warehousing and the maximum exploitation of docking positions. Thus, it is able to employ equipment and labour with flexibility 'where' and 'when' needed. The port restricts its responsibility and, consequently, it can be more concentrated in the effective development of its workforce.

A second type is that of *service ports*, which refers to cases where the port authority provides infrastructure while private companies provide superstructure and administer the provision of other port facilities. In this category one might include all ports that provide, apart from basic infrastructure, the 'tools', i.e. the equipment at the docks and all the facilities of the superstructure (sheds, buildings, warehouses, tanks, and equipment, such as cranes, quayside gantry cranes etc.). The port administration while not involved in cargo handling provides the necessary means for loading/unloading to private companies. Private companies are the providers of the largest part of port services in such cases. The view arguing that private enterprises and competition lead to the highest possible efficiency is among the main justifications why such port authorities do not undertake cargo handling. Moreover, having full responsibility for the cargo aboard the ship, the ship owner may hire or contract the loading/unloading to certain preferred stevedores.

The third type, *landlord ports,* refers to those cases where the responsibilities of port authorities are limited to the provision of land, basic infrastructure, and general and public welfare services. Basic infrastructure comprises navigational aids, the docks, docking positions, road infrastructure, and railways links to the port. The port authority is the 'owner' of the port and its property – which it leases, without, however, being involved in the entrepreneurial activities of its leaseholders (cf. ISL, 1990) – and is responsible for the future development of the port. This authority usually undertakes the initiative to develop an industrial zone, by leasing the relevant facilities to the interested parties, without again being involved in entrepreneurial activities. In other words, the port authority is responsible for the precise division between entrepreneurial activities and future development.

Apart from ports that correspond to one of the above categories, there are intermediate forms of port organisation, while European ports that have elements of all three categories can also be observed. The organisation of the port of Bremen, for example, lies between the categories of comprehensive and landlord port. The port of Rotterdam and the port of Antwerp approach the landlord model, while in France most ports approach the service port model.

European ports represent a dynamic economic industry. To the above-mentioned parameters which contribute to the diversity of the sector in question, the production factor 'labour' should be added, since it is possible to observe different forms of employment at the dock (Chapter 2.4, see also: Chlomoudis, 2001).

2.3　THE GEOGRAPHY OF EUROPEAN PORTS

The Role of the Geography in the Development of the Port Industry

The geography of the EU is particularly significant to the development of ports. Due to the characteristics of its coastline, no internal point is more than 350 kilometres away from the sea. There are areas of demographic concentration, and this is considered an essential element for the development of the neighbouring ports. The North Sea ports base their development on an area populated by 120 million people, while the ports in northern Italy and several ports located in the south of France are benefited by the development of the Arc of Alps (Switzerland and Austria) and the valley of the river Po.

The volume of the national traffic of goods depends significantly on the geography of each member state. In the case of a country where its territory contains islands of economic importance, or the maritime tradition is apparent, the use of maritime transport is encouraged. The member state exhibiting the highest volume of container traffic is the United Kingdom, since due to its geographical position all of its trade takes place via the sea. In the case of Greece, Italy, Spain, and Portugal the importance of coastwise transport is increased due to the need to provide transport services to the islands.

Socio-political events are capable of radically altering the geographical importance of some ports. The fall of the Berlin wall (in 1989) significantly increased the importance of trade between Eastern and Western Europe, parallel to the increase in trade between the North and South. Another example is the recent developments in the Balkans, especially in the countries of the former Yugoslavia, and their implications to the development of the ports in Eastern Italy and Western Greece. The restructuring and strengthening of the maritime transport system in the area are, at present, of crucial importance among the East–West routes, which connect the Balkan area with Europe. In this context, the role of ports is critical as essential links that permit the best utilisation of economic development opportunities through already dedicated corridors, and in some cases as poles of territorial and directional development (cf. Valleri, 2000).

The rapid development and widening of the transhipment process, in the sector of containerised cargo, significantly affects port geography. This process requires certain ports to assume the role of regional centres within a complex network of ports. A large port usually provides the necessary space and facilities to motherships, thus acting as the hub port of a network of satellite (spoke) ports that are connected to the central port via feeder ships. Furthermore, the more than doubling of the volume of this specific transport process, during the last two decades, has resulted in different growth rates and prospects for the container traffic sector. It creates favourable conditions for ports situated in certain regional areas (such as areas in the Atlantic and in the Mediterranean, Figure 2.2).

Apparently, geographical factors critically affect port competition. The role of European ports in the modern transport systems depends on their geographical position, especially their position in relation to the coast or other ports and their regional position (coastal and inland ports, estuary ports). Theoretically, due to the limitations imposed by the continuous increase in the size of vessels, container traffic seems to favour the coastal ports at the expense of estuary ports (Baird, 1996). In practice though, since they have carried out essential supplementary workings (such as dredging) estuarine ports are able and, in fact, do handle a large number of containers (e.g. Rotterdam, Antwerp). A further example is the difficulties associated with the transport of containers longer than 45 feet. The difficulty associated with road transport along the European corridors, and consequently their transportation to and from the intermediate and final links of the transport chain, favours estuarine ports rather than coastal ports.

Port Regions of Europe

Four port regions can be identified in the EU, on the basis of the traffic of goods and persons in the EU and to/from neighbouring countries, with distinct characteristics: (a) Baltic Sea, (b) North Sea, (c) the Atlantic and (d) the Mediterranean Sea.[1]

The first region refers to the Scandinavian ports and the ports of eastern Germany. The traffic of goods and persons is concentrated in the ports linking the Scandinavian countries to the EU and the Baltic in general.

The second region comprises the area between Hamburg and Le Havre, where the largest EU ports exist that can be regarded as the links of the EU to the rest of the world. It also includes the ports of eastern England where commercial traffic is directed to/from continental Europe and Scandinavia.

The third region includes the ports situated between Le Havre and Portugal and Spain, the ports of western England and Ireland, where commercial traffic is directed south to/from the Atlantic, France, North Spain and Portugal.

The fourth region includes the Mediterranean ports. In this case, the traffic of goods and persons is more complex. There is the traffic to/from mainland

Greece, to/from the Greek islands. There is the traffic to/from Italy and to/from the Black Sea. It also includes traffic to/from continental Europe to/from Africa, between Italy and southern France, and, finally, the Mediterranean islands to/from the Central Europe.

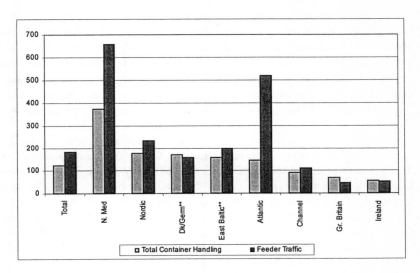

Notes
[a] Area Traffic (AT) refers to the number of containers handled in an area
(AT =Exports + Imports + Cabotage)
Channel: Channel France, Benelux.   *N. Mediterranean*: South Spain to Black Sea.
Nordic: Norway, Sweden, Finland.   *Atlantic*: Rest of Spain and France, Portugal.
Ireland: Irish Republic and N. Ireland
East Baltic: Estonia, Russia, Latvia, Poland, Lithuania.
[b] Whilst in 1996 data the former East Germany are part of the Denmark/Germany area, in 1986 they are part of East Baltic.

Sources: MDS Transmodal (1983, 1998)

Figure 2.2 Growth of European Short Sea Container Traffic 1982–1996

The ports of the *Baltic Sea* are going through a period of development – the result of the economic growth of a region where maritime links often provide the shortest distance between two points. The Baltic port system is made up of a large number of small and medium-sized ports. Its growth is likely to go hand-in-hand with improved intermodal connections.

North Sea ports handle approximately half of the EU maritime traffic, and about half of its transoceanic traffic. Nevertheless, the critical factor behind the success of these ports has been their closeness to the most developed industrial regions of Europe. Today, other things being equal, these ports probably owe their continuance and growth more to their acquired expertise, which in the future will lie mainly in the container sector. In all probability, the success of the ports in this region is also attributable to particular maritime traditions and can be observed in the form of more efficient port administration and activities.

The main problem for the ports in this region is the inland transport network, and more precisely its capacity to absorb traffic, rather than the absence or inadequacy of infrastructure: the remedy may be to boost the development of the existing road and rail infrastructure, but particularly that of the inland waterways. Some North Sea ports are also facing problems caused by tides, water depth – which is insufficient for large-tonnage vessels – and the width of the sea locks, which obstruct transport between sea and river.

The ports of the *Atlantic* have a large regional importance. They are closely associated with their hinterland, to which they are important as development poles of industrial activities. In many cases, however, their hinterlands extend no more than 200 kilometres from the coast, and, as a result, they have not developed the container sector but are used primarily for the transportation of bulk and liquid cargoes. The Atlantic ports suffer from the problem of not being linked to major land transport axes, particularly those running from east to west. This situation reduces their outlets and, as a result, limits their future development prospects.

The *Mediterranean* ports were, until a few years ago, lagging behind the ports of the other regions in the quantity and quality of their infrastructure, their tariffs, their administration, and their land links to the rest of Europe. In the second half of the 1990s, they have become more important and competitive, particularly in recent years when various national reforms have enabled them to abandon traditionally Mediterranean characteristics and take on a more 'Nordic' form. The growth of the ports in this region has taken place mainly in its western part, and in the container sector. The modernisation and improved efficiency of the Mediterranean ports has made them competitive with the North Sea ports for links between Europe and the Far East. A slow down of the economies of the Asian countries could also slow down the development of the Mediterranean ports.

Table 2.2, containing data on traffic for each of these regions, provides useful analytical tools for this purpose. The four regions differ greatly in their overall volume of traffic: the most important, the North Sea, accounts for 48.16% of the *total port traffic*, well ahead of the Mediterranean region in second place on 26.33%, while the other regions' shares are 10.6% (Baltic) and 14.9% (Atlantic). Trans-oceanic traffic is concentrated essentially in the North Sea and the Mediterranean (44.21% and 34.25% respectively), but the importance of this traffic to overall traffic in each of these regions is significantly different: 40.84% in the case of the Mediterranean and 29.65% in the case of the North Sea. This suggests that the Mediterranean is less integrated into intra-EU traffic, a view confirmed by the weak contribution made by the Mediterranean to inter-regional traffic, meaning long-distance intra-EU traffic: 14.9% of total inter-regional traffic and 22.1% of all Mediterranean traffic. The Atlantic region, by contrast, is highly integrated into intra-EU traffic, and the same can be said, allowing for its smaller scale, for the Baltic region: the 82.3% of its port traffic is directed to/from one of the other three European port regions.

Table 2.2 Goods Transport per Region (million tonnes)

Region	Trans-oceanic Traffic	Inter-regional Traffic	Intra-regional Traffic	Total
North Sea	359	494	355	1,209
Mediterranean Sea	270	146	245	661
Atlantic Region	136	219	19	374
Baltic Sea	47	121	98	266
Total	812	980	717	2,510

Source: CEU (1997a).

The commodities handled in all four regions range from bulk raw materials to all kinds of manufactured goods. An ESPO (2001) study of a representative sample of European ports suggests that 90% of them handle dry bulk traffic, 63% handle petroleum and petroleum products, 60% handle passenger traffic, whist the percentage of European ports handling containers is 57% and equals the percentage of ports handling roll-on/roll-off(ro/ro) traffic. Although all these ports exist to transfer goods and passengers, most of them also support marine-based industries.

2.4   INSTITUTIONAL AND ORGANISATIONAL FEATURES OF EUROPEAN PORTS[2]

Institutional Models

Various institutional models have been adopted by the Member States. These models are dynamic in the sense that they are subject to partial or total change. More specifically at the beginning of the 21st Century the following institutional models may be observed in the Member States:

In *Belgium,* the ports are municipally run, with the exception of the port of Bruges-Zeebrugge, administered by a private company with public participation under the supervision of the Flemish Community. In the municipal ports the bodies, which run the port, are the municipal authorities, and the Municipal Council elects a Port Director. The Port Director of Ostend, a port that is integrated into the civil administration, is appointed by royal decree.

In *Denmark,* there are four institutional types: municipal or autonomous ports, special statute ports, state ports and private ports; however, in all these forms the administration of the port is entrusted to a specific collegiate body chaired by the Mayor in some of the municipal ports, and by a Port Director on the administrative level.

In *Germany,* the majority of ports are not administered by bodies with legal personality: their territory, as well as the waters included within them, belongs to the Länder or other local authorities, whose services undertake the functions exercised elsewhere by the port authorities. As a result, importance attached to the various forms of organisation whereby these functions are carried out: there are ports in which they are undertaken by various departments of the authorities concerned, each with responsibility for some of the functions; in other ports a specific agency has been set up or administration has been entrusted to a private company; and there are also instances of private ports.

In *Greece,* ports have been classified into three categories: national, prefectorial and local, which local authorities may administer. The ports of Piraeus and Thessaloniki have been public corporations administered by a public port authority, whilst the other Greek ports have experienced different levels of autonomy subject to the control of the Prefectures. All Greek ports have been under the overall supervision of the Ministry for the Merchant Marine. This structure is currently under revision. This structure is currently under revision. Though the public sector retains the management and owes 75% of the shares, the Port of Thessaloniki is already listed in the Athens Stock Exchange, while the Port of Piraeus is soon to follow.

In *Spain,* the public interest ports are under the control of the state, while Regions control the others; in institutional terms the port authorities are public bodies that act autonomously, but for the public interest ports the public authority of *Puertos del Estado* [State Ports] performs functions integrating the individual ports into the national system.

In *France,* there are six autonomous ports and 11 non-autonomous ports of national interest; the former are legal persons with administrative and financial autonomy but subject to state control essentially as regards their financial administration; the non-autonomous ports are mainly those of national importance or those linked to naval bases, while others are under the control of local authorities.

In *Ireland,* the ports enjoy autonomy, although the law provides institutional links to the Ministry of the Marine; in general, they are answerable to the local planning bodies.

In *Italy*, the ports are directly administered by the state or by autonomous port authorities, or are of hybrid form in which state administration is flanked by companies which carry on various public interest activities.

In the *Netherlands,* most of the ports are administered by the towns, whereas others are privately run. The organisation of the municipal ports varies from town to town, but three models can be identified: direct administration by the municipal authority; the *Havenbedrijf,* a port authority separate from the municipal authority; and the *Havenschap,* in which a collegiate body representing the various levels of government administers the port, appointing a director for everyday administration.

In *Portugal,* the ports are state owned, with the exception of those in the Azores and Madeira, which are controlled by the appropriate autonomous regions; they may be administered by a port authority or by an 'autonomous council' in accordance with the provisions of the port statutes, which also regulate the functioning of the port.

In *Finland,* the ports are publicly or privately owned; the former are municipal in type and managed by a specific municipal institution, but each municipality has very extensive autonomy in the organisation of the port.

In *Sweden*, the ports are primarily managed by port undertakings, which are generally municipally owned, though private sector involvement is increasing; in many cases the infrastructure is owned by the municipality and the port undertaking runs it under an agreement. There are also ports managed directly by the municipalities.

In the *United Kingdom,* there are independent statutory ports (trust ports), municipal ports (generally small) and private ports; the internal organisation of the ports and their functioning are determined independently by statute.

Financial Resources of European Ports

As in any administration of economic activities, finance also plays an essential part in the development of ports. Competition between them has added importance not only to aspects of financial resources but also to their profitability and, hence, transparency of management.

The accounting rules applicable to ports, and especially to the compilation and publication of their balance sheets, depend on the legal form of the body administering the port and, in particular, will be those generally applicable to companies in all cases in which the managing authority is in the legal form of a company, irrespective of whether the shareholders are private or public.

In other cases, there is generally a budget compiled by the administrative body in accordance with the rules applicable to it and with budgetary autonomy; if the ports are an integral part of a municipality, the accounting principles that apply will determine whether or not they have budgetary autonomy. Absence of such autonomy has repercussions on management, both as regards approval of expenditure, which will depend on the municipal authority's procedures and may require approval by the political authorities even for sums which are insignificant in the management of a port, and as regards loans which, apart from structural loans whose purpose is indicated by the contract, form part of the municipality's general income. In any case, it seems more difficult to determine the profitability of the port.

If the port authority itself produces the budget, however, it is possible to determine its actual economic situation, and the port may be regarded as a genuine business undertaking, which has effects on its ability to negotiate loans with the banks. In such cases, a clear budgetary policy is also possible.

Regarding the variety of statutes by which the ports are governed, it is impossible to allocate all the ports within a single state to one particular type of accounting practice, though it can be said that specific profitability targets have been set in Spain alone; in other states, a profitability margin is calculated by the individual ports but not as a specific objective of the port, unless the latter is privately owned. With regard to loans, market conditions apply virtually everywhere, with a few exceptions or additions.

In *Ireland*, the ports may also have access to the Local Loans Fund, which grants loans for a period of up to 35 years, at a rate below bank rate.

In *Greece*, the sources of loans available to the ports are the Public Investment Programme, run by the Ministry for Public Works, and the Prefectorial Funds, which draw on the former source, both offering zero interest rates and advantageous repayment terms, together with the Deposits and Loans Fund, which provides loans at interest.

In *Italy*, the authorities can also obtain access to loans granted by special credit institutions for the medium- and long-term financing of public bodies at reduced rates.

In the *Netherlands*, the municipal ports can also obtain access to the *Algemeen Leningfonds,* reserved for local authorities, which charges rates determined on the basis of the weighted average for the year.

The constitution of the port also has an influence on tax matters. In general, ports, which are of public legal form, are not subject to income tax and in some cases enjoy exemptions from VAT. This is the situation with the non-private ports in Belgium, Denmark, Germany, Ireland, the Netherlands, Portugal and Finland, while in France they are subject to income tax only on income not deriving from port activities. In Spain and Italy, the ports, even if publicly owned, are subject to taxation.

The diversity of accounting rules examined here may have adverse effects on competition between ports, since a lack of budgetary transparency may conceal state aid, while the diversity of fiscal treatment and the possibility of access to special forms of credit are two forms of distortion, though the second is becoming less important as a result of the gradual reduction of interest rates in the states participating in monetary union.

As regards the sharing of the costs involved in sea access and access to the port infrastructures and superstructures, a general distinction can be made between state (or Federal) responsibility for structures located outside the port area as such, and the responsibility of the port, or other levels of government, within it. Nevertheless, there are many exceptions: the port authorities and regional or municipal authorities are involved in the access arrangements where the port has greater autonomy, and conversely there are cases in which the state intervenes in connection with the internal structures. Private intervention is exclusively confined to the internal aspects, where it exists at all. It could be said that the spreading of the financial load is based on two overlapping criteria: the criterion of location of the structure concerned and the institutional criterion – in other words, the status of the port. In some cases, this overlap results in responsibility for the financial burdens being shared between the various responsible bodies. State by state, the framework is as follows:

In *Belgium*, the state is responsible for decisions and investments relating to the infrastructures and shipping support equipment outside the port, including port access facilities, but the use of the latter is the responsibility of the municipal authorities or the port authority. They are also responsible for investment inside the ports, but with regional participation that may be as high as 60–80%. Private participation in the superstructure appears to be increasing.

In *Denmark*, the port authority is responsible for the infrastructure, the port access and port equipment, subject to state approval as far as the outer harbour walls are concerned, but the private sector is responsible for the costs of some infrastructures, especially those of the specialised terminals.

In *Germany*, the Federal Government bears the cost of sea access, while the infrastructures within the port are the responsibility of the Länder or municipalities; as for the superstructure, this is generally the preserve of private enterprise.

In *Greece*, the state has general responsibility for the construction of infrastructure both inside and outside the ports, while the prefectures have general responsibility for maintenance and the port authorities for administration. However, the port authority is responsible for the superstructure.

In Spain, the port authority bears the cost of the infrastructure and superstructures inside the port, and outside it as regards access and the coast within its zone of responsibility. The private sector finances certain infrastructure facilities whose use is more directly commercial, such as silos, warehouses, etc.

As far as *France* is concerned, a distinction has to be made between the *autonomous ports* and the *non-autonomous ports*. In the former case, investment connected with sea access is shared between the state and the port authority, 80% and 20% respectively, but maintenance is entirely borne by the state as regards the locks, access channels, outer harbours and outer walls; lighthouses and buoys are the exclusive responsibility of the state if located outside the port, while in the case of expenditure on infrastructure within the port state participation is 60% for warehouses, wharves and certain specialised terminals, whereas the port authority or private enterprise pays for the superstructures. Still in France (non-autonomous ports), the state's burden is reduced for infrastructures providing access to the non-autonomous ports; its participation is in the region of 30–50%, while the remainder is borne by the Chamber of Commerce. The state also participates up to 30% in the internal infrastructures, and, as far as the remainder is concerned, private enterprise provides support for the Chambers of Commerce, which are also responsible for the superstructures.

In *Ireland,* the port authorities are entirely responsible for sea access, the internal infrastructure and the superstructures, making additional use of EU funds; private enterprise provides the equipment, excluding cranes in some cases.

In *Italy,* sea access and the major infrastructures, including those within the port, are the responsibility of the state, the regions or the port authority, depending on the classification of the port. The body that was responsible for providing them normally maintains them as well; private enterprise may build infrastructures in the areas conceded to it, but it is generally confined to the superstructures. The situation is currently being restructured as a result of the 1994 reforms.

In the *Netherlands,* the distribution of investment and expenditure between state and port authority follows the line dividing sea access from port infrastructures, while the superstructures are generally privately owned. Specific agreements with Belgium divide the costs of the access channels when these are of value to both countries.

In *Portugal,* the state intervenes financially in works and expenditure connected with sea access and the port infrastructures if the resources of the port authorities are not sufficient and the use of credit is impracticable, while the port authorities are entirely responsible for the superstructures. The private sector contributes to certain specialised terminals.

In *Finland,* the port authorities are fully responsible for sea access and the internal infrastructure, with the sole exception of the access channels within territorial waters. The private sector is involved in some port infrastructures and equipment.

In *Sweden* and the *United Kingdom,* the port authorities are entirely responsible for sea access and the internal infrastructures.

From the standpoint of income, the way in which it is determined and collected matches quite closely the varying levels of autonomy between ports in the north and south of the EU. The greatest autonomy here exists in Sweden, where the state has relinquished any form of control over the finances of the ports in favour – as far as the setting of fees is concerned – of the local authorities. The lowest degree of financial autonomy is probably to be found in the Italian ports, where the port dues are set and collected by the state and then passed on, in whole or in part, to the port authority. Financial independence, where it exists, is generally governed by rules designed to ensure that the ports break even, at least as far as administration is concerned if not in terms of investment.

Fiscal matters and the determination of the tax base are more consistent: in almost all cases tax is levied on access to and time spent in the port, irrespective of the use of the infrastructure and services. While use of the infrastructure is still generally the subject of a charge, the other services are tending to become commercial and are sold on the basis of price lists.

In *Belgium,* the main revenue is from port dues, calculated as a function of tonnage on the basis of the international standards of tonnage measurement, payment of which allows ships to moor, make use of any locks and undertake commercial operations for one month; in addition to these dues, a further charge is made for specific services or for the use of land areas within the port.

In *Denmark,* the port dues are imposed on the basis of tonnage (ship dues) and cargo (cargo dues).

In *Germany,* the port dues are calculated on the basis not only of tonnage but also of the geographical area visited during the voyage, the type of cargo and the duration of stay. In the majority of German ports, the weight of the cargo handled is also taken into account. Other dues or revenue of various kinds include fees for pilotage and the use of the port's berthing structures.

In *Greece,* the port dues are fixed at the national level. Dues for entering the port, mooring and berthing are paid to the Port Fund, while the costs of laying up vessels form part of the general state revenue.

In *Spain,* there is a system of port tariffs, laid down by the state and forming part of an overall scheme for financing the port system, which provides income both for the ports and for a national fund that helps to finance them. The principle underlying the setting of the tariffs, which may be varied by the individual port authorities, is that the port should be financially self-sufficient.

In *France*, the port dues are laid down by law, are set, except for passenger dues, by the government, and are paid to the port authority or to the local financing bodies. They are charged: on ships entering and leaving port on the basis of their gross tonnage; on berthing on the basis of their tonnage and length; on cargo handled within the port on the basis of weight or number of units, depending on the type of goods; and on passengers embarked, disembarked and carried in transit.

In *Ireland,* the port dues are set and collected by the port authority on the basis of the gross tonnage of the ships concerned and the cargo handled within the port.

In *Italy,* the port dues are widely diversified, and are charged on berthing, based on tonnage, with a surcharge for deck cargo and other charges or surcharges levied only in certain ports on loading and unloading and on passengers. These are collected directly by the tax authorities and then paid, in whole or in part, to the port authority.

In the *Netherlands,* the port *dues* in sea ports are payable only by ships entering from or leaving for the open sea, as a function of gross tonnage, cargo loaded and/or unloaded and, in some ports, passengers. These dues and the *wharf and area dues* are determined, depending on the statutes of the port, by the municipal authority of the town, the port authority or – in the case of privately owned ports, wharves and areas – by the company which administered them. Wharf and area dues are calculated in accordance with infrastructure use based on various parameters. Fees *for pilotage,* a completely privatised service, are paid to the company which provides it, and depend on draught.

In *Portugal*, the harbour charges and dues, set and collected by the port authorities, are charged on entry and berthing and based on gross tonnage and length of stay, while the cost of tying up to a wharf is calculated in accordance with the same parameters plus the length of the vessel. Port dues, however, are charged on cargo handled within the port.

In *Finland,* port dues and taxes are decided upon by the port authority or local government and are calculated on the basis of cargo handled, apart from a charge for waste disposal. Other dues or tariffs relate to the actual use of the infrastructure or services. As a result of sweeping liberalisation decided on in 1981, the local authorities at their discretion set port dues in Sweden, and it is therefore impossible to produce a sufficiently specific overall summary covering the various port situations.

In the *United Kingdom,* the 1964 Act provides for a number of port dues based on use of the infrastructures and port services, which in the majority of cases are determined and collected by the port authority.

Port Activities

These are highly diverse, and may be divided into two broad categories: services to ships and services to cargo. The former may be further subdivided into those relating to ship handling (pilotage, towage, and mooring) and those provided to vessels after they have docked (emptying of bilges, revictualling, cleaning, etc.).

In the comprehensive authorities, these form part of the port administration and cannot therefore be identified as a separate area from the institutional aspects, but the situation is different in the landlord model, which now covers virtually the whole of the Union. Seen in this light, the type of market established activities within the port and the relations between the undertakings responsible for the activities and the port authority are becoming particularly important. The resulting framework is as follows.

Belgium: the situation varies from port to port; in general, the state provides the pilotage service at sea and in the estuaries, while other services relating to ship handling are provided – with significant exceptions involving the private sector – by the municipalities or port authorities. However, private companies administer the provision of services to moored ships. Also privatised, with some exceptions, are cargo-related activities.

Denmark: port activities relating to ship handling (including ice-breaking) are generally state-controlled, with certain exceptions relating in particular to towage, which is undertaken by private enterprises in virtually all ports; other activities, too, are undertaken by private enterprises.

Germany: port activities are generally undertaken by private enterprises, or by pilots' associations for that particular activity, which is provided under public, federal or regional control, depending on the port concerned.

Greece: pilotage is provided by the Pilotage Service, which comes under the Ministry for the Merchant Marine, except in certain minor ports where it is handled by private companies under the supervision of the port authority. Private bodies, not necessarily enterprises, are responsible for towage, while moorage is the responsibility of the port authority. Services to moored ships are provided by private enterprises, while those relating to cargo are undertaken by cargo-handling associations that use the equipment of the ships themselves and of the port.

Spain: port activities relating to ship handling are the responsibility of the port authorities, which normally put moorage services out to tender by enterprises and co-operatives; other activities are privatised.

France: pilotage is provided by pilotage stations which employ pilots hired as a result of public competition, and are subject to government control. Other port activities are handled by the private sector.

Ireland: services relating to the handling of ships are provided by the port authorities, which in the major ports assume the capacity of district pilotage authorities for the purposes of the application of the relevant law. The other activities are in the hands of private enterprise.

Italy: pilotage is the responsibility of pilots' associations, whose legal form (publicly or privately owned) is uncertain, though their activities come within the sphere of the Maritime Director and the rules and charges for the service are approved by the Minister of Transport. Towage is provided by private undertakings, which operate under franchises awarded by the port authorities that lay down their obligations. Moorage is supervised by the harbourmaster, except in a few ports where it is the responsibility of the port authority. Activities relating to moored vessels, some of which are subject to licences, are handled by private undertakings; those relating to cargo are the responsibility of the carrier, who uses his own resources or employs private companies, including the dockworkers associations.

Netherlands: pilotage is the responsibility of pilots' associations which are private in form and are established in each of the four maritime regions of the Netherlands. The remaining port activities are carried out by private enterprises, though in the case of moorage a distinction has to be made between berths in common use, which are administered by the port authorities, and those in zones allocated to a single user, which are administered by that user.

Portugal: pilotage is the responsibility of the National Pilotage Institute, a public body under the supervision of the Ministry of the Marine. The port authority or private enterprises, depending on the specific case, undertake other activities concerned with the handling of ships, while the remaining activities are generally undertaken by private enterprises.

Finland: pilotage is generally under state control, though some port authorities are responsible for pilotage within the port; other activities connected with the handling of ships are primarily undertaken by the port authority, the private sector being involved in towage in some ports. Other activities are privately run.

Sweden: the situation varies greatly from port to port. As a general rule, public authorities provide pilotage while other handling activities are generally publicly owned, the private sector being represented especially in towage. Activities connected with moored vessels are mainly private, while a hybrid situation exists in cargo-related activities.

United Kingdom: pilotage is the responsibility of the harbourmaster, which in general means the port authority, and is provided by pilots who may be either employees of the authority or freelances, though in either case they must hold a licence. Other port activities are undertaken by specialist private companies other than those that administer the ports, with the exception of towage within the port, which in some cases is undertaken by the port enterprise or by joint ventures between the latter and a specialist enterprise.

The situation, in general terms, is that pilotage has remained within the public sector or, when it is in the private sector (generally in the form of an association), it is nevertheless run as a monopoly. The other ship-handling activities are characterised by a strong presence (or even predominance) of port authorities, while the private sector is strongly represented in the provision of services to moored ships and cargo services. It should be noted, however, that many activities carried on by private enterprises are subject to more or less strict supervision by the port authority or public bodies.

Dock Working

This section refers to manual workers in port activities (generally described by the English word 'dockers'), whereas other workers employed within a port enjoy the legal status provided within each state for employees of the public authority that administers the port, or a contractual system based on the rules governing private labour in other cases.

Although this is not, from the strictly systematic point of view, an institutional aspect, the organisation of labour in the specific sector of ports has diverged from the form taken in other sectors and has acquired features which link it closely to the institutional model of the port. This situation is particularly apparent in the comprehensive authorities, which hold a monopoly on the provision of services to users and on the dock workforce, as a result of which the workforce is totally integrated into the structure of the authority. Even in institutional models of the landlord type, however, the negotiating power of the dockers had given rise to forms of trade monopoly that are unknown in virtually any other sector of production. The situation in the various countries is as follows.

Belgium: dock labour is restricted to qualified dockers, and an appropriate committee of workers and employers deals, by law, with issues arising in this area. The dockers are hired by the port undertakings by the day and work under a special unemployment benefit system, which is financed separately in each port.

Denmark: in the port of Copenhagen, the dockers have an open-ended contractual scheme; in other ports, working conditions are governed by a collective agreement concluded for each port separately. The dockers form a pool, and are required to report at a predetermined time to be hired by the day, a system for which no priority criteria are laid down; provision is made, however, for a docker who has been taken on to be transferred to another task once his original one has been completed, without going through the reporting procedure. The dockers are paid on a piecework basis and covered by an unemployment insurance scheme.

Germany: the dockers work under the normal contractual system laid down for the private sector, with the single special feature that the employers, in each port, have created and financed a pool *(Gesamthafenbetrieb)* which supplies additional or temporary labour and is subject to the same contractual arrangement as that which applies generally. The port undertakings have the option of taking on temporary personnel from those registered as unemployed at the job centre administered by the Federal Government.

Greece: apart from the ports of Piraeus and Thessaloniki, in which the dockers are employees of the respective port authorities, they are either on open-ended contracts or employed as temporary workers; the former are hired at the number laid down for the port concerned, and the latter are taken on temporarily as the need arises. A committee answerable to the Ministry of Labour is responsible for regulating work within the port, defining the number of dockers for each port, keeping nominal rolls, providing subsidies for unemployment and determining the charges for handling services.

Spain: the workers are employed by the private handling enterprises, and a company – in which the port authority generally owns a 51% holding while the handling enterprises own the remainder – administers a pool in each port which covers peak working periods; the pool workers are paid by the day.

France: under the rules of the Navigation Code, dock workers are covered by a national collective agreement and, in some ports, local agreements. They can be hired by the month by the handling enterprises or as casual labour, the latter being chosen from among those who have registered at the local employment office or, in some ports, have been organised as a pool; casual workers benefit from a special scheme which covers them for a maximum of 150 days' unemployment.

Ireland: the dockers are covered by a national collective agreement. Those in the port of Dublin are full-time employees of the handling enterprises, but in the other ports, except Limerick, they are hired on a casual basis, generally by the day.

Italy: the dockers are covered by a national collective agreement and their duties are reserved to those registered with the dockers' associations, and supervised by the port authority. The associations act as employers, providing the necessary labour to the handling enterprises; however, an exception applies to the employees of bodies and enterprises which operate within the port on the basis of an administrative licence.

Netherlands: the dockers are covered by a national collective agreement and most of them are full-time employees of the handling enterprises. In the ports of Rotterdam and Amsterdam, however, a number of dockers are employed by a dock employment agency, which allocates them by the day to the handling companies, on request, although their relationship with the agency is an open-ended one. It should be noted that workers who undertake the same tasks in terminals administered directly by an enterprise on its own account are covered by the collective agreement for the sector within which that enterprise operates.

Portugal: the dockers are covered by a national collective agreement and are employed by the handling enterprises or by special enterprises that, on a competitive basis, supply labour to the handling enterprises. An appropriate national body oversees dock labour and, in particular, runs the lists from which workers can be hired and grants the licences to the agencies that supply the labour.

In Finland dockers are employees of private companies and covered by the general system for employed workers. In *Sweden* dockers are covered by a national collective agreement.

Finally, in the *United Kingdom,* since 1989, when the special system for dockers was abolished, they have been covered by the general employment legislation.

Within this general picture, three different types of scheme can be identified. The first is the general arrangement covering work in any sector of production (Finland, Sweden, the United Kingdom and, in essence, Ireland). The second combines the general scheme with dock pools, run in various ways so as to be able to meet peak labour demands and, to a more or less explicit degree, to compensate for unemployment in the sector (Germany, Spain, France, the Netherlands, Portugal and, with certain special features, Denmark). The third type is characterized by variable degrees of regulatory intervention by government, which regulates work (Greece), reserves it to particular associations (Italy) or encourages co-operation between the parties (Belgium).

NOTES

1. A categorisation according to the plan on the Trans-European Transport Network, Section: Sea Ports (CEU, 1997a).
2. This section is based on the review of the European Port Industry presented in: European Parliament (1999).

3. European Ports in the Common Transport Policy Framework: Inexorable Integration

3.1 PORTS AND THE COMMON TRANSPORT POLICY IN A HISTORICAL PERSPECTIVE

During the historic course of European integration, and within the evolutionary framework of the Common Transport Policy (CTP), the progress towards an explicit European Union policy concerning the port sector can be distinguished into three periods, each exhibiting distinct features. The first period lasted from 1957 to 1973 and was characterised by *the exclusion of the transport sector from the framework of CTP*. The second period, which was characterised by *a policy of 'non-intervention' in the port sector*, lasted from 1974 to 1990. The third period, beginning in 1991 and lasting to the present day, is characterised by the resumption of initiatives and the formation of proposals within a steady course *towards a European Port Policy*. Table 3.1 illustrates the keystones of this process, all of them to be discussed in the forthcoming sections.

It is important to point out that the precise moment that determines the introduction of a new EU approach, and the simultaneous conclusion of a previous one is not usually apparent. The formation and progress of any EU policy is a result of a structured and complex sequence of events. As is the case for every process of policy development (Kingdon, 1984), it consists of several intertwined phases, including the stages of problem identification, the formulation of draft proposals, the adoption of official decisions, and the implementation of those decisions.

Hence, the distinctive moment of a new EU strategy may be determined either by the 'discourse' of a policy approach, i.e. the intellectual developments that the Commission initiatives and policy proposals put forward, or by the 'policy output', i.e. the legislative and political decisions that the Council of Ministers adopts.

Nonetheless, the selection of the 'policy discourse' as the indisputable point in time of the introduction of a new EU approach is not free of ambiguities. A specific policy output might influence the future approach of the Commission. On many occasions the conceptual innovations, informal discussions, and proposals necessary for actions are evident before the formal expression of the EU Institutions' new policy thinking. For instance, the Treaties and the successive enlargements of the EU, both 'policy outputs', have been identified as influential agenda setters affecting all EU policies (including the CTP).

Table 3.1 Towards a European Port Policy: Main Policy Developments

PERIOD	YEAR	DEVELOPMENT
1st Period	1957	Signing of the Rome Treaty (introduction of the CTP)
	1970	The first EU document with reference to the port sector (policy of non-intervention)
2nd Period	1974	Expansion of the CTP base to include maritime (and air) transport
	1979	Adoption of the 'Brussels Package'
	1983	EP takes the inaction of the Council to the ECJ
	1985	Commission Memorandum: The first proposals towards a Common Maritime Transport Policy (thoughts on the revision of the non-intervention policy in the port sector)
	1987	The Single European Act comes into force
3rd Period	1991	Introduction of the Horizontal approach
		Signing of the Maastricht Treaty of the European Union (Policy for the development of intermodal transport – TEN-T)
	1992	White Paper on the future of the CTP
		Green Paper on the impact of transport to the environment
	1993	Publication of the document concerning the common policy on safe seas
	1995	Publication of a policy document on short-sea shipping (first signs of a European Port Policy)
	1996	The two parallel strategy documents
	1997	The Treaty of Amsterdam
		Green Paper on Sea Ports and Maritime Infrastructure (Revision of the 'non-intervention' policy)
		Signing of the Amsterdam Treaty
	1998	Strategy documents integrate the CTP in the EU sustainable development and cohesion policies
	1999	New proposals by the EP towards a European Port Policy
	2000	The European ports become part of TEN-T (Common position of the Council)
	2001	Publication of the 'Port Package'
		White Paper on a European Transport Policy for 2010

It would be misleading, however, to determine *a priori* the moment they began to affect, at least intellectually, the nature of the ensuing EU policies. Specific proposals regarding the improvement of maritime infrastructure can be traced back to 1997 but as explained in other parts of this volume, earlier documents can be considered as predecessors of those proposals. On that account, although a ECJ ruling on the application of the rules of the Rome Treaty regarding maritime transport (1974) is commonly considered as the point that marked the beginning of the CMTP, this point could also be traced to a year earlier, when the first enlargement of the EU took place.

Since there usually is a time lag between the reaching of any political agreement and the moment that this agreement is implemented (for example the Treaty on European Union, which incorporates policies for the creation-development of the TEN-T and of combined transport, was announced in 1979, signed in December 1991, and ratified in November 1993), only the beginning of the legal influence of a policy decision can be precisely traced. Preferences ultimately depend on the conceptualisation of the policy-making process. For analytical reasons, and taking into account the existing practice, in this book the starting point of a policy is regarded the point of 'policy discourse' by the EU institutions (i.e. for the TEN-T starting point is considered the year 1979), without disregarding the importance of preceding or ensuing decisions.

3.2   1957–1973: THE ABSENCE OF MARITIME TRANSPORT FROM THE CTP

Article 3 of the Treaty establishing the European Community (Treaty of Rome, 1957) states that the Common Transport Policy is one field requiring action by the European Community. The aim of the founding countries of the EU (Belgium, France, West Germany, Italy, Luxemburg, the Netherlands) to emphasise the transport sector should not be surprising: the free movement of goods and persons was, along with the free movement of capital, the *raison d'être* of the Common Market. The first attempts for the formation of a supranational transport policy took place in the institutional framework of the European Coal and Steel Community (ECSC).[1]

A special chapter of the Treaty (Articles 74–85) officially recognised transport as an area in which action ought to be taken and provided the broad lines of what this policy ought to be. However, the transport injunctions of the Treaty were remarkably general and limited in scope (Bayliss, 1979). Article 3 did not have any direct reference to transport modes but Article 84(1) stated, 'the provisions of this Title shall apply to transport by rail, road, and inland waterways'. Maritime transport was mentioned only in Article 84(2) which provided that '[T]he Council may, acting unanimously, decide whether, to what extent, and by what procedure, appropriate provisions may be laid down for sea and air transport'. The interpretation of the latter paragraph led to the conclusion that maritime (and air) transport fell outside the scope of the CTP, as well as outside of other provisions of the Treaty such as competition.[2]

The first period of the CTP was characterised by 'disappointing performance' (Despicht, 1969; Button, 1984), and 'output failure' because 'the system was unable to translate a general commitment to participate in a collective decision-making effort into an acceptable set of policies of rules' (Lindberg & Scheingold, 1970, p. 165). The existence of different regulatory regimes in the national markets discouraged any policy progress (Gwilliam, 1990; Button, 1993). Lindberg & Scheingold (1970) argued that by trying to introduce far-reaching proposals the Commission found little support by the different national governments, since some of them (i.e. Germany) were advocating the 'social service philosophy' and others were endorsing the 'commercial philosophy' (i.e. the Netherlands). That situation led to the critical absence of any hegemonic attempt towards concrete policy developments. Other studies question, however, whether any category of policy actors, including the EU institutions, really perceived a CTP to be in their vital interests. Abbati (1986) and Vickerman (1992) suggest that the CTP was a component of the Treaty due to a commitment to a gradualist 'sectoral' approach of integration and not because the founding members were conscious that such a policy was an essential precondition of the common market.[3] According to Swann (1988) the introduction of a CTP was the result of a delicate political compromise between the Netherlands, which had significant interests in the Rhine transport, and the five other states.

The latter may explain why the founders of the EU, while having gained some experience in the area of international road haulage policy in the context of the ECSC, decided to include inland waterways in the provisions of the Treaty but opted not to include neither maritime nor air transport. Given the major difficulties that had already arisen, during attempts to reach a compromise formula for inland transport, it seemed preferable, at that point, to exclude these two modes from the *lex specialis* of the Treaty. The functioning of the EU and the shortcomings of the decision-making process, at that time, significantly affected any progress towards a common transport policy. More specifically, Erdmenger (1983) propounds that the 'strongly legalistic even dogmatic in nature' work in the field of transport during these early days could be interpreted as a result of a 'certain institutional dogmatism'. Decisions had to be taken according to the legal provisions in the framework of the Treaty and in no other way.

It is worthwhile to mention that the first, even if extremely premature, interest for the resolution of problems regarding European ports at a supranational level was demonstrated during the early 1970s. The first initiatives were the Commission's *Note on Port Options on a Community*

Basis, in 1970, and a report to the European Parliament, entitled *Report on Port Policy within the Framework of the European Community,* in 1972.[4]

3.3   1974–1990: THE 'NON-INTERVENTION' POLICY

The first EU enlargement in 1973 had an enormous impact on the content of the CTP. It increased the relative importance of sea transport and the new EU of nine Member States became more active in this sector. Issues regarding the maritime transportation of persons and goods began to be discussed, at the European level, as being an integral part of the CTP. The accession of three maritime nations (Denmark, Ireland, and the UK) remarkably changed the economic structure of European integration. Among others, it substantially increased the relative importance of the maritime mode. The bulk of the trade between the three new members and the rest of the EU was carried by sea. Maritime flows represented 25% of the intra-EU trade of nine members compared to 8% in the EU of six. The size of the EU-flagged fleet almost doubled, and the number of ports within the EU increased as well. The second enlargement (accession of Greece, 1981) and the third (accession of Spain and Portugal, 1986) furthered the importance of maritime transport to the EU economy.

A major policy reform was the extension of the EU interest to include the maritime mode within the common transport strategy. In 1974, the Commission took a test case to the ECJ attempting to resolve whether the provisions of the Treaty were applicable to the maritime mode.[5] The ECJ confirmed the EU policy-making authority. This was a ruling with significant legal and political implications: it incorporated this mode in the process of European integration, hence, it is considered as the most important ECJ case in the field of maritime transport (cf. Bredima-Savopoulou, 1990; Power, 1992).

Subsequently, the focus turned to whether the EU could help to bring about solutions to specific sectoral problems. Following a European Commission initiative in 1974, the Community Port Working Group was formed consisting of representatives of EU ports. That Working Group studied the institutional framework and the management characteristics of European ports in an attempt to identify potential actions that would improve the competitiveness of the port industry.[6] In 1975 the French government presented a memorandum on the development of EU action on shipping and in 1976 an interim EP report emphasised the need for further EU coordination and action in the field of shipping and maritime transport. After the previously mentioned ECJ ruling all EU institutions embarked on discussions on the prospects of a common policy regarding *all* transport modes. According to the then Commissioner whose portfolio included transport: '...the Community is working on the emerging problems in respect of which it seems profitable to examine whether the Community might be able to act more effectively than Member States individually; or indeed supplement Member States activity.' (Burke, 1978, p.13).

Until the end of the 1980s, a *policy of non-intervention* in port production and industry was followed: European ports were not being considered in the framework of the CTP. The European Commission accepted and adopted the view of the Community Port Working Group on ports that there were no sufficient reasons justifying the introduction and development of a specific policy regarding ports. At the same time, the Commission acknowledged the existence of issues that ought to interest the EU since ports comprised a vital link between maritime and inland transport modes. For that reason the Commission adopted the view that issues regarding ports ought to be taken into account when issues regarding maritime and inland transport were being examined. Consequently, the Commission proposed the examination of whether and to what extent national and European policies on charging and state aid were affecting port competition.

In a paper entitled *Progress towards a Common Transport Policy: Maritime Transport,* the Commission reviewed its work on ports up to 1985 in the following terms. Point 102 of that document stated:

> the Commission's services worked closely with representatives of the major port authorities of the EU in the production of two reports. The first of these set out the major differences in practice as regards the financing of infrastructure, superstructure and operations both between the ports of the various Member States and often between the ports of a single country. The second attempted to determine whether these differences led to serious distortions to competition. (CEU, 1985, paragraph 102)[7]

The reason behind the inertia regarding the promotion of measures or the initiation of actions in the specific sector seemed to be the fact that the majority of experts did not consider that the then existing differences required a specific Community port policy. Nonetheless the Commission argued that there existed various aspects of port policy for which Community action would be useful. According to the Commission's Memorandum, since Community ports constituted vital links in the transport chain between maritime and inland transport, it was considered necessary that issues of port policy be taken into account in the framework of the development of inland and maritime aspects of the CTP. Further, the Commission deemed it necessary to take into account the suggestions of the EP whose arguments were stressing the fact that issues regarding ports ought to be seriously considered. The Commission in order to define the possible fields of work at the EU level decided to explore two issues:

- The influence of national and EU transport policies on conditions of competition between the ports of Member States.
- The influence of charging policies and provision of state funds to ports on competition between the ports of the Member States.

With respect to the effect of national and EU transport policies on conditions of competition between the ports of the Member States the Commission recognised that the market structure of inland transport modes had a significant impact on the competition between the EU seaports. Evidently, it is not the only determining factor of the competitive strength of a port and of a customer's decision to use the services of a particular port rather than the ones offered by a competing port. The attractiveness of a port is unquestionably enhanced the more versatile the services it can provide in the way of transport links with the hinterland and the more flexible the rates charged.

The Commission also recognised that, at the same time, most of the EU's heartland could be regarded – particularly due to the constant improvements of the technical and organisational efficiency of inland transport modes – as a collection of geographical areas each of which could be served by several ports. Port competition to serve these areas could function optimally only if each of these markets was regulated along much the same principles, i.e. if ports and their customers were offered comparable terms from the point of view of quantity and quality in comparable circumstances.

Consequently, it was deemed necessary to resolve problems such as the competition between the German ports and the ports located in the area defined by the three ports: Amsterdam, Rotterdam, and Antwerp. Inland transport in Germany was, to a large extent, subjected to a system of regulated competition involving, in particular, a relatively rigid set of compulsory tariffs for road haulage and inland waterway transport, a rigid capacity limitation on commercial road haulers and all the intervention by public authorities that this entails. By contrast, inland transport to and from the area defined by the ports of Amsterdam, Rotterdam, and Antwerp was predominantly international in nature and enjoyed complete freedom of commercial activity in Rhine shipping and a freer regime, in respect of access and tariffs, in the road haulage market. There was evidence of similar discrepancies in other transport markets making up the hinterland of several seaports with overlapping catchment areas, for instance competition between North Sea and Adriatic ports. The rivalry between these ports led to a situation in Italy where goods that were being carried to and from Trieste were no longer subject to quotas and road hauliers were not obliged to obtain authorisation. The fact that the problem was affecting competition between all EU ports (i.e. those of the North Sea, of the Atlantic, and of the Mediterranean, but also competition between individual ports in each of those port regions) led the Commission to stress the importance of finding an appropriate solution to the issue, an assessment similar to the one previously expressed by the European Parliament.

A problem that came up was associated with the great difficulty of determining the effects of the various distortions on competition, since there was a multitude of factors influencing the volume of traffic at a particular port over long periods of time. Furthermore the various statistical figures could not be advanced to prove what the actual effects on competition were. Nonetheless, as a general principle, it was considered that a port with access to a variety of freely competing inland transport modes charging market rates could, *ceteris paribus*, have a competitive edge over rivals whose hinterland communications were regulated by state or quasi-public cartels governing market access and prices.

In the Commission's view, no satisfactory regulatory method could be applied to harmonise the conditions of competition in such different routes facing a considerably widespread set of conditions. The only genuine harmonisation possible would be that brought about by the free operation of the market. It was thought to be conceivable and practicable to abolish all restrictions on access, notably in the area of quota-fixing, and to abolish fixed tariffs in respect of the carriage of exports and imports to and from all EU ports, whether on international or on national routes. This so-called 'corridor approach' did not seem to pose any insurmountable technical problems and the system could also be monitored.

A solution of that nature was expected to stand the test of achieving fair competition between seaports. It was also stressed that such an approach was not designed to iron out any natural advantages or disadvantages in the competitive positions of the various seaports: according to the provisions of the Treaty of Rome the aim was to discard all artificial distortions stemming from discrepancies in market regulations and out-of-date measures. With this end in view the Commission initiated consultations and presented a proposal to the Council.

With respect to the second issue (i.e. how the various charging policies and the provision of state funds to ports were affecting competition between the ports of the Member States), the Commission did not deem it useful nor necessary, at the time, to embark on the complex task of harmonising the charging policies of the EU ports, despite the significant variation in those policies. The Commission based its decision on the work undertaken by the Port Working Group. In 1980, its final report revealed that about 5% of the total transport costs were attributable to port charges (however, that relationship varied for certain types of ships such as specialised offshore vessels, passenger cruise ships or ships calling to load or discharge part cargoes to take on bunkers or for repair). In addition, port charges did not seem to constitute the major determining factor in the selection of a port by a ship.

Finally, as regards national aids to ports, the Commission chose not to attempt to draw up guidelines for the application of the Treaty to the case of state aids to ports, but to deal with specific aids, if required, directly on the basis of Articles 92 and 93 of the Treaty. Yet another time, the conclusion of the Port Working Group that national aids to ports were not causing serious distortions in competition was adopted. Nonetheless the Commission decided in the future to review the general situation from time to time and study further the different port aid systems existing in Member States. Other aids, such as regional aids and aids to facilitate the development of certain economic activities, which could also have a bearing on competition between ports, would be taken into account particularly in the Commission's considerations regarding their compatibility with the common market.

This work of the Commission in the area of ports culminated in 1981 in the submission of a report to the European Parliament on its work towards a EU Port Policy. The EP endorsed the so-called 'Carossino Report' on 'the role of ports in the Common Transport Policy', on 11 March 1983.[8]

Legal factors also contributed to the adoption of a non-intervention policy in port industry and to the failure of the formation or progress towards a European Port Policy. The lack of any reference to ports in the Treaty of Rome (1957) and the ambiguous legal interpretation of the Treaty did not clarify whether the voting system in the Council of Ministers of the EU on issues regarding ports should be based on the principle of unanimity or on the principle of majority voting. The existence of different rules in relation to maritime and inland transport (issues regarding inland transport required majority voting while issues regarding maritime transport required unanimity), in conjunction with the diverse philosophies underlying port organisation and management in the Member States and the subsequently possible differences of opinion regarding the policies to be adopted, did not permit the inclusion of ports into one of the two categories and the clarification of the terms according to which a Member State could express its objections to specific political initiatives of the EU.

Until 1991, no directive or policy regarding an EU Port Policy had been announced or adopted. The Commission did not attempt to advance proposals that would face opposition and opted to continue its co-operation with the representatives of the port industry in order to identify the common positions, to create allegiances and to prepare the background work of future proposals.

The only important result of this process was the, previously mentioned, Carossino Report of the EP on the role of European ports in the CTP.

The Common Transport Policy during that period was focused on the prospects of harmonising the rules governing the inland transport systems of the EU in the framework of a common market oriented towards free competition. The initiatives towards a Common Maritime Transport Policy progressed along a different path in relation to the initiatives regarding the other transport modes. Maritime transport, regardless of the necessity of a similar policy of market harmonisation, due to the long-established national maritime traditions, had not been included in the framework of the CTP. National governments considered the shipping sector as a distinctive case, due to its international character and its significant revenue-generation potential, thus the Commission did not proceed towards measures for the creation of a common market in this sector. Moreover all the relevant policy actors were considering any EU involvement as an undesirable intervention in an efficiently operating market.

The integral CTP developments during that period were marginal. At the end of the 1970s, the EU was no nearer to a real CTP than it was twenty years earlier (Button, 1984). Whitelegg (1988, pp. 16–17) argued that in the mid-1980s the record of the CTP '…was characterised by little development of its basic thinking about transport and much repetition and bureaucratic non-activity which passes for a common policy', adding that '…its resilience to popular academic and critical transport policy is remarkable and exists in isolation from transport policies'. In the opinion of the then chairman of the EP Transport Committee it was a period of a 'theological strife' between supporters of liberalisation and supporters of harmonisation (Anastasopoulos, 1994). The former group insisted that liberalisation was the precondition of any policy harmonisation; the latter argued that harmonisation was a *sine qua non* for liberalisation. Thus, national governments were inclined to make only limited commitments with reasonably clear implications. Bayliss (1979) pointed out that, lacking any 'grand design', Member States thought that a compromise could only make each of them worse. Since they could not see any great political advantage stemming from an agreement on a CTP, failure to agree was not perceived as damaging to the European idea.

To some scholars, the diversity of the institutional priorities was critical. Ross (1994) suggested that whereas the Commission, and especially the EP, had realised the importance of the CTP at every stage, the Member States via the Council were reluctant to follow suit. The unanimity requirement was strengthening the position of the *status quo* oriented parties, which in the aftermath of the Luxembourg compromise were effectively defending their interests via the use of veto. Both the Dutch and the British governments used that power on a long list of transport issues in the 1970s, including infrastructure pricing and investment, and apparently apolitical matters became great stumbling blocks (cf. Bromhead, 1979; Gwilliam, 1980). Abbati (1986) concluded that the short-term interests of the Transport Ministers, and the fact that the Commission was seeing itself as an arbiter for a consensus, were clearly revealed in the framing of transport policies. In a similar vein, Gwilliam (1979) held that, when the Commission found it difficult to reconcile the antithesis between liberalisation and harmonisation, it decided on a change of emphasis away from the field of operation to the field of infrastructure. Still, the difficulties surrounding the decision-making process and the problems of implementing and administrating EU-level initiatives resulted in negative effects on the production of policy outputs.

However, the institutional framework itself provided the impetus for the progress towards a common policy in all transport modes. The absence of such progress led the EP to institute proceedings against the Council, alleging inaction in the field of transport. It did so in 1982, arguing that the Council had infringed the Rome Treaty '...by failing to introduce a common policy for transport and in particular to lay down the framework for such policy in a binding manner'.[9] In fact, the EP had already expressed its discontent with the slow progress towards a real EU transport policy, to no avail though. Perhaps at that specific point of time, the strategic objective of the first elected EP was not the slow progress of the CTP *per se*, but to test its mandate to press for further integration. Nonetheless, the ECJ confirmed the Council's inability to convert proposals to actions and ruled that the Commission was obliged to produce proposals for the establishment of a common transport market by 1992.[10] That was the first time in the history of the EU that the ECJ found the Council guilty of breaching the provisions of the Treaty of Rome. The EP action and ECJ judgement provoked the Commission's reactions, which included the publication of policy papers on maritime transport in March 1985 where there was extensive reference to the significant lack of adequate EU activity regarding port production and industry.

3.4   1991–2001: TOWARDS A EUROPEAN PORT POLICY

As the previous analysis makes evident, for a time period of several years, progress towards the formation and implementation of the CTP was slow, particularly so in relation to the importance of transport to the EU economy. Since the early 1990s, especially since the end of 1991 and onwards, a new starting point for the CTP became apparent. The CTP progressed at a fast pace owing to a wide range of measures, actions, and initiatives aiming to complete the single market in the sector of transport services. A result of this process is the creation of a new freer market with minimal restrictions and quotas.

Additional significant elements of the new reality are the more intensive policy efforts to enhance competitiveness, economic efficiency, and effectiveness of transport companies, and ensure the operation and quality of transport systems. Additionally, measures for the protection of the environment from the expanding transportation activities were adopted along with the first steps for research and development projects concerning transport infrastructure. Further, the EU institutions have started focusing on their 'transport' relations with third non-EU countries.

The signing, on the 7 February 1992, and enforcement, on the 1 November 1993, of the Treaty of the European Union (Maastricht Treaty) expanded the objectives of the CTP providing, at the same time, for a new momentum to the common policy in question. The needs for a comprehensive policy approach regarding the transport sector and measures aiming to improve transport safety were explicitly acknowledged. The legal provisions on the Trans-European Transport Networks (TEN-T), and the mobilisation towards the endorsement of further policy initiatives regarding the economic and social cohesion of the Union, provided the EU with a new base for the development of transport infrastructure. Simultaneously, according to the principle of subsidiarity, as defined in the Maastricht Treaty, the CTP would be oriented towards actions that the individual Member States were in no position to implement and, because of the scale or their implications, it was deemed preferable that the responsibility be undertaken by the EU.

Therefore, the year 1991 constitutes an important landmark in the development of the CTP. From a policy aiming mainly at the completion of the internal market, it developed into a more integrated policy aiming to achieve the optimum operation of the EU transport systems, in the framework of an internal market free of restrictions and distortions.

Since the early 1990s, and more intensely in the last few years, there are concrete steps towards the development of common policies with the objective of balanced and sustainable development of the EU along with the improvement of accessibility and economic development of the remote areas and the lagging regions of the EU. This is attempted through the identification of practices permitting the policies of transport and regional development to complement each other. In accordance with the special reference in the Treaty of Amsterdam (1997), on the subsidiary role of the EU framework to the promotion of social and territorial cohesion, EU actions are essentially based on the endorsement of the subsidiarity principle in the making of transport policies. Within this framework the EU attempted to emphasise, among other things, the re-balance of the various transport modes, in order to reduce the problems associated with congestion and reduce the impact of transport on the environment.

This prospect encompasses noteworthy EU policies, whereas some of the most comprehensive initiatives have as an objective the development of combined goods transport and the creation of trans-European transport corridors. These policies are analysed in detail in the following chapters of the present book, since they affect significantly the organisation and operational characteristics of port activity. Various other, highly significant initiatives have been launched focusing on the improvement of the safety of transport systems and of maritime transport in particular. Illustrative examples are the directive proposals on the implementation of international safety regulations regarding shipping.

The articulation of the previously mentioned objectives has steadily developed since 1991 and is reaching the completion phase through horizontal approaches to overlapping issues. At the strategic level, a revision of the progress, along with a proposal regarding the objectives of the Common Transport Policy, was presented by the Commission at the end of 1998 with the publication of two Communications to the Council and the EP. The first one regarded the relation of the Common Transport Policy to sustainable mobility and the prospects of the future (CEU, 1998a). The second was focused on the strengthening of economic and social cohesion, competitiveness, and sustainable development, through the coordinated working of the CTP and of the Structural Policies (CEU, 1998b). Eventually, a further realignment was published in 2001 (CEU, 2001b), and similar steps will certainly take place in the future.

Overall, on the basis of the preceding analysis and of the strategy recorded in the previously mentioned documents, various policies were formed that integrated, in a single platform, policies of multiple levels and issues directly and indirectly related to the port industry and production. The most important of the ones that appeared between 1991 and 2000 refer to the following:

- Transport infrastructure, financing and charging methods.
- Combined transport.
- Trans-European Transport Networks.
- Infrastructure and telematics for administration systems and pilotage.
- Sustainable mobility and transport.
- Safety issues.
- Systematic statistical recording of transport activities.

In parallel to the above initiatives, but also in many cases as a *result* of the above initiatives, the Commission and the European Parliament repeatedly drafted specific policy proposals and EU actions with direct reference to the configuration of the parameters of the institutional and operational framework of port production and industry. In 1993 the European Parliament stated the principles of a 'possible' *European Port Policy* (EP, 1993). Two years later, within the context attempting to promote Short Sea Shipping, and on the basis of the philosophy of the horizontal approach of the interlinked industries of the maritime transport system (1991), all policy actors considered EU actions regarding the restructuring of port industry as a key for the materialisation of the objectives of the EU.

The signs of the progress towards a Common Port Policy are confirmed by the reconsideration of the principle of non-intervention by the Commission in the Green Paper on Sea Ports and Maritime Infrastructure (CEU, 1997a), the new proposals of the European Parliament (1999), and the visible mobilisation of those related to the port sector (i.e. port authorities, users, social partners) and those affected by it (i.e. local authority representatives, haulers) towards the formation of specific proposals regarding the role and contents of the European Port Policy. The progress is also confirmed by the common positions reached in the Council of Ministers. The latter has adopted the above proposals put forward by the Commission and endorsed by the European Parliament, the relevant action programmes and the systematic preparation of new initiatives on behalf of the EU institutions. A current peak of these developments, which seems to sketch the prospects of the European Port Policy, are the Commission's recent proposals on the improvement of the quality of port services (CEU, 2001a).

While, at the beginning of 2001, a comprehensive all-embracing European policy aiming to regulate in detail all the issues concerning the port industry still does not exist, nor is considered desirable by several policy actors, a series of proposals, signifies and makes noticeable the substantial progress of the last decade towards a European Port Policy.

The following chapters examine this progress, as it has been shaped by the choices of the EU and the input of other policy actors during the last decade. The next chapter begins with an analysis of the common policies affecting the port industry, including a description of the policy framework and the implications of its implementation. Following, there is an analysis of the impact of the CMTP development to the European port system. Finally, there is the presentation and analysis of those initiatives aiming to achieve the formation of initiatives focusing exclusively on the port sector.

NOTES

1.　Specifically, the founding Treaty of the ECSC (Treaty of Paris, 1951) had explicitly laid out a number of basic requirements regarding transport charges for carrying coal and steel, publication of rates, and the use of discriminatory transport charges, during a transition period prior to eventual harmonisation.

2.   The Council Regulation 141/62, of 26.11.1962, excluded maritime (and air) transport from the common competition policy.

3.   The 'sectoral approach' of integration is a process '(i) limited to particular industries or sectors of the economy, or the economies concerned and (ii) gradual proceeding successively from sector to sector' (Machpul, 1977, p. 33).

4.   European Commission, Document 16/VII/71 (24/03/1970); and Doc.EP 10/72 (12/04/1972).

5.   Case 167/73 Commission v. France (1974) ECR 359, alternatively known as the 'French seamen case'.

6.   Report into the Current Situation in the Major Community Seaports drawn up by the port Working Group (CB-22-77-863).

7.   The two reports mentioned were: (a) the Report into the Current Situation in the Major Community Seaports drawn up by the port Working Group (CB-22-77-863), and (b) the Report of the Port Working Group (VII/440/80) (Internal Working Paper)).

8.   EP, 80/050/final, 11/03/1983.

9.   OJ C49, of 19.2.1983, p. 10.

10. Case 13/83. European Parliament vs. Council of Ministers (1985) ECR 1513.

4. Implications of the Contemporary EU Transport Strategy

4.1 THE CONTEMPORARY EU TRANSPORT STRATEGY

In the early 1990s, the EU introduced major political initiatives with a view to reversing a long period characterised by inertia and lack of progress towards the creation of an integrated Common Transport Policy (CEU, 1992a; 1992b). The EU institutions emphasised the fact that the competitiveness of the European transport sector constituted an essential condition for the successful completion of the internal market, thus they reaffirmed the strategic significance of the transport sector. To enable and facilitate the effective and efficient operation of the Single European Market, the EU decided to accelerate the liberalisation and harmonisation of transport markets and to develop a policy that would result in the interconnection of the European transport systems. Moreover, the EU proceeded decisively to incorporate into the contents of the CTP several provisions that intended to prevent and address existing and potential environmental problems caused by economic growth and the associated increase of transport activities.

The nature and underlying philosophy of the policy actions initiated by the EU throughout the 1990s were clear indications that the EU was aiming to adopt a holistic strategy towards the development of the CTP. That strategy was taking into due consideration all transport modes and parts of transport networks. It also addressed the entirety of the direct or indirect targets that the CTP ought to achieve. Those partial targets (such as the interconnection of local networks) and those parts of the transport system (such as the European ports) that had been ignored in the past would have to be included into the 'new' policy agenda. The far-reaching goal of that strategy was the creation of a EU framework that would ensure the achievement of sustainable mobility in Europe.

Those initiatives also adhered to the *principle of subsidiarity,* introduced in the EU practice by the Treaty of Maastricht (1992): the local authorities or national governments ought to undertake action for the achievement of the targets of any common policy. Policy action at EU level ought to be undertaken only if, and insofar as, the objectives of the proposed actions could not be realised adequately by lower levels of administration, i.e. local authorities or Member States individually, and therefore, by reason of their dimension or scale of effects, would be better realised by the EU.

In this vein, the Commission presented in late 1998, two vital initiatives regarding the future EU actions in the transport sector. The coming of age of the Single European Market constituted, due to the changes it had already introduced (i.e. removal of borders, liberalisation measures, including the liberalisation if intra-EU transport), the turning point for transport too (Butt Phillip & Porter, 1995). The reality of the single market created new social and economic requirements relating to the need to address the increasing demand for transport and to resolve associated problems, such as congestion and saturation of the transport networks and infrastructure. The Commission deemed necessary the liberalisation of transport services to be complemented by the harmonisation of the social conditions in the EU, as well as by common transport regulations and quality standards. Taking the above into consideration, the EU focused on the need to create a transport strategy that would contribute to the achievement of *sustainable mobility* by linking *social cohesion* and *transport*.

Those developments strengthened policy and market practices aiming, on the one hand, to reverse the fragmented nature of the CTP, with reference to how the policy was conceived and implemented in the past, and, on the other hand, to develop the CTP in conjunction with other EU policies. The content of the Commission initiatives marked the introduction of integrated proposals towards the renewal of the EU strategy, along with a partial reorientation of its objectives. They did so by defining the principles and the parameters regarding the relation of EU practices with all parts of the transport system, including European ports.

Advancing the Social and Economic Cohesion of the EU

The first of the previously mentioned Commission initiatives targeted the relation between social cohesion and transport. The objective was the development of EU policy measures aiming to strengthen the economic and social cohesion of the EU, improve the competitiveness of the European economy, and achieve the goal of sustainable development through the combined efforts of the CTP and the EU structural policies (CEU, 1998b).

The EU explicitly recognised, in the new Treaty signed in Amsterdam in June 1997, that market powers alone are not always adequate to achieve the societal goals; hence, the Treaty contains a direct reference to the significance of 'services of general economic interest' to the *promotion of social and territorial cohesion*. Based on this general principle, the EU proceeded to the advancement of the transport sector liberalisation, aiming to establish an open and competitive market. Moreover, it developed a legal framework aiming to create the conditions that would ensure the availability of efficient and affordable transport services to all EU citizens. Transport liberalisation without the establishment of a proper regulatory framework would probably result, on the one hand, in reduced provision of transport services in thinly populated, rural, or remote areas. It would also result in the establishment of a system of transport mode preference that would be ineffective and unsustainable in the long term. Such a situation would undermine the EU efforts to provide new opportunities to those EU areas in receipt of structural aid in the framework of the regional development programmes. Consequently, the EU considered it important, in terms of socio-economic cohesion, to ensure that the CTP would create and maintain the necessary frameworks that would permit the operation of relatively less-profitable transport services that were of high socio-economic significance.

To achieve that target, the Commission called the Member States to increase investment in the local and regional transport systems that were environmentally friendly. The latter consisted of maritime transport, railways, combined transport, and public transport. The Commission also noted that the Member States ought to pay special attention to the impact of transport infrastructure on regional development, ensuring the development of adequate links between large-scale TEN-T projects under construction (see: Chapter 5) and secondary regional and/or local transport networks. Recognising the need for further coordination between the two EU policies, i.e. the Regional and Transport policies respectively, during the planning phase of any large-scale projects, the Commission reaffirmed its will to incorporate the above aspects in the preparation of the future programmes undertaken by the EU structural funds.

Since then, three means have been in use in order to achieve the integration of the transport dimension in the EU regional policy. The first one is the continuous provision of direct financial assistance to the national and private projects aiming at the development of integrated transport systems. The second one is the uninterrupted contribution of the European Regional Development Fund (ERDF) and of the Cohesion Fund to the financing of the TEN-T. Finally, there is financial contribution towards the improvement of the interconnection of local networks. Apart from the ERDF and the Cohesion Fund, the European Investment Bank (EIB) and the European Investment Fund also contribute to the financing of transport infrastructures. The latter was established in 1994, according to the provisions of the Maastricht Treaty, with its main objective being the promotion of investment in transport and especially the completion of the TEN-T.

Nowadays, the priority of the EU policies lies in the effort to improve the effectiveness of the specific EU instruments, as well as the mobilisation of, either private or public, financial support for the development of the European transport systems. The existing policies include the increased use of loans, the strengthening of the corporate relations between the public and private sectors, and measures aiming at the better coordination of all the EU mechanisms financing transport infrastructure.

Both the European Parliament[1] and the Economic and Social Committee (Ecosoc)[2] endorsed the suggested policy framework. In their statements, the two EU institutions stressed the particular nature of the transport problems that were prevailing in the least-favoured EU areas, i.e. the islands and the remote regions. They also noted the significance of several existing public transport systems to the social cohesion of the EU and to the lessening of regional inequalities.

However, the reaction of the European Parliament critically focused on the lack of specific coordination measures between the CTP and the EU cohesion policy initiatives. Moreover, it stressed that the Commission and, by implication, the future CTP developments would have to take into account the particular conditions/characteristics of the transport sector in specific peripheral EU areas, along with the need to create an EU legal framework concerning the harmonised charging of transport infrastructure. The rationale behind the proposed practice was the need to avoid discriminatory charging of the provided transport services against the above-mentioned areas. Considering of vital importance the optimal coordination between (a) the transport policy; (b) the infrastructure policy; and (c) the EU structural funds, the European Parliament argued for the need to coordinate all EU actions affecting transport in the framework of an ambitious European Spatial Development Planning policy.

Moreover, the European Parliament stressed that some particular types of transportation, such as the transportation of goods by combinations of modes that included air and maritime transport, deserved more attention by the CTP. It also noted the need for supporting, through EU-level policy developments, all those public transport services that were of irreplaceable socio-economic importance. Finally, the European Parliament reminded that it was very important for the future prospects of the Union to improve the pan-European transport connections with the applicant countries and, generally, with the neighbouring countries.

The Ecosoc asked for a further clarification of the objectives described in the Commission's initiative. The core principle of the EU policies, according to the Ecosoc, ought to be multidimensional and ensure the compatibility between four long-term objectives. Those objectives were (a) the economic development of the peripheral areas, (b) balanced development within the EU territory, (c) the creation of favourable conditions for the forthcoming EU enlargement, and (d) sustainable and reasonably priced mobility. Towards that direction, the CTP ought to prioritise the promotion of investment in maritime, railway, and inland waterway transport, as well as the sustainability of the necessary public transport systems that serve remote, peripheral and island areas.

Towards Sustainable Mobility

A second Commission initiative, also launched in 1998, stressed the relation between the CTP and the sustainable mobility strategy of the EU (CEU, 1998a). The principles of the CTP that were submitted by the Commission in that context, as well as the action programme under way, were favourably received by the Ecosoc[3] and by the Committee of the Regions.[4]

The first decisive political impetus to the role of the environment in planning the socio-economic development of the EU had been given two decades earlier, when the Commission adopted the *First Action Programme on the Environment* (1973–77). The main concern was to ensure the proper functioning of the Common Market by, amongst others, introducing harmonised standards for consumer products. For the transport sector this programme provided explicitly for technical improvements in noise and gaseous emissions of motor vehicles, as well as for the maximum content of lead in fuel. It also provided for specific action in the area of marine pollution resulting from sea transport. The *Second Action Programme* (1977–81) continued the same line of action. It concentrated, as far as the transport sector was concerned, on marine pollution, measures to reduce noise from motor vehicles, motorcycles, and aircrafts. The *Third Action Programme* (1982–86), however, introduced a new dimension into the general philosophy. Environmental policy was to be motivated by the fact that the environment itself contains the limits to further economic and social development. This Action Programme stressed the need for a greater awareness of the environmental dimension in the area of transport. Vehicle emissions, aircraft noise, and the environmental impact assessment of infrastructure projects were earmarked as priorities.

It was only in the Fourth Action Programme (1987–92) that the interaction between transport and the environment was dully recognised as being of a wide-ranging nature. This new approach was the result of the Single European Act (1987), which in Article 130R provides that the environmental protection requirement shall be a component of the EU's other policies. This approach was endorsed in the Declaration by the European Council of June 1990, which stressed the need for sustainable and environmentally sound development as advocated in the 1987 Report 'Our Common Future' by the

World Commission on Environment and Development (the so-called Brundtland Report). In April 1989, the Commission gave a more specific response in this direction, when it considered it necessary to reflect on the relationship between environmental policy and other EU policies, in particular in the field of transport. The outcome of this exercise provided the guidelines for further work in this area with a view to examining the impact of transport on the environment in a global and coherent framework. This process resulted in the transformation of the transport sector to one of the five economic target subjects of the Fifth EU Environmental Action Programme (1992–2000).

The Commission adopted in 2001 the Sixth Environmental Action Programme (2001–10), which defines five priority avenues of strategic action: improving the implementation of existing legislation; integrating environmental concerns into other policies; working closer with the market; empowering people as private citizens and helping them to change behaviours; and taking account of the environment in land-use planning and management decisions (CEU, 2001c). In addition the work programme for the forthcoming years will include, among others, new proposals on the promotion of renewable energy, on air quality, noise, integrated coastal zone management, and civil liability for environmental damage

A few months before the publication of the Commission's document on sustainable mobility, in a report to the European Council (1998), the Council of Transport Ministers referred to the achieved progress with regard the sustainability of the transport system in Europe. This report nonetheless had recognised the need for a thorough short-term, medium-term, and long-term strategy that would include relevant intermediate and long-term objectives. The European Council in Cardiff (June 1998) welcomed the report, along with a Commission Communication entitled 'Partnership for Integration', aiming towards a strategy of integrating environmental dimensions into sectoral policies. Introducing the so-called 'Cardiff process', it invited nine sectoral Councils, including that of Transport,[5] to establish their own strategies for giving effect to environmental integration and sustainable development within their respective policy areas. Along with the Transport Council, the European Council invited the Commission to specify indicators and monitor the progress, taking account of the suggested guidelines. The Cardiff process is the main tool for the implementation, through a comprehensive approach for policy makers, of Article 6 of the Treaty, which states that all policies should integrate environmental concerns with a view to promoting sustainable development.

In this context, the main objective of the Commission's 1998 initiative on the relation between the CTP and sustainable mobility was the modernisation of the existing action programme and the creation of future policies covering the period between 2000 and 2004. The Commission, in the report on the implementation of the 1995–2000 action programme (CEU, 1995a), mentioned that the strategic targets adopted in the early 1990s ought to continue to be enforced. The continuation would address the challenges arising from the completion of the single market, the prospects of the EU enlargement, the issue of safety, and the consistent and systematic protection of the environment.

The action programme for the period 1995–2000 has been successful, since all EU institutions and all the stakeholders involved in the EU policy-making process have favourably assessed it. The extension of that action programme constituted a first-class opportunity for the Commission to propose an updated action framework, aiming to ensure the development of the CTP in accordance with the prospects of sustainable mobility for the period 1998–2000 and thereafter.

The action framework includes three major priority areas to which the main EU actions, that have been initiated, or are about to be initiated (at least up to 2004), must be aligned. These three priorities are aiming at:

(a) *Improving the effectiveness and competitiveness of EU transport.* Actions in five areas have been announced towards the achievement of this objective. The liberalisation of market entry, especially with regard railways and ports, is the first of these areas. The Commission explicitly expressed its intention to submit, after consultation, proposals for the liberalisation of the port services market. The second policy area is the establishment of integrated transport systems and the development of a trans-European transport network. Thirdly, EU initiatives are directed towards the application of fair pricing, based on the marginal social cost. The other two areas are the improvement of working conditions in the sector, and the better supervision of the existing regulatory framework respectively.

(b) *Improving the quality of transport services.* In this case, EU policy developments include initiatives concerning the safety of transport, especially with regard the maritime, air and road transport, and the protection of the environment.

(c) *Improving the effectiveness of the EU transport abroad,* through the signing of international agreements. The latter include agreements on the subject of transport safety and environmental protection.

That action framework reconfirmed the emphasis of the EU institutions on the balance between the various transport modes, and especially on the promotion of those modes that are more environmentally friendly: maritime, railway, inland waterway and combined transport. Having in mind a long-term perspective, the Commission proceeded to investigate the potential approaches to the advancement of the CTP at the beginning of the new century. Towards this end, it called all policy actors, whether policy makers or stakeholders, to contribute to the creation of a common European strategy.

The Ecosoc greeted favourably that announcement, although it stressed the absence of long-term objectives beyond the year 2010. Within a different perspective, the opinion of the CoR insisted in the significance of the regional and local authorities' contribution to the formulation of the CTP. It also emphasised the need to respect the different national and/or regional approaches and diverse realities existing in the EU with regard to the transport sector. Finally, the CoR opinion highlighted the role that EU action ought to play in educating the public, thus stimulating the revision of attitudes towards transport (i.e. intensity of use, choice of transport mode or route), the increase of experience exchange, and the encouragement of private investment.

Aligned with the views of the Commission and the other EU institutions, the European Councils of Vienna (December 1998) and Cologne (June 1999) called the relevant sectoral Councils to submit strategy proposals for the integration of environmental issues in all the other EU policies. This call was in agreement with the wider political priorities of the EU, as stated in the Treaty of Amsterdam (1997). Responding to this prompting, the Council of Transport Ministers accepted a new report on the incorporation of issues concerning the environment and sustainable development in the transport policy,[6] which was forwarded to the European Council at Helsinki (December 1999).

In that report, the Council of Ministers reconfirmed the EU objective to ensure economic development without increases in the negative impact of transport. At the same time, the Council expressed its concern about the danger associated with the continuous increase of road and air transport. Despite the positive assessment of the CTP achievements, i.e. a decrease in the negative impact of transport on the environment, the Council recognised the need for additional action in the areas of gas emissions and noise, increased transport traffic and modal distribution of traffic. The Council report also mentioned that the existence of measurement indicators and of adequate control, especially as far as a report submission mechanism on the relation between transport and the environment is concerned, were of paramount importance to the integration of environmental objectives in the CTP. The Transport Ministers agreed that the coordinated actions of the Member States, the Commission and the Council would lead to further improvements towards the desired direction.

It can be inferred, and it is further confirmed by the subsequent analysis, that having adopted these views, as well as all the principles included in the two Commission initiatives, all decision-making and consultative EU institutions are formulating, proposing and adopting measures, within the CTP, that promote the stated objectives. In this process, there is an apparent contribution of the stakeholders involved in the production (or use of) the transport services.

The ongoing program of the CTP includes policy actions concerning a lengthy list of issues: the charging of transport services and infrastructure; the spatial planning of the transport process; the maintenance of the existing infrastructure; the use of telematics and telecommunications; passenger transport, railways; combined transport; the non-mechanic mobility; the continuous improvement of vehicles, motors and fuel; the provision of economic incentives for the use of vehicles that have low fuel consumption and use clean fuel; the research on new technologies; the enlargement of the EU; and the raising of public awareness.

Notably, whilst the progress of the Cardiff process has been uneven, transport is among the policy areas that have come furthest insofar as the integration of environmental targets in sectoral policies is concerned. In June 2001, the European Council in Göteborg concluded that the process has only begun and should continue and deepen, not least in view of the need to follow up and build upon the results achieved so far in the sectors. It suggested that the Cardiff strategies are important tools both for the implementation of the environmental dimension of the sustainable development strategy and the forthcoming Sixth Environmental Action programme. The latter, which is under adoption by the Council and Parliament, will set out the environmental priorities for the next ten years. The Council constellations responsible for the sectoral strategies got a renewed mandate in Göteborg. On a general level, it is also recommended that decision support systems such as Strategic Environmental Assessments (SEA) be used as an effective tool for safeguarding integration in decision making and that the internalisation of external costs in market prices be considered crucial.

Considering the setting of clear time limits the Council stated that an important lesson is that this process takes time. Sectoral integration requires new attitudes, new co-operation methods and new understanding from all parties in the process, so a satisfactory outcome may also hinge on satisfactory co-operation between environmental experts and those who formulate sector policy. A dialogue with sector stakeholders and non-governmental organisations could also make the process more effective. Moreover, EU policies may in many ways be linked to, or have consequences for countries outside, or currently outside the EU. The Council needs to pay attention to the external dimension in its future work, especially in view of the enlargement process.

4.2   FINANCING TRANSPORT INFRASTRUCTURE

EU-level discussions on the resolution of issues and problems relating to the transport systems of Europe have been 'omnipresent' in the course of the European integration, without however, at the same time, the materialisation of these discussions into relevant action (Turró, 1999). Against this trend, the last decade of the 20th century was characterised by the intensification of EU action towards the achievement of viable long-term solutions to two critical problems of the transport sector. These are (a) the adequate financing of the construction of new (or the upgrading of the existing) infrastructure of all transport modes, and (b) the formulation of effective methods for charging and distributing the costs of this infrastructure, respectively.

European Transport System: The Need for Adjustment

During the 1980s, the need for more systematic work on behalf of the EU, on issues regarding the upgrade of infrastructure and other general problems concerning the transport sector, became more necessary than ever. Throughout the period 1970–90, the intra-EU traffic of goods was increasing by 2.3% annually (in tkm), while the respective traffic of persons was increasing by 3.1% annually (in pkm). The gradual saturation of certain transport networks and the predictions suggesting certain increases in the volume of transport between the Member States, just before the commencement of the SEM (1992), were signalling a potentially worrying situation. The relevant statistical data were indicating a decrease in Investments in Transport Infrastructure (ITI), in relation to the Gross Domestic Product (GDP), from 1.5% in 1975 to 1% in 1990. The problem was exacerbated due to the geopolitical developments and the subsequent market liberalisation in Central and Eastern European countries, areas where transport infrastructure was, in general, less developed.

The additional problem to be resolved was (and remains) the distribution of transport activity per mode of transport and its implications. The increase in goods and passenger transportation up to 1990 was not the same for all transport modes (Figure 4.1 & Table 4.1).

In fact, the increase in goods transport resulted mainly in increases in the volume of road transport. The volume of traffic in road networks more than doubled between 1970 and 1990, exhibiting annual growth rates of 4.1%. On the other hand, rail transport decreased by 15% in absolute terms, and in relative terms from 28% to 25% of the total transport activity. The volume of inland waterways transport, during the same period, presented a slight increase in absolute terms (4%) but, in comparison to the total transport activity, it decreased by a third, to 9% of total traffic.

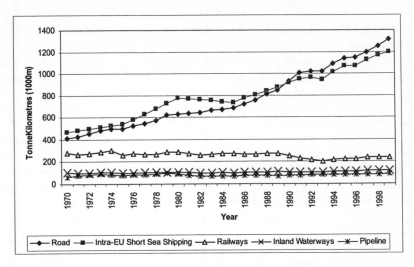

Figure 4.1 Evolution of Goods Transport by Mode 1970–99

Table 4.1 Average Annual Growth of Freight Transport (% per year)

Average Annual Change (%)	Road	Railways	Inland Waterways	Intra-EU Short Sea Shipping	Total
1970–80	+4.2	+0.2	+0.3	+5.1	+3.5
1980–90	+4.0	-1.2	+0.1	+1.7	+1.9
1990–99	+3.9	-0.8	+1.2	+2.9	+2.9

Source: European Commission. *Transport in Figures.*

In fact, the increase in goods transport resulted mainly in increases in the volume of road transport. The volume of traffic in road networks more than doubled between 1970 and 1990, exhibiting annual growth rates of 4.1%. On the other hand, rail transport decreased by 15% in absolute terms, and in relative terms from 28% to 25% of the total transport activity. The volume of inland waterways transport, during the same period, presented a slight increase in absolute terms (4%) but, in comparison to the total transport activity, it decreased by a third, to 9% of total traffic.

In relation to the volume of transported goods, maritime transport has always been the major mode with regards the longest, mainly transoceanic, routings. Following a significant increase in the volume of this type of transport in the aftermath of the second oil crisis (1979), the volume of goods transported by sea to/from other continents did not present any significant variation in relative terms. However, the growth rate of short sea shipping during the 1980s was disturbingly lower in relation to the respective growth rate of road transport (1.7% compared to 4.1%). 1990 marked the first year when the volume of intra-EU seagoing transport was, in absolute terms, less than the volume of road transport.

A characteristic of the 1970s and 1980s was that road transport absorbed most of the increase in the demand for transport services. Moreover, in the early 1990s forecasts indicated further increase in transport traffic. Addressing this modal imbalance emerged as a necessity. Besides, road transport capacity was already under significant pressure, and this resulted in many negative implications. This pressure was attributable to the following factors:

(a) Road users were not charged according to the total costs of the services they used; in particular, the final charges for road transport did not internalise the external costs.

(b) During the 1980s, fiscal problems coerced the decrease of public investments in road infrastructure (in real prices), even though transport activities were increasing.

(c) Planning requirements and public opinion had imposed complex restrictions on the development of new projects concerning transport infrastructure.

In short, the EU transport system found itself exposed to modal inequalities (some are still present) and to inadequacy and lack of infrastructure modernisation with regard to the requirements of the users of transport services.

Favouring Transport Modes

Whilst the problem of capacity under-utilisation of some transport modes (or their combined use) has been raised, for all the above reasons, since the late 1980s, comprehensive attempts to address the problem at the EU level became apparent at the beginning of the 1990s. What was the reason, though, that between 1960 and 1990 goods and passenger transport was predominantly served by road transport while, at the same time, the potential of railways, inland waterways and maritime transport was ignored?

The reasons should be sought in three directions: first, is the peculiar characteristics of the demand for transport services. These peculiarities have certain implications on modal competition and modal complementarity.

Second, is the existence of a selective internalisation of the external costs caused by transport activities. Third, the imbalanced modal distribution of the investments in transport infrastructure.

Complementary Modes and Peculiarities of Transport Demand

The role of the peculiarity of the demand for transport becomes evident by the analysis of the range of factors that determine the selection between transport modes. According to the relative importance of these factors, ensue the relevant data concerning a user's selection (Erasmus University, 1991).

In the case of *goods transport* the selection by a user is influenced by multiple criteria among which stand out:

1. The value and weight of cargo.
2. The transport costs, including the cost of loading/unloading, transloading and the cost of transportation itself.
3. The speed and reliability of delivery.
4. The quality of services, including the safe transport of goods.
5. The administrative efficiency and the availability of information concerning the location of cargo.
6. The distance and duration of door-to-door services (including the time devoted to loading/unloading).
7. The available alternatives.
8. The availability of infrastructure and the accessibility to it.
9. The availability of relevant services (packing, distribution, etc.).

The transportation of goods, though, is an indispensable part of the supportive framework of the production and distribution process. This support varies for distinct stages of transporting according, mainly, to the nature of cargo.

As far as *raw materials* are concerned, transportation takes place, usually, 'from point to point', i.e. between a limited number of suppliers and customers. This case refers mostly to maritime, road and inland waterway transport, while railways hold only a small market share. Transport cost is the determining factor for the selection by the user.

As far as *intermediate and semi-manufactured or unfinished* goods are concerned, transportation is 'convergent', generally between a large number of suppliers and a small number of customers. The transport of such products usually takes place by road, and the supportive framework is that of the 'just-in-time' process. The speed and reliability of delivery are the main factors determining the selection of transport mode.

As far as *final products* are concerned, transport is usually 'divergent' between a large number of suppliers and customers. The transport of such products takes place mainly by road and, to a lesser degree, by air. The combination of the quality of the service provided, the speed and reliability, as well as the availability of relevant services, determine the selection of transport mode.

As far as *consumer goods* are concerned, transport is usually 'hyper-divergent' between a very large number of suppliers and customers. The transport of such products takes place usually by road. The speed and reliability of the transport process are the basic factors determining the selection of transport mode.

As far as *passenger transport* is concerned, the modal choice is determined by three groups of factors: (a) the characteristics of the various transport modes, (b) the socio-economic status of the decision maker, and (c) the nature of the trip.

The *characteristics of the various transport modes* include the duration of travel and cost. The duration of travel may be distinguished in the time aboard the transport mode and the time off the transport mode. Cost usually comprises direct expenses (transport charges, cost of fuel, toll charges, and parking fees). The fixed expenses, such as amortisation and interest, insurance, annual licence fees, affect little, if at all, the short-term selection process of a customer. Additional determining factors are the transparency of the transport system, comfort, safety, validity-prestige and time accuracy.

Factors such as income, age, occupation, education and the type of residence comprise the *characteristics of the social and economic status* that determine the selection by a customer. For material, economic or social reasons certain groups may be more sensitive than others to specific peculiarities of the transport modes. As an example, the low-income groups are more sensitive to the issue of travel costs. Finally, the *nature of travel* is characterised by the purpose (e.g. work), the distance, the time of departure and arrival, the day of the week, the season during which the travel takes place.

In markets characterised by competition between all transport modes, the process of selecting transport mode involves multiple criteria. Probably, the most important are: (a) flexibility, (b) speed, (c) reliability, (d) frequency, and (e) price. In the case of goods transport, the increase in the percentage of the high-value and low-volume merchandise and the wider use of information technology, in production and distribution, favoured the use of transport modes able to fulfil the first four criteria, which could be named as *qualitative*.

Nonetheless, the selection by a customer also depends on certain limitations of which the most important is the availability of alternative transport modes and the knowledge of these alternatives. Apparently, the fact that the option of using road transport has always been readily available in most cases was significantly affecting the final modal choice. That was clearly not the same for the other transport modes. Overall, this reality has resulted in serious restrictions and distortions in competition between the various transport modes, especially in cases of short-distance transport.

Selective Internalisation of External Costs

Furthermore, road as well as air transport were favoured by the pattern of development in Europe during the last forty years, to some extent, because the external costs associated with their use (whether these are operational costs, costs of infrastructure, traffic congestion, environmental costs or the costs of accidents) were not included in the final price of the provided services.

The external costs associated with the various transport modes differ significantly. When these differences result in respective price differentials, transport users adjust their demand accordingly. In these cases, transport users are likely to opt for the least-expensive alternative, which is the mode that offers the lower price by not internalising the external costs it causes. Consequently, the demand for the same service by the other transport modes that have internalised either part or the whole of the external costs they cause is being reduced. Any changes in the level of the additional expenses for the transport users, due to internalisation of external costs, result in a redistribution of the modal split.

All relevant data indicate that certain sectors of the transport industry were not recovering the real cost of their operation, if external costs were to be taken into account. This reality made and still makes road transport more appealing. At the same time, it limits the incentives for the development and exploitation of the potential of other parts of the transport system that could contest a market share from road transport. To a notable extent, the high percentage of utilisation of road transport is attributable to the steady decrease, in relation to other transport modes, of the total external costs that the users were asked to cover.

Modal Distribution of Investments in Transport Infrastructure

The imbalanced modal distribution of the investments in transport infrastructure constituted the third factor contributing to the privileged expansion of road and air transport. Disregarding the existence of any annual variations, during the 1980s, some 66% of Investments in Transport Infrastructure (ITI) was devoted to projects improving road transport infrastructure, while investments in air transport infrastructure increased from 3.9% to 5.6% of total ITI in the late 1980s. On the contrary, investments in port infrastructure reduced from 5% to 3.5% of total ITI, while the respective investments in railways infrastructure remained unchanged.

Meanwhile, the effective response of the transport system as a whole to the increased (quantitatively and qualitatively) demands begun to significantly depend on the quality of infrastructure of each individual transport mode. This development was attributable to three factors. The first factor was the development of transport activities that demanded the use of (but also generated competition between) more than one transport mode. The second was the increasing transportation of containerised cargo. The third was the application of information technology and the implementation of logistics. Within these new conditions of operation and competition, the ability of each mode to participate in transport chains was largely defining the modal distribution of transport activity as well as the methods of transport that were being used.

Therefore, increased investment in infrastructure of specific transport modes, not only facilitated their users but, also, attracted (in conjunction with other circumstances: geographical and economic conditions, availability of alternatives) additional traffic. The faster, in relation to other transport modes, adjustment of the European road system, insofar as infrastructure upgrade is concerned, resulted in increases in the use of the specific mode. As the preceding discussion regarding the characteristics of transport demand highlighted and the empirical data confirm (cf. Jansson, 1993) the demand for any transport mode is not entirely exogenous, but it is also affected by the qualitative characteristics of the specific transport mode.

Financing Transport Infrastructure: Searching for a Viable Solution

Both the representatives of the European industrialists[7] and those of the transport industries[8] had long since stressed the problems associated with the lagging levels of ITI as well as the subsequent shortages and inefficiencies that it was causing. The need to address the possible imbalance between the volume of transport and the investments in transport infrastructure was soon after realised by the EU institutions. In December 1988, the Council of Ministers adopted the view that the possible continuation of the trend of reducing investments in transport infrastructure would undermine the objective of free movement of persons, goods, and services, an objective that was a precondition for the completion of the Single European Market. Thus, the Transport Council decided to examine, in cooperation with the Commission, various ways to increase investment in transport infrastructure and to reverse the visible trend.

The EU had already established the Transport Infrastructure Committee, an instrument aiming to contribute to the balanced development of a transport infrastructure network of EU interest.[9] In 1975, the Commission had submitted the proposal for its creation but did not receive any response by the Council that decided to 'consider it in the future'. Finally, following demands by the Commission and the EP, in 1978 the Advisory Transport Infrastructure Committee was established, having as the only objective the exchange of information about national plans and programmes of EU interest in road transport. The scope for action and effectiveness of the newly established committee were extremely limited, not only in relation to the objectives but, also, in relation to transport modes (only road transport was concerned).

It was not until 1982 that the Council approved a Regulation, whose period of enforcement was to be one year (with a budget of only 10 million Euro), on the financing of transport infrastructure. The positive aspect of that initiative was that it mobilised, to a certain extent, the coordination of the relevant national policies. However, the annual renewal of this Regulation, until 1990, did not permit the development of a medium- or long-term action strategy (Gwilliam, 1990). That same year the EU budget recorded financial measures to encourage certain investment projects in transport infrastructure by Member States, investments that in the absence of EU intervention would not have been undertaken, at least not with the same priority. As it became evident after 1990, the long-term programme proved to be more suitable, especially due to the long periods devoted to preparatory work and implementation of transport projects.

In the early 1990s, the EU deemed it proper to broaden the scope of the long-term programme and to include all transport modes. In December 1990, the Commission formulated a EU Support Programme for the development and interconnection of trans-European networks, as well as the connection of the EU regions through effective land transport modes (CEU, 1990a). Already, since October of the same year, the Council had submitted to the Commission a proposal for the creation of a high-level working party for combined transport, while later it also submitted a similar proposal for the road sector and inland waterways. The efforts of this workgroup were extended to the maritime and air sector, in order to take into due consideration the under-utilised potential of the combined use of transport modes.

At the same time, the signing of the Maastricht Treaty (1991) introduced new elements into the legal base and into the decision-making process for the implementation of the previously designed projects concerning transport. The financing of projects on transport infrastructure had already been the object of EU policy according to Regulation 3359/90. A Regulation whose period of enforcement was three years, which would cease to be effective on the 31

December 1992 and among others it provided for the upgrading of the advisory Transport Infrastructure Committee to a committee with the power to submit legal proposals on issues within its jurisdiction (thus becoming a Regulatory Committee).[10] Because of the possibility that certain projects already under way would be undermined, due to a lack in the legal framework, the Commission proposed the extenuation of the Regulation until the ratification and implementation of Chapter XII of the EU Treaty.

In this context and based on the subsidiarity principle, the Commission pursued the further promotion and encouragement of national plans of EU interest. Towards that aim it submitted to the Council and the EP a proposal for the amendment of Regulation 3359/90 and three proposals concerning network plans on: (a) combined transport, (b) road transport, and (c) inland waterway transport. Those proposals were supplemented by an announcement on the general principles governing the development of the TEN-T (CEU, 1992c; 1992d). Similar project plans regarding the other transport modes had also been prepared. However, for different reasons concerning each of them, the Commission opted not to include those plans in its final proposals (the reasons that maritime transport was exempted are discussed in Chapter 5).

Thus, within a year (1991) the Commission had at its disposal network plans for all transport modes.[11] The new financial framework for the period 1993–97 extended existing budget lines for European infrastructure investments, especially in the framework of the EIB and the ERDF. In addition, it developed guidelines regarding the operation of the Cohesion Fund in providing financial resources to cover the infrastructural needs of the lagging EU regions. Apart from direct co-finance of the projects, these attempts implicate the subsidisation of the interests, budget guarantees, improvements of the fiscal environment, and means to promote self-finance of these projects.

During the formulation of these network plans, the advantages of the various transport modes and their potential for contribution to the EU activity became apparent. It was a turning point that created a framework for a more rational use of the existing, under construction, and planned transport infrastructure, offering the potential to reconcile increasing mobility with the needs of the environment. Thus, the EU deemed it necessary to find ways to connect ports and sea corridors with the other parts of the transport network, so that maritime transport could be integrated into systems of combined and intermodal transport.

The remaining problem, though, was the mobilisation of sufficient funds to cater for the needs of implementing the above-mentioned objectives. Towards the resolution of that problem, various proposals for potential, even if partial, solutions are still in discussion. One of these proposals refers to the need to secure the increase of the available funds for investments in transport infrastructure through the participation of the private sector.

European nations have a long-standing tradition of public sector financing of transport infrastructure and of related services, although practices exercised in Member States tend to differ. However, in the course of time a trend involving higher private sector participation has been observed. This trend reflects the will to introduce to a larger extent the logic of the market, sometimes through privatisations, with a view to relieving the public budgets and increasing the viability of the projects through the combined efforts of public and private funds and administration. Given the existence of multiple scenarios (see: Table 4.2), the participation of the private sector depends on the prospects for profit making within accepted limits of risk. It also demands the thorough examination of the distribution of risks between the public and the private sector.

Table 4.2 Scenarios of Financing Transport Infrastructure

Financing	Risk Taking		Marketing
	Construction	Operation	
Private	Private	Private	Private
Private	Private	Public	Private
Private	Private	Private	Public
Private	Public	Public	Public
Public	Public	Public	Public

Source: ECMT (1990).

Nonetheless, the new investments and the new instruments of financing are just a part of the solution. All other issues considered, it would be wise to examine methods to make use of the under-utilised capacity of the other transport modes (apart from road transport), including maritime transport. This should take place, however, without compromising the user's freedom to modal selection.

Indeed, this dimension of the transport policy is increasingly discussed at the EU level, in particular the fact that in small-scale maritime transport, inland waterway and railway transport did, in fact, have under-utilised capacity. Consequently, the EU recognised that the efforts of any policy measures, ought to advance the 'attractiveness' of the said transport modes and promote their combined use (see: Chapters 5 and 6). Combined transport could provide wider solutions to the problem, due to the capacities of the various types of combined transport, especially those of railways/maritime and railways/inland waterway.

4.3   CHARGING TRANSPORT INFRASTRUCTURE

Theorising the Parameters of the European Policy

An important tool to address the problem of unused, existing or potential, capacity of some transport modes was thought to be the more rational cost recovery of transport infrastructure use and the harmonised application of the system throughout the Union, in order to secure the rational implementation of this policy.

Whilst the EU institutions have stressed these necessities at several stages of the CTP strategy design, no steps have been taken towards that direction. Although not mentioned in the Treaty of Rome (1957), issues on cost recovery of transport infrastructure appeared soon: in 1961, in the first EU document on the CTP (Schaus Memorandum), these issues were considered as being the guiding principles towards the integration of the transport systems of the Member States (CEU, 1961). In 1968, the Commission submitted a proposal on the harmonisation of the tax systems applied to commercial vehicles aiming, among others, at the recovery of at least the marginal cost of using transport infrastructure.[13] The different priorities of the Member States at that time did not permit any relevant decision to be taken. The Council initially agreed on a proposed Directive in June 1978, but the specific Directive was never officially adopted. Nothing positive resulted from the common position of the Council, apart from the acknowledgement that a policy concerning the charging of transport infrastructure ought to be an indispensable part of the CTP (Bromhead, 1979).

In 1988, the Commission submitted a new proposal on the charging of road infrastructure use by heavy lorries. That proposal was essentially an attempt to avoid the problem of double charging by the combined application of national taxes on *vehicles* and the application of charges based on *territoriality*. Towards this end, a proposal was submitted on the introduction of a system that would be based on the principle of territoriality. The lack of statistical data on the cost of road infrastructure, at the time, for the whole of the EU territory led to the adoption of a gradual approach, with the initial deadline being the 31 December 1994. Moreover, there were clear signs of the prospect to implement a final EU system concerning the charging of transport infrastructure (cf. CEU, 1990a).

In the late 1990s it was acknowledged that the mechanism of the CTP would have to examine the implications of transport price changes to/from the peripheral, or less developed, regions of the EU (CEU, 1998b). The burdens of transport cost would have to be differentiated, so that the regions with low congestion and pollution would be affected the least. In cases where the higher costs imposed on the users of transport services were likely to undermine the economic development of the peripheral or less developed regions, the EU policy could allow for the gradual implementation of the charging reforms.

Thus, guidelines had to be formulated with regard to the conditions permitting the provision of financial contributions according to the EU legislation. The financial support to new investment projects, especially those regarding the operation of new and innovative transport systems, and financial support provided for the removal of environmentally hazardous traffic from the road network towards other transport modes, had to be carefully examined.

Consequently, the issue of funding methods reappeared: the cost relationship between the transport modes would be altered using public financing as an instrument. The use of public funds could reduce the cost of those transport modes (e.g. maritime) that could potentially relieve the great pressure on other transport modes (e.g. road). However, policy makers deemed irrational the application of a generalised common policy directing capital resources towards specific types of passenger and cargo transport. The justification was that such a policy practice would relieve the interested parts from competition and, at the same time, would place their competitors at a disadvantage. Moreover, it was rather unlikely that such a policy would lead to viable, efficient and long-term solutions. Nonetheless, it was evident that the provision of state aids had yielded some positive results. Not only was it altering the cost relations between the transport modes, but also it was creating the conditions for some of those modes to become more attractive to the existing or potential users.

At macroeconomic level, the more efficient use of the total transport system leads to reduced transport costs for the society as a whole (societal costs). At the micro level, this efficiency advances the competitive position of specific producers. In those cases where all transport modes are not optimally developed, the total transport costs might be, *ceteris paribus*, higher than otherwise. This is certainly true in the case of producers located in remote peripheral areas that depend on only one transport mode, and attempt to distribute and/or sell their goods to distant markets, like the major markets at the core of Europe, and try to compete with the local producers of that central area. Thus, the administrations of some peripheral regions are likely to use measures to promote the competitive position of such producers by helping them to restructure their production towards products with higher value/weight ratio. Foremost, they do so by improving the quality and variety of the basic transport systems with the support, when necessary, of the Structural Funds and the Cohesion Fund.

All the above measures ultimately affect transport costs with direct implications on the competitiveness of the transport systems and, not least, of transport companies. Given the increased internationalisation of trade and other economic activities, the unilateral national or local-level endorsement of these policy practices would be rather impossible. This is because, national and local authorities acting individually towards that direction, would distort competition and breach the EU competition rules by advancing the competitive position of the enterprises located within their jurisdiction at the expense of those enterprises located in other areas. To ensure a level playing field, the relevant measures are decided and adopted at the EU level. Still, neither is the intention of these EU actions to replace the role of national governments, nor the competence does rely solely to the EU. As they continue to develop and maintain their respective networks, national or local authorities need, according to the subsidiarity principle, to implement and administer this EU framework, taking into consideration the particular local conditions, such as when they decide on the application of specific toll charges.

Internalising the External Costs in Infrastructure Charging

The definition of 'what the real transport cost is' and the formulation of a suitable method for the internalisation of the external costs in charging are further critical parameters of the prospects for a viable EU cost recovery system of transport infrastructure. Hence, they both constitute themes currently under discussion by stakeholders and policy makers. A common policy on the internalisation of the external costs, on the one hand, would affect the demand for the different transport modes. On the other hand, it would increase the charges imposed to the users of some transport modes, thus reversing the trend of burdening the society with expenses due to the fact that their users were not previously paying the full cost of the services they enjoyed.

There has already been mention of the effects of non-internalisation of costs to the competition between the transport modes: road transport has a comparative advantage in relation to the other transport modes. The example of ports further highlights the social dimension of the problem. As is the case with every other transport mode, the transportation of freight via ports has some negative aspects/implications, such as the wear and tear on port infrastructure and the infrastructure of the networks permitting access to the hinterland, congestion, accidents, or pollution. These consequences bear a cost, which at present is largely ignored by the charging system of port services and by the tax systems as well. As a result, other social groups, not related to the port activity, are burdened. Consequently, it is the European economy and society as a whole that bears the total costs resulting from the operation of transport via ports, or transport in general.

The problems of transport infrastructure cost recovery, as well as that of minimising external costs produced by the contemporary split of the transport pie are characterised by complexity, and they are intertwined with a wide spectrum of issues. Any attempt to reverse this situation requires action at two levels. The first one relates to the adoption of policies that incorporate in the price for transport services both the cost of infrastructure and all the external costs produced. This approach would contribute to the reduction of cost differentials between the transport modes, especially as the currently employed pricing schemes rarely incorporate the costs associated with these two factors.

The second level consists of measures aiming to improve the quality of the services provided by alternative transport modes, especially combined transport. Unquestionably, the availability of feasible alternative solutions is a prerequisite in order to reverse the present situation. This is not always possible though, especially in the case of short-distance transport. In the case of medium- and long-distance transport, the presence of potential alternative solutions is normally given, a fact that has advanced not only the competitiveness of the road transport sector but of the other modes as well. Consequently, any relevant EU policies should aim to secure the fair distribution of the transport infrastructure costs and of external costs, through the equivalent development of the transport modes.

Two more arguments seem to support the specific orientation of the EU actions. Even if the users of road transport covered all costs associated with the use of the road network, it is not possible to increase indefinitely the capacity of the latter in order to address the increasing needs for transport. Especially in congested and environmentally sensitive areas, the potential to expand the road network is extremely limited. In fact, whenever a road transport network is reaching its limits, various demand-regulation mechanisms are applied. The various charges that motivate or even force the users to reconsider the necessity of a specific trip or to search for alternative solutions provide an illustrative example. Then, the application of charges or tolls essentially entails the use of a market mechanism. This allows for some customer choice, while it ensures the better use of the various transport modes in terms of time and space.

In this discussion, the counter-arguments are not absent. One of these states that the increase in transport costs, especially in the case of road transport, is uneconomical not only for transport companies but, also, for the economy as a whole. A possible solution, that has been proposed, demands the restriction of increases in transport costs, reducing at the same time the costs imposed on enterprises that use combined transport systems and increasing the level of the other charges with particular effects on the individual/private or road transport.

The Proposed Framework of Charging Infrastructure

Benefited by the preceded discussion, the EU institutions have been involved in the search for a framework that would ensure a fair and efficient determination of transport prices. Aiming to formulate final plans and determine a uniform long-term EU policy, the endorsed approach to govern the harmonisation of transport infrastructure charging systems (as well as the systems of enforcing the relevant charges) complements another vital principle: *the same fundamental principles should be applied to all transport modes in all EU Member States.*

The publication of a relevant Commission proposal, in 1995 (CEU, 1995b), advanced the debate on how the adoption of common charging methods would contribute to the resolution of critical transport problems (such as traffic congestion, accidents, pollution). The Commission subscribed to the view that the internalisation of the external transport costs, i.e. when every user pays for all social costs associated with transport services used, results in a reduction of transport problems and, consequently, in improved competitiveness of the European economy. The aim of the proposal was not to increase transport costs *per se*, but to motivate users and manufacturers to review their attitudes with a view to soften the adverse side-effects of transport activities. Among others, the Commission argued, such a choice would rationalise the terms of competition between the different transport modes to the benefit of port services.

In this spirit, and having the support of both the EP[14] and of the CoR,[15] the Commission proposed the establishment of a system of price differentiation linked as closely as possible to costs and designed to recover the full infrastructure and operating costs. According to the Commission's view on policies concerning the charging of infrastructure, the search for a system determining the prices of transport services must take account of the twin concepts of equity (i.e. fair cost allocation) and efficiency. Further, the Commission thought that a radical reform of this system would be unfeasible without the prior assurance that equitable conditions of free competition prevail within and between the various transport modes in the common transport market. Although the Commission recognised that local or regional authorities are often best suited to deal with transport-related problems,

European action was justified to deal with transfrontier externalities or the effects on the internal market and to capitalise on possible economies of scale and policy spillovers.

Via the application of a EU-wide system of transport infrastructure charging, where prices are approaching the real cost of transport, the calculation of all external costs resulting from port activities will also be achieved. An additional target to be achieved is the determination of the methods allowing the expression of these costs in prices and, subsequently, the submission of proposals regarding the means to achieve the fair distribution of the said prices. For example, maritime congestion in certain European ports or the increased traffic in the surrounding areas constitute a significant external cost. To address such issues various systems of information sharing, electronic traffic management or electronic charging can be developed and applied. However, in the long term the only means of reducing maritime congestion is to establish explicit charges for the use of port infrastructures.

The 'User Pays' Principle

Parallel to the proposals concerning the establishment of a EU system determining transport prices, the EU institutions have tried to identify potential ways of fairly imposing the relevant charges for the use of transport infrastructure. The Commission proposed the gradual harmonisation of the systems of charging for transport infrastructure according to the *'user pays'* principle (CEU, 1998c). Under development is the adjustment and harmonisation of charging systems of a part of the transport sector (road and rail transport), the ultimate aim being to create an EU framework to be applied to the entire transport system.

According to the 'user pays' principle, all the users of the transport infrastructure must pay for the full costs they cause, i.e. both the internal and external costs. According to the principle of territoriality, the payment must be made at the place of infrastructure use, or at the nearest possible point. Predecessor to this principle, that facilitated the private funding of transport infrastructure, was the endorsement within the CTP of the concept *'services/charging'*. According to this concept, the user is willing to pay for the provision of a high-quality transport service (CEU, 1990b).

In 1998, the Commission submitted a proposal, in the form of a White Paper, whose aim was to stress the need to harmonise, at EU level, the principles governing the distribution of costs applied to the various types of commercial transport. This was necessary because escalating congestion and pollution were raising serious doubts about the sustainability of the contemporary European transport system. Transport charges could help address these issues since they influence prices, which in turn can change the pattern of transport use. Transport companies that are forced to calculate their prices based on the true cost of their activities, have an incentive to review their options concerning the selection of transport mode, and ultimately increase the demand for port services. In conditions of equivalent pricing by the various transport modes, all those involved in transport are selecting routings and organising their activity with a view to reducing the wear and tear of the transport network, traffic congestion, the impact on the environment and the number of accidents.

The application of the new and harmonised approach to all transport modes is expected to rectify many of the significant negative implications that have resulted from the extremely diverse national charging systems. Such an approach naturally is to be introduced gradually, in a way that gives the users and providers of transport services adequate time to adjust to the new reality.

The Commission, therefore, proposed a step-by-step approach to implementation, to be accompanied by an advisory committee from Member States' experts and with the full involvement of all stakeholders. The Committee could begin its work base on the available evidence, allowing the first steps towards the full introduction of the principles to be taken during the first phase. This phase, which would run between 1998 and 2000, would see the introduction of charging systems in rail and airports, complementing the charging system in road haulage and ensuring that a broadly compatible structure is in place in the main modes of transport. Charging of external costs grounded on an agreed EU framework would be allowed, but total charging levels would be capped by average infrastructure costs (which was the current rule). The second phase, between 2001 and 2004, would see greater harmonisation and adaptation of charging systems, especially for heavy goods vehicles and rail transport where a kilometre-based charging system, differentiated on the basis of vehicle and geographical characteristics, would be instituted. As of this period, charges should not exceed marginal social costs (including external costs). The third phase would see an updating of the EU framework in the light of experience gained during the first two phases.

The absence of European ports from the pilot planning of the first two phases does not mean their exemption from this system and philosophy of charging after 2004. The review of the final implementation will only be positive if it is applied to all transport modes, including ports. It is important that the Commission's initiative, apart from the creation of harmonised methods of charging and accounting, includes actions concerning *all* transport modes. Especially for ports, the Commission refers to the need for EU measures improving the transparency of the funding of ports. Indeed, there are wide variations in charging for the costs of port infrastructure, not only between the Member States but, also, between ports in the same member state. These variations are already an objective of the EU agenda in order to complete the integration of the CTP, which is under development.

The creation of a specific, more cohesive, system of charging of infrastructure will eventually lead to a reduction in total transport cost, while it will also allow the infrastructure administrators to recover a significant part of the cost of infrastructure from the users without the imposition of additional costs to the latter. Consequently, the system will result in the more efficient use of the existing infrastructure, and will facilitate investments in infrastructure both for the modernisation of the existing and the creation of new.

The European Parliament,[16] the Ecosoc,[17] and the CoR[18] have approved the adoption of the 'user pays' principle. The EP has commended favourably on the introduction of a harmonised charging system for all transport modes based on the marginal social cost. The Ecosoc and the CoR argued that, in order to make the system of price determination more fair, in other words a system that respects income neutrality, complementary actions are required prior to the determination of the cost. These actions need to concern the partial cost factors and the issue of calculating the various externalities, especially the environmental, caused by every transport mode. However, as both these advisory EU institutions have stated, the existence of alternative transport modes is a prerequisite for the viability of the European transport system, since charging itself will not result in the expected change of attitude as envisaged by the Commission.

Transport, Financial Transparency, Competition

A European Court of Justice (ECJ) decision confirmed in 1984 that the operation of the common market in the transport sector is not only governed by the provisions of the Treaty of Rome relating to the CTP (Title IV) but, also, by the competition rules (set out in Articles 85 to 92) and the more general provisions of the same Treaty.[19] That decision resolved critical legal ambiguities regarding the vague provisions on transport in the Treaty of Rome, the standing-out case being the regulatory framework concerning competition, and the belief of some commentators that the latter did not apply in the case of transport.

In fact, the financial and technical characteristics of transport were posing obstacles to the application of EU rules concerning competition. In certain cases, the existence of transport systems based on the exploitation of isolated networks have allowed just one, or only few, transport companies to gain a dominant market position. Then, the implementation of integrated systems would most probably require cooperation agreements between the various economic entities. The undertaking of the obligation to provide services of a public benefit nature in many cases entailed the granting of special or exclusive rights of operation to them. At the same time, transport companies often depended on state financial support, such as the provision of subsidies that were not compatible with the operation of the internal market.

All the above examples highlight the critical importance of the application of competition rules to the efficiency of the transport sector, once the particular characteristics of this economic activity have been taken into account. Structural changes took place in the transport sector, such as the entry of new companies in some markets. New relations among the transport companies as well as various types of partnership schemes have appeared. The EU had to secure that the adjustment process of the transport sector would discourage distortions in competition, create a level playing field, and enable the users to benefit from the competition between the transport companies. The application of such a framework in transport services creates substantial positive changes when enterprises attempt to adjust to the scale and requirements of the single market. Otherwise, the most dynamic transport enterprises would attempt to reap the potential for economies of scale and expand the range of their operations, something that has actually taken place.

Nowadays, as a measure to strengthen transparency, the Commission has proceeded to an inventory of all state aids given to every transport mode with a view to assess periodically the scale and nature of the provided state aids. In order for this inventory to reflect accurately the various types of state aid the Commission has proposed measures increasing, where necessary, the transparency of accounts of infrastructure and transport companies. Whilst the specific EU action has first examined the case of the railway companies, the other sectors will follow gradually. The whole process follows the Commission's, and also the stakeholders', advocacy that financial transparency is indispensable for the proper application of any system of public (whether EU, national or local) sector financial contribution.

Ports have been, and in some cases still are, among those parts of the transport system where public authorities have undertaken investments in infrastructure that are not compatible with the EU competition rules. Consequently, the application of the above-described measure to ports was deemed necessary in order, among other things, to increase the transparency of their accounts. However, the lack of adequate data, and the unwillingness of some market players to contribute to this process, posed significant difficulties to the calculation of the scale and impact of state aids on ports in particular, and the total transport sector in general. Thus, the progress of this issue has been limited and, as discussed in detail in Chapter 9, it was only in

2001 that the Commission managed to publish the results of this public inventory regarding the port industry.

NOTES

1. Official Journal, C 279 of 1.10.1999.
2. Official Journal, C 258 of 10.9.1999.
3. Official Journal, C 258 of 10.9.1999.
4. Official Journal, C 374 of 23.12.1999.
5. The nine sectoral Councils are: Transport, Energy, Agriculture, Enterprise, Internal market, Development cooperation, Fisheries, ECOFIN, General Affairs.
6. Bulletin of the activities of the EU 10-1999, paragraph 1.3.77.
7. The European Round Table of Industrialists had mentioned, since its inception in 1981, the need for policies to address the expected increase of transport activity (ERTI, 1981).
8. See the proposal for a European network of high-speed trains (Comité des Constructeurs Français d'Automobiles, 1989) and the plan for a road network for Europe (International Road Federation, 1990).
9. Decision 78/184/EEC of 20.2.1978.
10. Regulation 3359/90 of 20.11.1990.
11. Sec (91) 2274, of 29.11.91 (Internal Document of the Commission).
12. Official Journal, C95 of 21.9.1968
13. Official Journal, C 55 of 24.2.1997.
14. Official Journal, C 116 of 14.4.1997.
15. Official Journal, C 219 of 30.7.1999.
16. Official Journal, C 116 of 28.4.1999.
17. Official Journal, C 198 of 14.7.1999.
18. Case 209-213/84 Ministere Plic vs. Lucas Asjes (The Nouvelles Frontieres case) [1986] ECR 1425; [1986] 3 CMLE 173.

5. Advancing the Interoperability and Interconnection of Transport Modes and Networks

5.1 THE CONCEPTS OF INTEROPERABILITY AND INTERCONNECTION

Apart from measures aiming to improve the performance/potential of individual transport modes, a significant part of the CTP encompasses initiatives promoting those conditions allowing the increase in the combined use of transport modes. The ultimate end is to increase the efficiency of transport services through the utilisation of the full potential of the overall transport system. Efficiency that will come about from the development of a common policy concerning the interconnection and the interoperability of the existing networks, but also taking into account the capacities and inherent problems of each mode, as stated in the Maastricht Treaty of the European Union (Article 129B).

The term *interconnection* refers to the creation of the necessary international and multimodal connections to facilitate the use of networks of different transport modes and different countries. This process will bring about the positive effects of cooperation and higher efficiency of the transport system (Erdmenger, 1996).

The term *interoperability* refers to the administrative, technical and organisational compatibility of the transport system for the mutual satisfaction of transport traffic in a way that eliminates barriers to uninterrupted network access (Button, 1998). These are complementary policies affecting, by definition, all possible methods and modes of transportation, as do the EU actions on the development, consistent with existing networks, of new networks integrating landlocked, island or isolated regions, wherever their absence causes isolation or hampers the development of part of the EU territory.

5.2 COMBINED TRANSPORT

The first EU policy actions having a multimodal perspective were those involving the development of combined transport, even though they were restricted only to rail and road modes during the initial stages. *Combined transport* is, in general, the transportation of goods with the use of multiple (more than two) transport modes without the unloading of cargo during the journey. The policy concept is that the part of the journey carried by road must be as short as possible, and the advantages of the other transport modes must be explored. Such a transport method is a key factor for the creation of a modern and efficient transport system.

The initial EU legal document that attempted to address the issue of combined transport was adopted in 1975. Directive 75/130,[1] in relation to certain types of combined transport between Member States, decreed specific EU rules on relative transport liberalisation and defined combined transport in a way that precluded maritime transport. If multimodal transport was to be favoured, the restrictions imposed on the detachment of traffic from the road transport system had to be overcome.

Economic and technological developments imposed the continuous revision and rephrasing of the specific Directive. Up to 1991, the Directive 75/130 had been amended five times.[2] Among other things, the developments required the field of combined transport to include maritime transport. The amendment of 1982 incorporated in the definition of combined transport the transport of containers of more than 20 feet length with the use of inland waterway and/or maritime transport modes, i.e. the transport between Member States within a radius of 50 kilometres from the estuarine port of loading or unloading. The amendment of 1991 extended the limit of the part of the journey carried by road to 150 kilometres in a straight line.

In September 1990, the Commission created a high level Working Group for the promotion of combined transport. However, at the time maritime and air transport were not included in the EU definition of combined transport. The next step was the adoption of a new Directive in 1992 aiming to reduce road transport through the development of transport combining the road, rail, inland waterway and maritime transport modes.[3] Article 1 of the Directive stated that:

> "combined transport" means the transport of goods between Member States where the lorry, trailer, semi-trailer, with or without tractor unit, swap body or container of 20 feet or more uses the road on the initial or final leg of the journey and, on the other leg, rail or inland waterway or maritime services where this section exceeds 100 km as the crow flies and make the initial or final road transport leg of the journey;

- between the point where the goods are loaded and the nearest suitable rail loading station for the initial leg, and between the nearest suitable rail unloading station and the point where the goods are unloaded for the final leg, or;
- within a radius not exceeding 150 km as the crow flies from the inland waterway port or seaport of loading or unloading.

A logical consequence was the decision on the creation of a trans-European network of combined transport.[4] The Decision 93/628 was an important step towards the inclusion of maritime transport in the chain of combined transport that the CTP was promoting. More specifically, it set the target aiming to improve freight transport through the interconnection of the various transport modes throughout the EU. It defined that the basic trans-European combined transport network would comprise rail, inland waterway and road junctions of great significance to the long-distance transport of goods and serving all Member States. Most significantly, for this study, it also included the transloading facilities between the rail, inland waterway, road and maritime networks.

Throughout the next years, all the EU documents and policies developed at national and local level used the definition of combined transport as stated in the Directive 92/106 (CEU, 1996c). As recorded in the Commission's report on the outcomes of the specific Directive up to 1995 (CEU, 1997b), almost all Member States had incorporated the Directive into their national legislation. However, the majority of the Member States had not implemented the tax provisions of the Directive.

Moreover, the aforementioned report observed that during those years an increase in the combined transport of containers through inland waterways, as well as through the combined use of the road and railway transport has been observed. In 1994 7.6 million TEU were carried by combined transport networks, a number representing a 60% increase in four years (1990–94). Combined transport expressed in tonne-miles accounted for 5% of road transport and 23% of railway transport of goods. However, combined transport was not always able to challenge long-distance road haulage due to distortions in competition arising from the operational framework of road transportation (such as lack of internalisation of externalities, duration of driving hours, overloading), as well as from structural problems of combined transport itself. Thus, the Commission expressed its intention to undertake further initiatives for the improvement of combined freight transport.

Even the definition of 'freight transport between Member States' itself started causing problems. If taken literally, the phrasing ought to include the transport within the territories of the Member States and between a member state and third country, even in cases where the largest part of the journey was carried by inland waterway or by short maritime or railway routings. In 1998, the Commission, advocating in accordance with this concept, submitted a new proposal amending Directive 92/106 (CEU, 1998d), aiming to address the limitations of the previously adopted policies. Therein it proposed a new phrasing, in alignment with Article 75 of the EU Treaty, precisely because the single transport market was including combined transport within the confines of a single Member State (cabotage). Taking into consideration the new parameters, the Commission specified that the road leg of the journey could exceed 150 kilometres but under no circumstances, could this exceed the 20% of the journey carried by the other transport modes. Thus, a new definition of combined transport states that:

> "combined transport" means the transport of goods to or from or within a Member State where the lorry, trailer, semi-trailer, with or without tractor unit, swap body or container of 20 feet or more uses in successive sections several modes of transport, among which are rail and/or inland waterway and/or maritime services and/or road, provided that:
> - each individual road section shall be no more than 20% of the total kilometres of the journey by the other mode or modes mentioned,
> - there is an equivalent road transport possible for the sea or inland waterway section.

In order to promote the types of transport that the above definition incorporated, a new Directive was adopted in 1999. According to the latter, Member States ought to enforce, or extend the enforcement of, the necessary legal, regulatory, and administrative provisions (and notify the Commission about the adopted measures) so that fiscal relief would be applied to all vessels engaged in combined freight transportation. The taxes and various charges applied to the transport vehicles (lorries, trailers, semi-trailers, with or without tractor units) employed in combined transport were to be reduced or returned, possibly as a lump sum, or exempted, on the basis of specific EU rules.[5]

Meanwhile, a Regulation, adopted in October 1998, had mobilised EU financial support for actions of an innovative nature that would advance combined transport.[6] That Regulation established a mechanism for granting financial assistance to pilot projects aiming to promote the combined transport of goods (PACT programme – Pilot Actions in Combined Transport). The duration of the programme was for a period of five years (1 January 1997 to 31 December 2001) and the total budget available was ECU 5 million. The objectives pursued were as follows:

(a) to increase the competitiveness of combined transport both in terms of price and of service quality *vis-à-vis* road transport from start to finish;
(b) to promote the use of advanced technology in the combined transport sector;
(c) to improve the range of combined transport available.

Renewing the Pact Programme, the Commission approved in June 2001 twenty-one actions on the improvement of carriage of goods by combined transport. Six of these actions aim to improve the commercial attractiveness of short sea shipping (see Chapter 8.1) and it is estimated that they will reduce road traffic (in favour of more sustainable modes of transport such as maritime transport) in the specific corridors by approximately 3.5 billion tonne-miles per year.

5.3   STRATEGIES FOR THE DEVELOPMENT OF AN INTERMODAL EUROPEAN TRANSPORT SYSTEM

Apart from actions concerning the increase in the use of the combined transport modes, the CTP provides for the development of measures concerning the creation of a European intermodal transport system. Aiming to adopt a systemic framework approach promoting intermodal freight transport, the Commission proposed in 1997 the creation of a EU policy (CEU, 1997c). The European Parliament[7] and the Committee of the Regions[8] approved those directions in 1999.

An essential characteristic of a successful transport network is its ability to combine different methods of transport in a cohesive system that enables the satisfactory carriage of passengers and goods. *Intermodality* is a quality indicator of the level of integration between the different modes: 'more intermodality' means more integration and complementarity between modes, and provides a more efficient use of the transport system. The economic basis for intermodality is that transport modes, which display favourable intrinsic economic and operational characteristics individually, can be integrated into a door-to-door transport chain in order to improve the overall efficiency of the system. This integration needs to take place at the level of infrastructure and other hardware (e.g. loading units, vehicles, telecommunications), at the level of operations and services, as well as at the level of the regulatory framework.

The Commission's understanding of 'intermodality' and 'intermodal transport' (CEU, 1997c) extends beyond earlier definitions that other EU institutions have proposed. The Council of Ministers restricted intermodal transport to unitised transport, while unitisation is but one possible, though important, means to facilitate the transfer of goods between modes. In this vein, the Council of Ministers had defined intermodal transport as the movement of goods in one and the same loading unit or vehicle, which uses successively several modes of transport, without handling of the goods themselves in changing modes. Respectively it had defined combined transport as intermodal transport where the major part of the European journey was by rail, inland waterways, or sea, and any initial and/or final leg carried out by road was as short as possible.

According to the wider intermodalism concept that the Commission's initiative endorsed, intermodal transport is the movement of goods whereby at least two different modes are used in a door-to-door transport chain enabling, due to an overall systemic approach, the more rational use of the available transport capacity. The modal combination advanced by this concept does not intend to impose a particular modal option. It advocates, however, a higher participation of railways, inland waterways, and maritime transport in transport chains, when none of these modes individually can provide a door-to-door service. Most importantly, it does so when many users tend to consider door-to-door services as a precondition for the use of a transport mode.

Opportunities, Prospects, and EU Policy Actions

The Commission identified opportunities for the development of intermodal transport, which could offer new options to companies and transporters and higher cost efficiency in the case of long-distance transport. It also noted that many points of congestion of the European transport system were having a direct impact on the peripheral areas of the EU. The geographical position of most of the poorest Member States often requires the need to use more than one transport mode to secure connections with the economic centre, especially for the carriage of goods.

The cost of production logistics, storage, handling, processing, and transportation of goods accounts for as much as 30% of their price, while transport cost itself accounts for a significant part of the final price (CEU, 1992c). In the case of the peripheral regions, the cost of goods transportation to the central regions is higher than the respective cost in the central regions themselves. Given that the systems of combined and multiple transport result in lower costs for long distance transport in relation to other options, such transport systems can play an important role in addressing the geographical disadvantages of the peripheral regions. Moreover, the peripheral regions have additional disadvantages due to dated equipment and infrastructure, given that large-scale and long-term investments are required to achieve cohesion with the central regions of the EU. In the case of the central regions of the EU, the most important problem concerns traffic congestion and its indirect implications for the environment. Thus, in this case, the redirection of part of the transported volume from road haulage towards less-congested and more environmentally friendly transport modes is clearly beneficial.

Nonetheless, given the conditions prevailing in the transport sector, the use of multimodal commercial transport presently faces certain obstacles.

Primarily obstacles exist because of lack of interconnection at three levels. The first one is between the available infrastructures of transport means. The second one is that of transport operations, i.e. between the provision of services and the use of infrastructures, especially terminals. The third level is the lack of interconnection between modal-oriented services and regulations. The change of mode within a journey involves a change of system rather than just a technical transhipment. *Friction costs*, i.e. the costs arising from the lack of combination and interconnection of transport modes, significantly affect the competitiveness of combined transport. These costs are expressed in the form of higher prices; longer journeys, longer delays or less reliability in terms of time; lower availability of quality services; limitations on the type of goods that can be transported; higher risk of damage to the cargo; more complex administrative procedures.

In the EU, intermodal transport is rather limited due to the gap between the shippers' expectations and the actual quality of the services provided by intermodal routings. As a result, the market for intermodal routings remains stagnant. In 1996, the market share of intermodal transport did not exceed 8% of total tonne-miles. The reason is various inadequacies at all three previously mentioned levels.

The first level concerns the infrastructure of transport modes. The development of infrastructure is still mode-specific, while uninterrupted intermodal transport requires the planning of transport networks based on the interconnection and the interoperability of transport modes. Additionally, the use of intermodal transport increases the variety of loading units, thus; as a result, cargo handling becomes more complex and costs increase.

The second level concerns transport operations. The level of handling quality at the terminals exhibits wide variation. Variation also exhibits the performance of the different transport modes, in part due to the various degrees of service liberalisation and the pressures of competition, and in part due to various degrees of customer response per transport mode.

Finally, the third level concerns the routings and the regulatory framework. Intermodal transport entails the participation of many actors, which exchange data and information vital for the efficient administration of routings and networks. Open information systems on intermodal transport do not yet exist. Further, the largest part of transport legislation is mode-specific whilst intermodal transport has its distinctive dynamics and requirements. The fragmented and mode-specific nature of resolving the problems further hampers the development of intermodal transport.

However, the higher degree of integration of the EU economies and the establishment of the internal market, result in economic development, in turn increasing transport intensity,[9] and creating a wider scope for intermodal transport. The average distance of freight transport exhibited exponential increase between 1985 and 1995. In the United Kingdom the average distance of freight transport increased by 24%, in Sweden by 37% and in France by 36%. The average distance of freight transport in the EU was increasing at an annual rate of almost 2% between 1970 and 1997. Long-distance freight transport is particularly suited to intermodal transport, the longer the transport distance the higher the competitiveness of intermodal transport.

As regards transport intensity, empirical evidence suggest that trends in individual Member States have exhibited a substantial amount of diversity throughout the last three decades. Still, the rate of increase in transport volumes is unambiguously outstripping the rate of improvement in environmental technology for transport (Stead, 2001), resulting in increasing environmental problems for the transport sector. This trend in transport intensity leads to the increase in the demand for effective and efficient intermodal container transport. Secondly, it requires the upgrading of the managerial organisation and administration of the distribution chain. The demand for intermodal transport increases because it is more cost efficient than road haulage in the case of long-distance transport. Policies and actions in the transport sector aiming to improve efficiency also include passenger demand management policies (cf. Meyer, 1999) – whilst policies and actions outside the transport sector include energy taxes and land use planning.

The increasing importance of managerial organisation and administration is explained by the fact that the demand for transport is essentially a derived demand. The use of transport is determined by the requirements of industrial organisation. While transport intensity increases, the industrial circles realise that it is possible to reduce transport and administration costs through the better use of transport within the operational framework of the logistics chain. In turn, the administration of logistics is aiming to optimise all the flows (financial and material information) from source to the final customer. The objective is to align the external flows of the various economic actors (suppliers, manufactures and distributors) in order to reduce costs and benefit the customers.

The objective of intermodal transport is the further integration of the transport modes in order to upgrade the quality and reliability of routings and value added services. Intermodal transport is mainly based on the wider cooperation between transport stakeholders. This cooperation would allow for the optimal use of the existing transport capacity and could lead to a more balanced demand for transport. Thus, intermodal transport is one of the most important propulsive forces behind the attainment of continuous mobility. It also allows for the better use of infrastructure and routings and it is more environmentally friendly in relation to the widely used road haulage.

The Commission, adopting the view that the integration of transport modes would improve the weaknesses of interconnection at the various levels, initiated actions promoting intermodal and multimodal transport in Europe. In fact, if intermodal services were to develop on a large scale it would be necessary either to readopt a 'derigistic' approach to freight transport and to direct certain types of traffic to rail, waterways and maritime; or to intervene in favour of intermodal systems with the minimum short-term assistance measures necessary to ensure future success in a free market. With the Commission advocating that the later possibility was the sensible one to adopt in order to achieve the desired widespread use of intermodal transport, the proposed and final endorsed strategy is based on four central issues:

(a) Development of infrastructure networks of all trans-European transport junctions.
(b) Harmonisation of the legal requirements and competition rules.
(c) Identification and abolition of the obstacles to intermodal transport and of the relevant friction costs.
(d) Application of advanced information technologies to the transport sector.

This choice is political and complementary to EU policies concerning transport, the development of TEN-T, the promotion of fair and effective charging and the application of advanced information technologies to the transport sector. A part of the attempt to further promote intermodal transport is the Commission's proposal on the inclusion of seaports, estuarine ports and intermodal terminals in the TEN-T (CEU, 1997d). The rationale is developed in the context of the EU initiatives concerning explicitly the port industry (hence it is analytically discussed in Chapter 8).

In 1999, the progress report on the application of the action programme concerning intermodal transport (CEU, 1999a) added to the future EU actions four new initiatives. These are: (a) the development of integrated applications of Intelligent Transport Systems that exploit the potential of advanced telematics; (b) the creation of applications of electronic commerce for intermodal transport; (c) the continuation of the work on the administration of the distribution chain, the hardware support of intermodal and combined transport; and (d) the diffusion of information on the potential benefits of combined transport to the distribution chains.

Accepting the content of this progress report, the Council of Ministers decided, in December 1999, to invite the Commission to include issues concerning intermodal transport in future amendments of the Regulation on the TEN-T. It also called the Commission to submit proposals on the application of telematics in intermodal transport; to study the aspects of intermodality relating to the supply-chain management system; to promote the harmonisation of standards and units of measurement of cargo; and, finally, to clarify the issues of liability and competition in the course of the transport process.[10]

5.4   INTRODUCING TELEMATICS AND INFORMATION TECHNOLOGY

It is worth mentioning that the implementation of telematics applications and electronics systems in the transport sector has been recognised not only as important means to achieve higher interoperability between the transport modes but, also, as precondition for the adjustment and quality enhancement of every transport mode individually.

In October 1995, a Council Resolution was published with a view to encouraging the Commission to promote the introduction of compatible telematics systems in the transport sector that would contribute to the creation of European information infrastructures.[11] The resolution stressed the importance of introducing interoperable automatic road traffic information and warning systems in the Member States, the need to define and use compatible specifications in air transport, the need to introduce a European ship-reporting system and the importance of applying compatible telematics systems in railway transport. The Council called the Commission and the Member States to cooperate in order to determine the necessary measures in relation to rail and road transport, to submit recommendations on a EU policy that would promote satellite sea navigation, and to support the efforts promoting standardisation in the air traffic sector.

Promoting the views of the Council of Ministers, the Commission adopted an action programme aiming to define measures for the development of telematics and electronics systems infrastructure in all transport modes so that further proposals for the deployment of specific policy actions would be formulated (CEU, 1994a).

In order to attain the effective administrative and organisational decision-making strategy when using an intermodal freight transport system, shippers require access to real-ime information as well as the presence of single standards in all transport exchanges (such as movement, storage, and handling reservations) To shippers the importance of real-time information has been upgraded, as the logistics function has widened its scope from the distribution of finished products to the end-to-end supply chain and has been elevated from an operation to a wider corporate strategy (McKinnon, 2001).

However, in Europe the lack of real-time information on intermodal transport is evident. The reason is that the existing information systems have been established according to the needs of each individual transport mode.

Moreover, most transport providers use customised information systems. These obstacles restrict the interconnection and interoperability of the information systems. The same is the case for the existing informatics regarding modal interchanges during the transportation activity. The availability of such systems is limited only to certain modal connections, thus allowing only certain exchanges. A transport exchange standardisation does not exist. Consequently, the application of e-commerce to intermodal transport is, generally, impossible.

The creation of information and exchange systems for intermodal transport will improve the efficiency of the service providers in this sector; it will help to maximise vehicle load factors, minimise empty running, and achieve an optimal allocation of freight between modes. Along with the standardisation of handling systems, they will help them make effective use of vehicle and warehouse capacity (European Logistics Association, 2000). Apart from reducing the cost of transport as a whole, these systems enhance e-commerce. Then, the accurate and timely information provision as to the cargo nature from the port of departure to the port of the (next) arrival is of primary importance for the safe handling of 'dangerous goods' cargoes, provides a basis for minimisation of errors and even elimination of potential misunderstandings. By enhancing the monitoring capabilities of the process, it increases the safety of operation of the maritime transport activity (cf. Giannopoulos & Koukouloudi, 2000). For all these reasons, the existing EU Research and Development action framework is taking into account these facts and developing actions aiming to create models for possible open-systems architectures applicable to the transport sector.

5.5   TRANS-EUROPEAN TRANSPORT NETWORKS

The Single European Market Requires a Common Transport System

Transport sectors in Europe have exhibited quite different growth rates. This is mainly a result of the diverse strategies and policies of national, regional, or local institutions, and the vague preferences and divergent opinions regarding competition between the various transport modes. This differentiation has resulted in unbalanced and uneven cost and price structures, as well as differing accounting practices, regulations and standards concerning safety and the environment.

The aforementioned reality is incompatible with the fundamental objectives of the European process of political and economic integration. The Single European Market needs to be served by an integrated common transport system governed by common rules that ensure a competitive environment throughout Europe. The practices of the system ought to enable the citizens, and the economic entities to benefit from the creation of a common economic and monetary space, without internal borders, where a plethora of transport service providers and transport users act according to common rules.

The markets of passenger and goods' transport use, largely, common infrastructures. In turn, these markets are subdivided into local and regional markets, serving the local demand for transport activities, and into trans-European markets, serving the respective demand for long-distance transport within Europe. The latter also serve national needs.

However, in the late 1980s national governments continued to plan most, if not all, the transport networks in Europe at the national level. The emphasis was on the development of single-mode transport networks (particularly road networks) rather than on integrated multimodal transport planning. That approach has caused several problems. The acceleration of the integration process was accompanied by the lack of efficient connections between the national networks, congestion, and significant friction costs where obstacles to interoperability and interconnection were causing serious inadequacies.

Furthermore, the particular geographical location and economic history of the Member States had already created significant national differences as regards the level of sufficiency and quality of transport infrastructures. In general, the developed central and northern regions of the EU were better equipped than the peripheral regions and the southern Member States. The successive EU enlargements that took place in 1981 (accession of Greece) and 1986 (accession of Spain and Portugal) widened those regional inequalities, while the first EU regional funding policies (e.g. the Integrated Mediterranean Programmes), developed in an attempt to narrow the apparent economic divergences, did not seriously consider (thus, affect) the transport sector. In addition to the above problems, an increasing concentration of traffic in certain routings, transport modes and destination terminals was emerging as a core characteristic of the system that ultimately threatened the total efficiency of the transportation system in Europe.

The realisation that the existing incoherent pattern of individually developed planning, organisation, and administration of transport networks could not address and reverse the above situation, resulted in EU action towards the creation of an integrated Trans-European Transport Network (TEN-T) that would constitute the basic infrastructure of the European transport market. The impetus of the TEN-T concept is the prevailing view that a piecemeal development of the transport sector in Europe causes isolation of parts of the Community's territory, hampers the competitiveness of the European economy, has negative effects on the environment, and increases energy consumption (CEU, 1994b). In order to be efficient, this network aims, on the one hand, at the integrated development of the infrastructures of the various transport modes and, on the other hand, of the adoption of those administrative strategies allowing the best possible use of the network. Thus, the planning and development of the TEN-T entailed the participation of authorities at all decision-making levels: European, EU, national, regional, and local.

The Creation and Progress of the TEN-T Policy

Although nowadays the presence of EU policy concerning the connection of European networks is quite intensive, until 1990 the involvement of the EU in this issue was rather limited. As already mentioned, the EU proceeded to the first, though limited, *ad hoc* financing of 'investment programmes of EU interest' in 1982, and to the first medium-term budget (three-years) only in 1990. More significant, in terms of volume, was the supranational financial contribution of investments in transport infrastructure that was provided in the context of the EU Structural Funds. The reform of these Funds in 1988 marked the abolition of the financing of individual projects and the support of the less-developed Member States assumed the form of integrated development programmes concerning the relevant regions.

The provisions of the Maastricht Treaty of the European Union concerning the TEN-T created a new basis for EU action, defining more accurately the objectives and the limits of EU participation, as well as a new approach towards the financing of these actions. Chapter XII of the Maastricht Treaty (Article 129) explicitly stated the importance of the Trans-European Networks to the SEM. Under the terms of Chapter XV (Articles 154, 155 and 156), the European Union must aim to promote the development of TEN-T as a key element for the creation of the Internal Market and the reinforcement of Economic and Social Cohesion. All these developments singled-out *interconnection* and *interoperability* of national networks as the fundamental and interlinked means to achieve the integration of such networks.

Incorporating economic, social, and environmental justifications, the EU embarked on a project to establish a unified trans-European transport network. In this vein, the Commission is developing guidelines regarding projects of common interest. The European Parliament and the Council approve these guidelines after the consultation of the Ecosoc and the CoR.

This strategy implicates the interconnection of the transport modes through the completion of the missing links, and the interoperability of the existing links through their technical harmonisation. Its success demands the rational and balanced development of the different modes, so that the transport system will become gradually integrated in operational terms in a wider context, i.e. the Community, and beyond that, the continent of Europe.

The strategy also insists upon the expansion of those modes whose operation produces the lowest demands in energy and the least possible negative effects to the environment, albeit without disregarding any other advantages resulting from the use of the different modes for passenger and freight transportation. The aim is that the sector will 'meet the present needs without compromising the ability of the future generations to their own needs' (definition of sustainability by: World Commission on Environment and Development, 1987). Those provisions clarified the application of the subsidiarity principle to the transport sector and, consequently, the way that the EU ought to join its activities with the activities of the responsible authorities at the other levels (national, regional, local).

The parallel activities of the Commission, especially the document entitled *Towards the development of Trans-European Networks* (December 1990 – CEU, 1990b) and the White Paper on the CTP (CEU, 1992b), created the conditions for the upgrading and precise determination of action concerning the specific sector. The emphasis of EU policy shifted to the economic and qualitative performance of the whole network, the protection of the environment, the stimulation of research and technical development, and the improvement of the EU relations with third countries as far as transport is concerned.

In 1993, the European Council decided to accelerate the TEN-T project. Towards this end, it appointed a group of representatives that, under the presidency of the then vice-president of the Commission H. Christophersen, attempted to prepare proposals on the priority projects during the first phase. In December 1994, the European Council at Essen approved 14 priority projects for the transport sector, after a proposal by the Christophersen Group (CEU, 1995c). Despite the fact that the European Council had asked for a specific timetable and financing plan concerning each of the 14 priority projects (included in the Annex III of the Decision 1692/96/EC on the EU Guidelines towards the development of the TEN-T), problems had arisen in relation to the initial estimations. In the 1998 progress report, the Commission attributed those difficulties to the complexity of certain projects, to technical, legislative, legal, and financial problems, as well as to the need to address the complex environmental impact on each of these projects (CEU, 1998e).

The creation and development of the TEN-T ought to take place in the framework of a system of open and competitive markets. The aim was not the improvement of the transport infrastructure in general, but the completion of the EU transport system through the integration of the networks and, at the same time, considering the needs of the peripheral or most remote regions too. Recently the Commission advocated that the extension of the TEN-T to the neighbouring countries could directly contribute to the enhanced and continuous improvement of their growth and competitiveness (and consequently to employment and social welfare) due to decreased transport costs, as well as to the promotion of the exports capacities of the EU member countries and of the applicant countries (CEU, 1997e).

The Absence of European Ports from the Initial TEN-T Planning

The initial approaches and plans concerning the TEN-T did not include ports and airports. This stance was reflecting the views developed during the first stages of the European integration process and the particular competitive characteristics of ports and airports infrastructures. Whilst in the case of airports it was possible to categorise their infrastructures (connection points, local points, access points) in order to facilitate their faster inclusion in the TEN-T, in the case of ports even such a basic solution was not possible. In any case, the need to improve port infrastructure was profound. An EU Task Force on Ports and Maritime Transport, which was formed to address that aim, could not decide on the character of EU intervention in a sector that appeared to operate under conditions of competition, but was actually characterised by significant organisational differences and was the recipient of state aid.

Among the strengths of the port sector is that comparatively moderate (in terms of capital requirements) projects may have a disproportionately large impact on the development of transport activities that can be handled by a commercial port. Additionally, in most cases such projects are identified, materialised, and implemented in a shorter time span (compared to other transport modes). At the time, however, the EU philosophy was influenced by the argument that any effect on competition ought to be avoided. Thus, it did not attempt to set up a final selection of 'ports of EU interest'. Any initial thoughts on the creation of a specific relevant list were abandoned. For these reasons, as well as because of the fierce competition between European ports, neither a plan concerning a port network was conceived, nor any specific target for the adjustment of ports within a specific period was set.

The discussions of issues concerning ports during the initial consultations on the TEN-T were restricted to 'projects of common interest'. Port- and port-related projects of common interest could concern sea and estuarine port access infrastructure, port zone infrastructure, inland transport infrastructure within the port zone, and inland transport infrastructure connecting the port with the other parts of the TEN-T. The special condition that was set for those projects concerned their economic viability. The viability of the project ought to be proven on the basis of financial analysis or, if that was not possible, a proposal had to be made based on a cost/benefit analysis. The EU institutions thought that way they would ensure the effectiveness of the EU financed projects. Further specific conditions concerned specifically projects promoting short sea shipping.

Ports become part of the TEN-T: The Determining Role of Transport Modes Complementarity

Core elements of the planned TEN-T, in the mid-1990s, were the modal exchanges of combined transport chains, the terminals and the interconnections of transport modes that allowed the uninterrupted change in mode, or the transport of passengers and goods to their final destination. In that context, it became necessary to examine the potential role of the ports, since they constituted the interconnections between the maritime and the other transport modes. .

In the mid-1990s, proposals appeared concerning the reconsideration of the exemption of ports from the TEN-T. The new thoughts and proposals resulted in the inclusion in the plans concerning the TEN-T of issues such as the improvement of port infrastructure and the integration of the European port system with the other parts of the transport process. This was formalised after an agreement at the Council of Ministers in June 2000 (the whole process is presented in detail in Chapter 8). However, it is worth mentioning that even if such a development was not desirable, because of the complementarities of modes in the transport process, *ports essentially already were an indispensable part of the TEN-T*. The specific role of complementarity was determining, since it can be argued that the Council's decision essentially regarded not *if* but rather *which* ports would become part of the TEN-T.

A characteristic example was the effects of the political agreement of the Council on the trans-European network of commercial railways (December 1999). The proposals concerning the completion of the specific network included a list of ports (CEU, 1997f). The potential and existing complementarities of the various modes demand an integrated approach, encompassing all transport modes, to be employed for the planning and financing of the TEN-T. Moreover, these complementarities directly affect competition and the practices of transport companies in general and those providing port services specifically.

An example is the subsidies granted to the two intermodal railway terminals in the port of Rotterdam. Those subsidies were deemed compatible with the EU Treaty (Article 73), under the condition that they would not be used for the financing of infrastructure and equipment concerning connections to/from ships, but only for infrastructure that would facilitate the transport of cargo by railways rather than road haulage. Without the subsidies, which ought not to exceed 20% of the total construction costs, the price of transhipment to/from the port by railway would not be competitive in relation to the respective price of road haulage. This fact made the Commission realise that the specific subsidies seemed to rectify rather than cause distortions in competition between the transport modes.

The implications of this political decision of the Council were significant and four-fold. Firstly, the adequate development of access infrastructure in ports, which are included in the plans of the network of commercial railways, is considered of paramount importance. The second implication derives from the fact that each Member State may provide financial support for the construction and operation of the infrastructure of the railway network to any company that has an interest in the specific activity (and not exclusively to public or private railway companies). Such granting can be provided within the limits of a Member State. Most importantly, as the Council document explicitly states that national governments may grant this support to public authorities, transport companies and all the stakeholders involved in combined transport, this is a provision that also applies to port authorities.

The third implication is the introduction of a harmonised infrastructure charging system of the total network, a system governed by the principles of transparency and non-user discrimination. Finally, an indirect implication is the improvement in the position of ports due to reduced congestion of the railway network connecting them with the hinterland.

Evidently, the complementarity of the transport modes creates *de facto* conditions that demand a new policy orientation at the European level, namely the inclusion of seaports, inland ports, and intermodal terminals in the TENs. The inclusion of these interconnection points emerge to be critical to the functioning of intermodal transport within a multimodal infrastructure network, not least because it increases the options in terms of alternative door-to-door intermodal logistics chains available to transport organisers and users. In turn, this inclusion will eventually result in a more competitive environment faced by alternative logistics chains, where distortions of trade flows between Member States resulting from different systems of financing and charging for port (related) infrastructure and services become, or could appear, more competitive (Verbeke et al., 2001).

EU Guidelines for the Development of the TEN-T

The European institutions have expressed their position regarding the TEN-T in the form of various decisions. The EU guidelines for the development of the trans-European transport network assumed their final form in July 1996 in a Decision approved by the European Parliament and the Council.[12] The Decision 1692/96 identified, among others, the following objectives of the TEN-T:

1. Ensure mobility of persons and goods.
2. Offer users high-quality infrastructures.
3. Combine all modes of transport.
4. Allow the optimal use of existing capacities.
5. Be interoperable in all its components.
6. Cover the whole territory of the EU.
7. Allow for its extension to the EFTA Member States, countries of Central and Eastern Europe and the Mediterranean countries.

The Commission publishes an annual progress report on the development of the TEN-T presenting an outlook of each sector and ideas on future revisions of the guidelines and the setting of priorities for the future.

Notably, while the issue of port participation in the TEN-T was still under debate, the 1998 Progress Report (CEU, 1998f) stated that work was also being undertaken on the inland waterway network and inland ports with a view to upgrading waterways, increasing their depth in order to improve reliability of navigation and enlarging locks. Investment in seaports up to that point (1998) accounted for 5% of total TEN-T infrastructure expenditure, or ECU 1.7 billion. Those funds were allocated to the construction of new port infrastructure (35%), improvement of connections with the trans-European land networks (40%), transhipment facilities and multimodal connections within the port area and improvement of sea access to ports. The total cost of projects up to 2010 is estimated at ECU 14 billion.

Key to the materialisation of the specific policy choices was considered to be the reform of the general rules concerning the granting of EU financial support, by the amendment of Regulation 2236/95.[13] Based on the experience gained by the three-year implementation, the revised criteria concerning the selection of funding of TEN-T projects were identified by the new Regulation 1655/1999.[14] According to the existing legal framework, the EU contribution is granted on a priority basis to projects contributing to the achievement of the objectives and priorities of the Treaty. EU funding is reserved for projects exhibiting potential economic viability but whose present economic effectiveness is deemed inadequate. The decision to provide an EU contribution also ought to take into consideration: (a) the maturity of the project, (b) the stimulation of public and private funding, (c) the health of the financial framework of the projects, (d) the direct or indirect socio-economic impacts, especially those concerning employment, and (e) the implications to the environment. The duration of the EU policy extends to the end of 2006. The assessment report, to be presented by the Commission that year will constitute the basis for the examination of the scope for continuation or amendment of the applied measures.

Earlier, in 1997, promoting the connection of the EU network with the networks of the neighbouring countries, the Commission had presented an action programme (CEU, 1997f) aiming to advance the vital level of policy-makers cooperation for the establishment of pan-European transport networks. The adopted means of cooperation included the coordination of programming, the study of the regulatory measures and the facilitation of financial agreements. As regards the cost of infrastructure investments and the mobilisation of the essential financial resources, the Commission underlined the necessary efforts of the applicant countries in order to address the expected problems arising from the increased volume of transport exchanges and tourism. In this vein, the programme incorporated in the other EU priorities, the initiation of action for the coverage of the networks in the neighbouring countries by the Global Navigation Satellite System, the implementation of a uniform ship-monitoring system in all European waters, and the enhancement of European cooperation in the field of research and development.

In its 1999 progress report, the Commission stated that the implementation of the approved TEN-T plans was satisfactory. At the same time, the legislative framework was enhanced by the adoption of Regulation 1655/1999. That Regulation provided for a funding framework of Euro 4.6 billion for the period 2000–06 to be used for large-scale transport infrastructure projects in the candidate for accession countries. These funds will be used by the mechanism of the pre-accession structural funds and are divided into annual budgets of Euro 520 million. The sum of the available funds must also include the EU funds reserved for the Fifth Research and Development Framework on the creation of *commercial cooperation plans between public–private stakeholders for the improvement of transport infrastructure.*[15]

The European Parliament (1999) estimated that it was necessary to increase the budget for the TEN-T and that the financing of the TEN-T required integrated measures.[16] For that reason the Parliament commended favourably on the previously mentioned amendment of Regulation 2236/95, aiming to secure the highest possible private sector participation in transport, the promotion of partnerships between the public and private sectors in financing TEN-Ts.

Financing the TEN-T: Problems and Prospects

A critical tool for the successful completion of the ambitious TEN-T policy is the ability to finance the total necessary transport infrastructures. In 1995, when the TEN-T did not include port infrastructures, the Commission estimated the needs to be approximately Euro 400 billion (CEU, 1995d).

Although Investments in Transport Infrastructure (ITI) in Europe are financed by various complementary funds, the main source of financing has always been national budgets. Investment activity in transport infrastructure throughout Europe in the early 1990s was mainly the responsibility of the public sector. This had caused scepticism concerning the ability to raise the necessary funds for the creation of the TEN-T (Johnson & Turner, 1997).

However, several projects undertaken within the TEN-T framework are now including the participation of the private sector. An illustrative example is the participation of the private sector in the financing of port infrastructure in the form of public/private partnerships. This development was the product of the view that the EU financial initiatives should not aim to replace Member States or the private sector as the main sources of financing. Nonetheless, it was deemed necessary to initiate EU action towards the resolution of problems concerning the combined action of the public and private sectors, especially regarding entrepreneurial risks, with a far-reaching goal being the self-financing of the projects. Of course, even if the EU so desired, it still could not be the main source of finance due to the lack of necessary funds. According to the initial plan of the TEN-T, the EU would not be able to contribute more than Euro 20 billion annually, of which Euro 8 billion would be raised by loans.

The Commission, having the acceptance of the Council of Transport Ministers, created a Task Force concerned with the financing to TEN-T projects by private–public partnerships (September, 1996). This Task Force comprised representatives of all stakeholders involved in transport infrastructure and representatives of the public sector appointed by the Transport Ministers. Following the suggestions of its final report on the financing of TEN-T projects by private–public partnerships, published by the Commission in May 1997 (CEU, 1997g), the contribution of the contemporary EU policy consists of provision of financial stimuli so that infrastructure projects, initially financed at the national or regional level, are included in the wider planning and priorities defined at the EU level. The needs in transport infrastructure are being addressed, largely designated, and partly funded at the Union level. The EU is taking the initiatives and providing the financial incentives. National governments need to implement these transport and environment strategies as they continue to develop and maintain their respective networks. They have a significantly larger role with respect to national planning and network design, distribution of capital resources, financing of ITI, and the monitoring of such funding. The second level of the contemporary EU policy concerns the mobilisation of private-sector capital, as an essential precondition in order to accelerate the pace and achieve the materialisation of the TEN-T projects (Kinnock, 1998).

The European Parliament favourably received the conclusions of the Commission regarding the financing of the TEN-T projects by *private–public partnerships*, and agreed that this form of financing was the key for the creation of the trans-European networks. The Commission, in order to ensure the uninterrupted continuation of the process is examining the clarification of certain EU rules (e.g. transparency) concerning, mainly, the public contracts on transport infrastructure. The previously mentioned 1997 Commission report had already provided clarification concerning the application of competition rules to the general objectives of the transport policy attempting to reconcile the need to maximise the economic viability of the plans and the free and indiscriminate access to infrastructure. Moreover, the Commission had also specified an evaluation process of the TEN-T plans.

The creation of private–public partnerships emerges to be critical for the success of the plan. However, it is also essential to address certain problems such as the distortions caused by political intervention in the projects, the framework governing investments and the construction of transport infrastructure projects when two or more Member States participate, the alterations in the competitive position of transport companies caused by market liberalisation, and not least the changes caused by technological advancements. Most important though, are the stabilisation of the regulatory framework as well as the specification of EU principles concerning the employment of all the actions reducing the 'risk of public policies' that the private sector faces, thus creating the conditions for undertaking the 'financial risk' by the private sector (Ross, 1998).

In April 2000, the Commission specified that the EU legislature, including the privileges concerning the operation of public services, is applicable to the private–public partnerships (CEU, 2000a). These privileges refer to the cases where public authorities grant to third parties the rights and obligations to create and/or upgrade the infrastructure while the third party undertakes the risk of operating the infrastructure. European ports are included in this category, since several private companies provide services of a public nature (i.e. technical and navigational services). The Commission specified that these privileges be based on the principles of non-discrimination, transparency, equality, proportionality, and mutual recognition. All these constitute fundamental principles of the EU legal system. Apparently, to the extent that there is still no specific policy concerning the liberalisation of the port sector (see: Chapter 8), these principles also concern the port sector. Indeed the specific principles govern all actions concerning the development of the TEN-T.

According to the principle of subsidiarity, the financial role of national governments remains very important to the materialisation of the specific programme. The same holds for the progress of the common policy on the

TEN-T as a whole (e.g. the creation of an institutional framework, development of the necessary relations with neighbouring countries – Siselschmidt, 2000). Member States are responsible for the planning and development of the local networks, the distribution of the available funds and the control of financing. To the extent that national policies – something that, according to empirical evidence, has been observed in Greece (Chlomoudis & Pallis, 1997) and, to a lesser albeit significant extent, in Spain, Italy and Portugal (Chlomoudis & Pallis, 2002) – do not adopt the EU priorities for the creation of the necessary conditions (e.g. regulatory framework) for the mobilisation of additional capital or the rational distribution of the available funds per transport mode, the progress towards the completion of the TEN-T will face further obstacles.

NOTES

1. Directive 75/130, of 17.2.1975.
2. Those were: Directive 79/130, of 19.12.1978; Directive 82/3, of 21.12.1981; Directive 82/603, of 28.7.1982; Directive 86/544, of 10.11.1986; and Directive 91/224, of 27.3.1991.
3. Directive 92/106, of 7.12.1992; Corrigendum: Official Journal, L 72 of 25.03.1993.
4. Decision 93/628, of 29.10.1993.
5. Directive 1999/62, of 17.6.1999.
6. Regulation 2196/98, of 1.10.1998.
7. Official Journal, C 150 of 28.5.1999.
8. Official Journal, C 198 of 14.7.1999.
9. Transport intensity per product refers to the number of tonne-miles per unit of economic outcome. For statistical data confirming the relationship of economic integration and the increase of transport intensity: Eurostat (2001).
10. General Report on the activities of the EU, Bulletin 10-1999.
11. Official Journal, C 309 of 05.11.1994.
12. Decision 1692/96 of 23.07.1996.
13. Regulation 2236/95, of 18.09.1995.
14. Regulation 1655/1999, of 29.07.1999.
15. Official Journal, C 359 of 11.12.1999.
16. General Report on the activities of the EU (1999), paragraph 1.3.105.

6. European Ports and the Common Maritime Transport Policy

6.1 INTRODUCING THE HORIZONTAL APPROACH TO THE CMTP

As the longitudinal analysis of the CTP progress demonstrated (Chapter 3), until the late 1980s maritime transport was unquestionably the part of the transport sector in which EU developments were the slowest and essentially unimportant. The content of an extremely limited and developing common shipping policy had been concentrated on the attempts to reverse the phenomenon of flagging-out and progress the liberalisation of cabotage trade in the Mediterranean Member States against a policy of flag restrictions. In the late 1980s, the debate included issues regarding the possibility of creating a European Registry of Shipping – Euros (CEU, 1989) – and a visible concern (though a decision to initiate any EU action was not taken) about safety issues. However, issues concerning the port industry, as well as the rest of the maritime transport industries, were not included in the policy-making agenda (Cafruny, 1991; Power, 1992).

A change of direction became apparent in 1991. It was advanced by the growing importance of the economic, environmental, and political aspects of the maritime transport system to the EU. This shift was also a result of the greater emphasis that was beginning to be placed on the transport sector. The Commission's initiatives on the introduction of a horizontal EU policy, referring explicitly the overall maritime transport system (CEU, 1991a), can be considered as the starting point of that change. The Commission, estimating the then existing and foreseeable new challenges affecting the international maritime transport system stated that the EU ought to answer the question whether national-level policies were still adequate in a changing context with increased international demands. As a partial reply to its own question, the Commission expressed the opinion that the EU ought to:
- Integrate in its action the necessary measures, which would guarantee that the totality of the various issues regarding all maritime industries would constitute dimensions of a common EU policy, and

• Identify the appropriate means to promote, at the European level, the maritime interests of the EU citizens.

When compared to the traditional practice of emphasising sector-specific issues, the above was clearly a case of introducing an 'unorthodox' approach. By deciding not to follow the traditional approach, but to consider the dimensions of the whole maritime transport system as interconnected, the Commission essentially attempted to incorporate the common shipping policy into the framework of the common maritime transport policy. The policy output of this incorporation encompasses both the dimension of a transport policy and the dimension of an industrial policy. Towards this end, various other directorates of the Commission, apart from the DG-VII (Transport), became active in advancing relevant policy actions, such as DG-I (External Relations), DG-II (Economic and financial affairs), DG-IV (Competition), DG-V (Employment, industrial relations and social affairs), and DG-XI (Environment).

The new approach elucidated the policy areas where common policy ought to be developed. Among the several issues explicitly raised by the Commission, particularly significant to the port industry, were the direct reference to the EU interest for the development of short sea shipping and the interest in the connection of maritime transport and inland waterways with the policy regarding the formulation of TEN-T's plans. In that period, the said policy was still at the stage of preliminary proposals. Additionally, the Commission stated that the efficient provision of port services, the application of new technologies for container handling, and the integration of the maritime sector in intermodal transport ought to become core elements of an effective European transport system. As presented elsewhere in his study, during the late 1990s the promotion of short sea shipping was already part of the CTP strategy whilst the year 2000 was marked by a Council of Ministers' political agreement on the criteria regarding the inclusion of European ports in the EU plans on the TEN-T.

The introduction of the 'horizontal' approach altered the agenda and strategy of the EU. No issue was to be addressed on an *ad hoc* basis in the future. All EU initiatives ought to be incorporated into wider, integrated strategies, aiming to improve the overall maritime transport system. The interdependence of certain important maritime services, and the significant size of the industries providing them, required the emphasis to be placed on the creation of an integrated EU strategy able to resolve problems of capacity and competitiveness of those maritime industries.

A crucial parameter of the Commission's strategy was the creation of the Maritime Industries Forum (MIF) '...based on cooperation between the different industries concerned, research institutes, universities, Member States administrations, and the Commission' (CEU, 1991a, p. 22).

The objective of the MIF was to secure the active participation of all stakeholders and other interested parties into the exploration, formulation and detailed determination of EU actions oriented towards the creation of a competitive market of European maritime transport. Via the MIF, the EU institutions were expected to create formal and informal networks of cooperation, thus achieving systematically an efficient dialogue and a cooperative relation with the maritime industries. The latter would become and 'feel' a part of the debate that was taking place (similarly to what was happening in other sectors within the EU) in the context of the CMTP decision-making process. National governments would have a higher degree of involvement; at least insofar as the 'exploration' level of essential EU actions was concerned. Finally, the existence of the MIF would provide the potential for a higher degree of participation in the decision-making process of the EP and the Ecosoc, institutions aiming, by definition, to the acceleration of the process of integration.

The MIF commenced its operation in January 1992 by proposing, among others, the cooperation between the Commission and the port sector for the launching of programmes linking ports, as well as the widespread use of the Electronic Data Interchange (EDI) system in the port sector. These proposals were a component of the next step of the EU towards the improvement of the competitiveness of the port industries (CEU, 1992d). One year later (1993), a new report by the MIF[1] pointed to the significant implications of the inefficiency of EU ports and called for 'more and better' port services, widening of competition in the provision of these services and greater transparency in their pricing policies. Moreover, the MIF called for EU action in the field of research and development in order to facilitate the adjustment of the port industry (and other parts of the maritime transport system) to the new types of demand. That report constituted the basis for the assessment of the first tangible results of the horizontal approach by the Commission (CEU, 1993a). In the specific report, the Commission expressed its intention to prepare new proposals regarding the competitiveness of maritime industries including the port industry.

6.2   THE 1996 STRATEGY DOCUMENTS ON THE MARITIME FUTURE OF THE EU

In March 1996, the European Commission published two interconnected documents. The aim of these two documents was to revise the EU policies, by accelerating all the necessary actions regarding the future developments of European shipping and maritime industries. In these two 'maritime strategy documents' the Commission identified three strategic priorities of the EU towards the development of collective maritime transport policies with regard to either the shipping sector or any other maritime transport industry: safety, open markets, and advancement of competitiveness. The contents of these three strategy priorities were endorsed by both the European Parliament[2] and, in December 1996, by the Council of Ministers.

Advancing the Competitiveness of Maritime Industries

The first of the two maritime strategy documents (CEU, 1996b) highlighted the significance of maritime industries to the EU and examined the contribution of the EU industrial policy to the advancement of their competitiveness. Maritime industries comprise a wide spectrum of products and services, including port services (as well as shipbuilding, maritime equipment, fishing, energy, etc.), and constitute a sector with great potential for further development and application of technological developments. The utilisation of this potential would result in job creation throughout the EU. Moreover, while the EU policy promoting short sea shipping had just been accepted by the Council of Ministers (March 1996), maritime industries were expected to grow even further, due to the continuously growing saturation of inland transport modes and the fact that maritime transport could be the most cost efficient and environmentally friendly transport mode.

Implementing the horizontal policy approach, the Commission, in the strategy paper on the competitiveness of maritime industries, identified four fields of action for the EU industrial policy.

The first field regarded the *promotion of investments in intangible resources*. The Commission expressed its intention to continue the efforts in the field of research and development especially with regard to information technology and telecommunications, coordinate the respective European and national programmes and enhance vocational training.

The second field involved the *development of industrial cooperation*. The Commission stressed the need to increase the said cooperation within the EU, as well as with relevant industries of third countries.

The third field of policy action regarded the *securing of fair competition worldwide*. The Commission explicitly emphasised the need for EU policy measures regarding the ship-repairing industry, especially the need for proper implementation of the relevant OECD agreement on the conditions of competition, and the abolishment of obstacles to the free circulation of European maritime equipment in third countries. Nonetheless, the implications of the EU action in that field did in fact spread in all other maritime industries.

The fourth field referred to the *modernisation of the role of the relevant public authorities*. The Commission estimated that maritime infrastructure ought to become more prominent as far as financial aid provision was concerned. Consequently, it expressed the intention to contribute to the upgrading of port and other maritime infrastructure, mainly through the programme of the TEN-T.

Reforming the Common Maritime Strategy

The parallel second 'maritime strategy document' reviewed the outlook of maritime transport and concentrated on the future prospects of EU shipping, with a view to formulating the new guidelines of the common shipping policy. At the same time, it declared the official abandonment of the earlier (1989) proposal for the creation of the Euros (CEU, 1996b).

The analysis of the specific initiative had as a starting point the radical changes that characterised shipping in the preceding years: intense internationalisation, globalisation of services, multiplication of free Registries of Shipping, acceleration of flagging out, ageing of the fleet, shortage of sailors. Thus, the expressed proposals had as their objectives the advancement of the competitiveness of shipping, the securing of fair competition in the application of international regulations and the achievement of a high safety level.

Apart from its importance to the shipping strategy, the widening of objectives concerning shipping incorporated the 'systemic' character of maritime transport in the EU action. The Commission's paper proposed, among others, a series of common policies affecting the port activities:

- The elaboration and mandatory implementation – on behalf of ships of the EU fleet and ships under the flag of a third country arriving to and departing from EU ports – of safety and environmental rules, considering that non-compliance was an important source of unfair competition.
- The enhancement of the control authority of the port state, and of the sanctions against shippers that, on purpose or not, chartered or employed substandard ships or ships that were not properly insured.
- The examination of the possibility of connecting a ship's arrival at a European port with mandatory liability coverage in the maritime transport sector.
- The support of agreements between shippers and labour unions on issues concerning the onboard working conditions of ships regularly travelling to and from European ports.

6.3 PORTS AND THE COMMON POLICY ON SAFE SEAS: DISTRIBUTION OF THE COSTS

Certain aspects regarding the implementation of the common policy on safe seas and prevention of sea pollution critically affect, directly or indirectly, European ports and port competition. The creation of the common policy framework on safe seas took place in 1993 and included four focal points of EU policy: (a) the convergence of the implementation of international regulations; (b) the uniform supervision of the implementation of international regulations; (c) the development of maritime infrastructure; and (d) the contribution of the EU to the creation of the necessary international regulations (CEU, 1993a)

The initial framework and the revised action programme of the Commission (1996d) assumed a specific form by the publication of several EU Acts after 1993. The major part of that activity had as an objective the implementation of international agreements, decisions and recommendations, especially those adopted by the International Maritime Organisation (IMO). It also included initiatives concerning port control, some of them having an important impact on the competitiveness of port industries. More specifically, decisions have been adopted that unavoidably caused increases in port administration costs. However, the aim of those decisions was to reduce operational pollution caused by the maritime carriage of polluting or dangerous substances.

In conjunction with the Code of Environmental Practice, which has been adopted by the European organisation of seaports (ESPO, 1995b), the EU initiatives transform ports to the nodal points on which the regulatory framework, governing maritime safety, focuses (Lak, 1998). Those initiatives aim to complement the apparent loopholes in the existing regulatory framework regarding ship and port safety or phenomena of inefficient implementation of that framework.

In fact, a specific EU policy regarding the protection of the port environment does not still exist. Nonetheless, port activities are now part of the multimodal transport networks and, thus, they are included in the objectives of sustainable mobility. Sustainable port development may be defined as the creation of the conditions providing for the needs of a port without undermining the future needs of the port in question (ESPO, 1995a). Unavoidably, the expansion of port activities, or the development of a port, is linked to the balanced relation between environmental, social and economic targets (Finney & Young, 1995).[3]

EU Enforcement of Port State Control

The EU has adopted Directives on the harmonisation of the ship inspection rules used in the EU ports for the stricter application of Port State Control (PSC). Until 1995 the application of PSC in the EU was voluntary according to the Memorandum of Understanding (MOU) signed in 1980 in Paris by all Member States. This fact resulted in the absence of any specific criteria concerning the inspection or the detention of ships arriving in European ports that did not comply with international regulations. Council Directive 95/21/EC of 19 June 1995 enforced the application of international standards for ship safety, pollution prevention and shipboard living and working conditions, in respect of shipping using EU ports and sailing in the waters under the jurisdiction of the Member States. Three years later, in 1998, after a proposal by the Commission, the Directive 98/25[4] was adopted concerning the enforcement of port state control according to the standards set by recent amendments of certain international maritime agreements. The new Directive specified the obligation of the national maritime administrations ('competent authorities') to verify that the International Safety Management Code was being applied to all ships.

Complementary EU policies attempt to create systems of compulsory controls and/or harmonisation of the regulations governing certain transport activities (i.e. transport of dangerous goods and bulk cargo) or the use of specific vessels (ferry boats and high speed passenger vessels in frequent routes).

A far-reaching aim of the EU actions is to secure the safe provision of transport services and at the same time the abolition of the obstacles to the free circulation of these services. However, the rapid rate of change of the conditions of the transport sector supersedes the policy-making process and, as a result, the implementation of EU Directives becomes outdated very quickly. It is sufficient to mention that the previously mentioned Directive 98/25 was under revision just one year later when, as a reaction to the wreck of the ship Erika (1999), the Commission initiated the examination of possible measures for the improvement of EU rules on safe maritime transport (December 1999 – CEU, 2000b). In the same vein, the Directive on the minimum requirements of ships sailing to and from EU ports carrying dangerous or polluting cargo (1993)[5] has already been amended three times to incorporate the rapid technological developments and the changes in the relevant international agreements.

The fact that EU legislation is dynamic and results in frequent modifications of the existing legislature and creation of new laws deems unnecessary any detailed reference to the techno-economic contents of the above initiatives. Nonetheless, this reality accentuates the intensifying and

ships. However, it was against laying down percentages at this stage, arguing that the Member States themselves should be allowed to set the fixed and proportional amounts.

Following conciliation, the Council and the European Parliament reached an agreement on a joint text for the directive (September 2000) that did not specify the exact percentage but stated that this percentage must be 'significant'. A new, amended proposal endorsed the provisions of this agreement (CEU, 2000c). As all EU institutions agreed, the Commission issued a declaration annexed to the final act in the Official Journal, stating that this meant no less than 30%.[9] It is expected that in 2003 the Commission will undertake an assessment of the operational impact of the system. In the case that it proves to be inadequate for cost recovery, the Commission will submit a proposal on increasing the percentage contribution of ships to the 1/3 of the total cost of port reception facilities.

A Differentiated Charging System of Oil Tankers

A further aspect of the implementation of the EU policy on safe seas is the impact of specific actions on the revenue of European ports. An example is the policy adopted in 1994,[10] enforcing the implementation of the IMO Resolution A.747(18) on the privileged charging of Segregated Ballast oil Tankers (SBTs). The objective of the EU initiative was to provide incentives for the use of environmentally friendly ships. It had a negative impact on the revenue of several European ports since it required lower charging of SBTs.

Most port authorities expressed their opposition to the trend of using as tools ports for the resolution of problems between the regulatory authorities and other maritime industries such as shipping. European ports opposed, though unsuccessfully, the EU initiative considering it as a direct intervention in their financial affairs. They also pointed out that port charges usually constitute a low percentage of the total costs of the shipping industry, thus such reductions would not motivate shippers to use environmentally friendly ships.

Due to the diversity of European ports the intensity of the impact and consequently of the reactions varied considerably. The level of participation of public authorities in port authorities turns out to be of vital importance. The ports of Hamburg and Rotterdam proceeded in the implementation of the above measure, before it was adopted as a common policy, following an initiative of the regional authorities that play an active role in the management of these ports. The Greek Ministry of Mercantile Marine (MMM) is the supervisory authority of shipping and port policy. Consequently, the only impact of the specific legislation relates to the reform of possible economic incentives (i.e. taxation) that the state could offer to shippers in order to promote investments in environmentally friendly oil tankers.

Since 1996, when the legislation was enforced, the port industry is aiming to secure that the policy of differentiated charging will not include other categories of ships. During the last months of 2000, the EU policy was focusing on the sensitive issue of banning Single Hull Tankers (SHTs) from European ports according to the regulations applied on the other side of the Atlantic (Oil Pollution Act, 1990). The issue of the differentiated charging system of tankers arriving in European ports became timely after a proposal by the Commission (CEU, 2000d). With regard to the proposed measure, the port authorities have expressed their support for an EU policy of 'voluntary' differentiated charging, rather than 'compulsory' differentiation of port charges.[11]

The European Parliament has expressed the fiercest opposition to that measure. The reactions were consistent with the approach of the EP that considered the European ports as 'enterprises' (see Chapter 8). The EP report (October 2000) regarding the Commission's proposal for the banning of SHTs from European waters included a proposal for the withdrawal of the measure enforcing the differentiated port charging system. The increased charges for SHTs would place an additional financial burden on their owners, thus delaying their replacement. The lower charges for the, seemingly safer, Double Hull Tankers would certainly reduce port revenue, especially when the prospects for the use of such ships are increasing significantly.

An additional negative impact, according to the EP, was the fact that European ports would have to change their charging policy often, in fact as often as the changes in requirements regarding the age or other characteristics of tankers.

6.4   MARITIME STATISTICS

The White Paper of 1992 on the future development of CTP stressed the need for the relevant authorities to have access to information regarding the operation of the transport market. At the EU level, that information was largely available only for inland transport. There was a lack of information regarding air transport, maritime transport, port facilities, combined transport, and transport safety. The statistical data of the Member States were incomplete or not comparable due to different national practices.

To address this problem the Commission submitted a specific Directive proposal (CEU, 1994c), on the availability in the EU of statistical data on maritime transport, harmonised among the Member States and in coordination with the existing statistics on road, rail and inland waterway transport of goods. These statistics were expected to contribute to the development, the monitoring, and evaluation of the development of the internal market in the maritime transport sector.[12]

The final Directive 95/64 on statistics relating to the carriage of goods and passengers by sea, adopted by the Council in December 1995,[13] seeks to harmonise the definitions, categories, terminology, and methods of data collection, analysis and reporting that will be used by the port users, the EU institutions, the national, regional and local authorities, the international organisations, and the research institutions.

The Directive specified the requirement that Member States ought to establish and collect EU-level statistics on the carriage of goods and passengers by ships calling at ports in their territories. Moreover, the Directive specified the rules governing the selection of the ports in which the data ought to be collected. The characteristics of data collection and processing of the results were determined at the EU level in order for interested parties to be able to obtain comparable statistics guaranteeing a high level of data accuracy, which ought to be disseminated periodically.

On the basis of the experience gained during the first three years of statistical recording, the Council issued a new Decision[14] in 1998. That Decision determined the details of the application of statistical recording for maritime transport of goods and persons stipulated by the Directive 95/64 (e.g. compulsory quarterly report by all Member States of their port traffic). The Directive came into effect in 2000.

NOTES

1. MIF (1993), Results of the Plenary Session of the MIF, Athens, 27&28/6/1993.
2. Official Journal, C 150, 19.5.1997.
3. According to the UNCTAD approach, the main concerns of port management are: (a) the efficient economic operation, (b) environmental sustainability, and (c) social satisfaction (UNCTAD, 1993).
4. Directive 98/25 of the 27th April 1998.
5. Directive 93/75, of the 13th September 1993.
6. Official Journal C 150, 28.5.1999.
7. Official Journal C 10, 13.01.2000.
8. EU Bulletin 4-2000.
9. Directive 2000/59, Official Journal, L 332, 28.12.2000.
10. Regulation 2978/94, of the 21.11.1994.
11. ESPO News, 6.8, September 2000.
12. Conclusions of the first European Research Round Table on Short Sea Shipping (Winjnost *et al.*, 1993).
13. Directive 95/64, Official Journal, 1 320 of 30.12.1995.
14. Decision 98/385 - Official Journal L 174, 18.06.1998.

7. Defining a European Port Policy: The First EU Initiatives

7.1 A SIGNIFICANT STEP TOWARDS A EUROPEAN POLICY: THE 1993 EUROPEAN PARLIAMENT REPORT

In 1993, two years after the introduction of the horizontal Community approach concerning the problems of the maritime transport system, and after two years of preparation,[1] the European Parliament presented an analytical report regarding the importance, the general framework and the orientation of a 'potential' European policy concerning the port industry (European Parliament, 1993). Following an initiative of the Transport Committee, the report of the European Parliament included detailed information on the financial and technical trends characterising the port sector and a respective analysis of the potential guidelines for a Community policy. Through the study of scenarios of the contemporary and future developments of the institutional form of ports, port competition and integration of the Community port policy to the CTP, the EP report culminated to the presentation of the main prospects, proposals and recommendations for a European Port Policy.

The Principles of a 'Potential' EU Policy

According to the specific report, the recommended choice was '...a realistic combination of communitarian impulses and information actions' for '...insuring the requirement of flexible intervention' since '...the Community ... does not lack powers to steer, stimulate and even intervene directly' (European Parliament, 1993, p. 18). The report identified four basic principles implicitly suggesting the guidelines that ought to be developed to direct the various possible types of Community intervention:
(a) *Availability and modernisation of port capacity* – to allow a market-led response to changes in shipping and port structures.
(b) *Free and fair competition among ports and undertakings operating in ports*, in agreement with Community rules.

(c) *Integration of ports in a Common Transport Policy*, with a view to creating a European transport system.
(d) *Social acceptance of the Community policy and port development*, through measures at the training and organisation levels and environmental protection aimed at favouring the required changes.

Those principles were accompanied by specific recommendations and proposals with some of them referring, at the same time, to more than one target. Overall, the following guidelines could facilitate the implementation of the basic principles:

- Orienting investments in a non-compulsory way.
- Defining an infrastructure and superstructure policy.
- Applying the rules of free and fair competition.
- Adopting a systematic approach towards seaports.
- Promoting a better balance between North and South.
- Managing employment problems.
- Promoting safety rules and environmental protection.

Availability and modernisation of port capacity

The primary goal of the European Parliament suggestions was a Community port policy that would advance the availability of an adequate and modern port capacity, in order to handle the necessary import and export flows of the Community on a competitive basis with other markets. A common policy in this field ought to be flexible enough to allow a market-led response to changes in shipping and port structures.

Given that to a large extent the demand for transport services is a derived demand, it should not be surprising that the document of the European Parliament emphasised the trends of market development up to 2010, focusing on the changes in trade patterns and the shipping sector.

With regard two distinct categories of cargo, crude oil (and its products) and steam coal, it was estimated that the existing port capacities and the level of modernisation of European ports were adequate. Based on estimations predicting no significant variation in the trade pattern of these products, the European Parliament stressed the need to focus on questions of safety and environmental protection during the transport process. Two factors contributed to the existence of quite different estimations on containerised cargo: first, the trend of strong growth of container traffic (a forecast growth of some 158% between 1990 and 2010); and, second, the trend of steady increases in vessel sizes serving this type of transport. The prospects of introducing post-panamax vessels created urgent needs for large-scale infrastructure and superstructure investments for operating such vessels (e.g. water depth of at least 14 metres and an adequate number of high speed berth cranes).

According to the European Parliament, the objective of the Community policy ought to be the faster adjustment and, by implication, the increased profitability of ports to the new conditions requiring higher administrative efficiency, expensive equipment and higher efficiency and quality of services through the development of automation. This could happen at three levels:

- At the port equipment level, with a higher degree of automation of its various elements (such as berth cranes).
- At the terminal level, where informatics could allow a more efficient management and planning of cargo and areas – provided that suitable infrastructures were present.
- At the transport chain management level, where the availability of information systems could offer the potential to connect and integrate ports in the combined transport network.

This policy would help to overcome the negative quality effects on port services whenever the latter were not integrated into communication networks, due to managerial or other problems. In such cases, ports usually face significant problems regarding their responses to the increased (quantitatively and qualitatively) demand for port services.

The increasing significance of the structural changes was already forcing ports to proceed to vertical integration, in a movement aiming at the creation of adequate conditions for the provision of competitive port services. Thus, the European Parliament suggested that the most important future problem would not be the organisation of ports as undertakings but the creation of conditions for undertakings to be organised within ports. Towards this end it proposed:

- The creation of relevant competition rules.
- The promotion of research projects on the development of transport undertakings.
- The tuning and testing of innovative projects of organisation based on informatics support.
- The training of ports' and port undertakings' management.

Those measures would contribute to the resolution of a further issue in need of action by a future European Port Policy. Namely, the adjustment of the workforce in the light of the observed diversity of the characteristics of the workforce employed in ports: for example, the need to familiarise the workforce with the organisational process in which it participated and its ability to operate the informatics systems. That would also satisfy the fourth basic principle of the European Port Policy: the social acceptance of the adjustment process of ports to the new era.

Declaring the availability of adequate and modern port capacity a primary target, the European Parliament proposed the creation of a 'Community Centre of Responsibility', answerable for the construction of infrastructures and the return of investments, which would be assisted by a national port managing body from every member state with the responsibility for constructing and financing port infrastructures. The European Parliament did not advocate the adoption of a centralised system for the provision of infrastructure funds, but the active guiding role of the common policy through decisions based on the following criteria:

(a) All investments in port infrastructures ought to be made on the basis of a positive internal rate of return.
(b) The users ought to pay the full cost, internal and external, of the transport services they consume.
(c) Through a generally accepted and clear distinction between infrastructure and superstructure, conditions ought to be set determining that private ports would receive no funding from state or local authorities, while private operators ought to bear the entire cost of superstructures.

With reference to the need for an unequivocal and general distinction between port infrastructure and superstructure projects, the EP proceeded to the formulation of specific definitions (represented in Table 7.1). According to these definitions, three categories ought to be established:

(a) Access and defence infrastructure projects for which both responsibility and costs ought to belong to the public sector.
(b) Port infrastructure projects for which the responsibility ought to belong to the public sector, but the costs ought to be borne by the users.
(c) Port superstructure projects for which both responsibility and costs ought to belong to each operating company.

One of the most difficult issues to address was the trend towards possible overcapacity and excess investment in the port sector in conjunction with the need to avoid any central planning. Considering as given the unreliability of any strong central planning, the EP document suggested that in order to avoid overcapacity the Community ought to provide the widest possible information to port planning bodies. At the same time, and according to the previously mentioned line of thought, the European Port Policy ought to ensure that the provision of public funds ought to be made under the condition that investments in infrastructures ought to be made on the basis of a positive internal rate of return. An additional proposal of the European Parliament concerned the need to focus the Community policy on the problems faced by the main European ports and on the improvement of these ports.

7.2   INSTITUTIONAL FRAMEWORK AND CONDITIONS OF PORT COMPETITION

Institutional framework: A Common Philosophy as Part of the CTP

The institutional framework, the operation, and the management of ports constituted the second set of issues on which the European Parliament focused its attention. These issues were decisive factors in the resolution of adjustment problems of the port sector to the new era, as well as to the determination of the conditions of port competition. The scale of the diversity of European ports was so large that the European Parliament concluded that it would not be reasonable to promote the uniform organisation of ports at the Community level.

However, according to the European Parliament the fact that any formal standardisation seemed unnecessary ought not to be interpreted in the sense that any Community initiative would be inadmissible or irrelevant. In fact, several institutional aspects of ports could bear significant consequences from a Community point of view, because of the effects they could have on ports' competitiveness:

(a) The different philosophies of port management about the role of the public and private sector implied a different degree of public interference in financing and building port structures, in their organisation and in the management of port activities.
(b) The different types of port administration would make it difficult to identify the financial flows addressed from the public powers to the ports.
(c) The pattern of labour organisation could potentially limit the competitiveness of ports and open the way to public subsidising of several port activities, justified by social needs.
(d) The existence within the ports of 'exclusive rights' to provide specific services or to operate cargo-handling activities could result in abuse of dominant position, i.e. a clear violation of the EU competition rules.

Table 7.1 Proposal of the European Parliament for the Definition of Port Infrastructure and Superstructure Projects

A	**ACCESS AND DEFENCE INFRASTRUCTURE PROJECTS** All those infrastructure projects that allow sea and land access to a port area; the latter may be defined as a limited area (a complex of water basins and land areas) where port activities are carried out; the latter are defined as services to ships (pilotage towing, berthing, bunkering, catering, supply of utilities such as water and power, repair, etc.) and to the cargo (loading/unloading, storage, stuffing and stripping, container repair, etc.). Maritime access and defence
A.1	Navigable channels, locks, dikes and breakwaters, navigation aids (beacons, buoys, etc.) up to the boundaries of the above defined port area. Land access
A.2	National road and rail network and connection with the local network of the port areas as defined above.
B	**PORT INFRASTRUCTURE PROJECTS** Civil works within the above defined port area that facilitate the supply of services to ships and cargo: berths, channels, yards, port road and rail network, port information and EDI system. The boundary for port infrastructure projects can be defined as the extremes of reinforced-concrete structures; canalisations would, thus, be included and pavements and surface arrangements excluded.
C	**PORT SUPERSTRUCTURE PROJECTS** Surface arrangement, buildings (warehouses, workshops, office buildings), as well as mobile and fixed equipment needed to produce services. Information and automation systems of the terminal activities.

Source: European Parliament (1993, p. 29).

Thus, the European Parliament stressed the need to adopt common criteria regarding the role of the private and the public sector in every port activity and to encourage and enforce the evolution towards a basic port management philosophy that could accommodate various aspects in relation to specific cases. The European Parliament argued that the most appropriate philosophy seemed to be '...in favour of a Port Authority *lato sensu*', i.e. '...a *specialist body* with coordination and planning tasks. Concerning the powers and the functions of this regulatory body, the most suitable organizational model is represented by a *Landlord Port Authority*, provided with *financial autonomy*, having *autonomous accounting* and operating only in the fields of *planning* and *managing* the port area' (European Parliament, 1993, p. 7).

The specific choice would facilitate and promote the control of financial flows to the ports, a higher degree of competition, clear identification of the state financial flows according to comparable criteria for all port activities – even when the port was administered by a national, local or municipal body –

and the potential to establish cooperation among the various modes of transport. The need for EU contribution to overcoming the anachronistic situations in the organisation of labour and for promotion of the necessary reorganisation was also stressed.

According to the above-presented philosophy the Community policy ought to focus on improving the main European ports, thus it was considered necessary that the proposals on the institutional framework ought to concern only the ports that were an 'essential' part of the Single European Market.

The Competition Issue

The creation of a regulatory framework governing the operation of European ports was closely related to the issue of port competition, and constituted the third set of proposals expressed by the European Parliament.

The basic guiding principle of *promoting the free and fair competition through the adjustment of the legal, operational, and organisational framework* was further specified according to three intervention principles:

(a) The control of subsidies to ports through the application of the EU Treaty provisions concerning state aid.
(b) The adoption of measures on the transparency of port accounts.
(c) The creation of a common policy concerning infrastructure projects.

The second principle referred to the elimination of practices that were incompatible with the Articles of the Treaty of the European Community concerning competition. The proposed measures were aiming at the encouragement of Member States to adjust their legislation in order to remove legal or actual conditions facilitating behaviours conflicting with Articles 81 and 82 of the Treaty concerning the abuse of dominant positions. Moreover, they concerned (a) the setting up of competition rules between ports, within ports, as well as between ports and other modes of transport; (b) the resolution of the transparency issue; and (c) the elimination of subsidising port administration, or inadequate labour organisation and inefficiencies, through state aid theoretically aiming to promote regional development in certain areas of the EU.

The third principle related to the views arguing that action at the *institutional framework and competition levels ought to be 'coordinated and integrated'*, and that the promotion of a common philosophy of port organisation would be a positive development. To the issue of competition was also linked the need to establish market rules in port planning, through a common policy on infrastructure projects. The aim was to create administrative/managerial systems that would significantly increase the competitiveness of a port and the enterprises operating in its context.

However, the resolution of competition issues was far from easy. The diversity and difficulty of identifying the practices, the multiplicity of institutional structures, the difficulty of identifying the extent that existing practices were affecting port competition, presented major difficulties in the attempt to infer conclusions and develop a common policy. Acknowledging the specific complications, the European Parliament proposed the adoption of a set of principles, taking into consideration particular aspects of individual cases.

State aid could, for example, assume the following detrimental forms: the setting-off of operating losses, loans on privileged terms (a practice especially widespread in the case of public or municipal ports), forgoing of a normal return on public funds used, non-liability to profit tax, leasing of land at privileged conditions and free provision of administrative and technical services. The difficulties associated with the monitoring and restriction of such practices were attributable to the fact that the specific phenomena could not be identified without in-depth investigation, while it was all the harder to identify such practices in cases of ports (e.g. Bremen, Hamburg) whose accounts were interconnected with the municipal accounts.

On the other hand, the administrative authorities could potentially favour specific enterprises either by transferring to the users the favourable conditions obtained by the state (e.g. providing services free of charge through setting-off of operating losses), or by granting 'exclusive rights', thus facilitating the abuse of a dominant position by the providers of certain port services.[2]

The European Parliament stressed that practical difficulties ought to not permit ignoring the problem and called the Commission to use its powers to a greater extent than it had done until then to compel Member States to align their regulations with the common rules. Furthermore, the EP mentioned the legal provisions of the *acquis communautaire* and specifically the increased powers stipulated in Articles 86 and 226 of the Treaty.

Integration of Ports in the Common Transport Policy

The third set of proposals by the European Parliament recognised the need to overcome the doubts derived from Article 80 of the Treaty regarding the position of the port system in the context of the CTP (Chapter 3). The reference to this point was not only based on the relevant ECJ ruling of 1974 (legally interpreting the specific Article), the emphasis was on the economic dimension, explicitly on the fact that 'ports are essential parts of the European transport system and are therefore involved both in the *common transport policy* and in the creation of *trans-European networks*' (European Parliament, 1993, XIV). The Commission had already identified the need to promote the maritime part of the network and reinforce it *vis-à-vis* road transport (CEU, 1992a; 1992b). The European Parliament argued that EU actions ought to be influenced by the fact that measures improving a part of the European transport system, in this case ports, ought to be in total agreement with the overall CTP.

The European Parliament proposed a more systematic policy approach towards ports in the context of the common transport system, despite the lack of a definitive and permanent list of ports of Community interest, given that the role of the various ports could be different in relation to both their position within the Community and to the different goals that the Community would choose to pursue. The integration of ports in the TEN-T ought to be based on the significance of ports as links between maritime and land transport and as functional elements of a wider European logistics system. The problem that remained unresolved, though, was how to integrate the European port policy and the individual national port policies, since it was not considered suitable to establish a definitive and permanent listing of ports of Community relevance.

A second reference point in relation to the integration of ports in the CTP was the contribution of the port policy to the promotion of a more balanced North–South situation. Obviously the significance of that effect of the port policy was high both to the improvement of ports as vital parts of the economic activity in the less-developed regions of the EU, and to the improvement of the position of the Southern European ports *vis-à-vis* the ports of Northern Europe. The European Parliament recognised the development of Mediterranean transhipment, through Community programmes of common interest, as an action improving the competitiveness and reliability of the specific ports. Finally, it stressed the need for initiatives, respecting the subsidiarity principle, aiming at the achievement of a European development plan concerning Mediterranean transhipment as a starting point for recovering traffic in the Mediterranean Sea.

Social Acceptance of the European Port Policy

According to the European Parliament, the promotion of social acceptance of the European policy and the operation of European ports depended on three factors: (a) the management of employment problems, (b) the improvement of safety, and (c) the protection of the environment.

Employment issues referred to the need for the port industry to adjust to the new reality parallel to the identification of methods ensuring the protection of employment without obstructing the modernisation process of ports. Thus, further Community action was proposed, such as specific initiatives regarding programmes enhancing professional mobility and retraining to facilitate the adjustment to the new era.

Due to the nature of modern ports (e.g. equipment, chemicals, containers) a precise Community response concerning port safety was deemed necessary. The application of uniform rules would reduce the strong pressures of unfair competition to ports. Specifically, the EP considered it necessary for the EU to discourage the differentiated application of rules, reduced expenses in equipment and trained personnel, or reduced inspections of vessels and ports. International standards and rules concerning the ships safety controls and port work (e.g. MARPOL 73/78) were assessed by the EP as essential, since their universal application would increase the general level of port safety (port access, ship safety, port work, port environment).

The European Parliament considered it necessary to remove commercial concerns from the safety procedures and the protection of the environment, through a process of detailed monitoring of port safety and environmental protection systems and the standardisation of regulations. The application and supervision of such systems ought to remain at the local level. The common policy would be restricted to the provision of financial support for the completion of insufficient port infrastructures, as well as the quality improvement of the labour force, including the extent of training of personnel specialised in controlling safety and meeting environmental emergencies. All these in view of a wider transport activities integration in case of international operations. Moreover, the collective EU initiatives ought to provide for a monitoring framework of the protection standards offered by individual Member States.

As far as safety aboard ships was concerned, the EP mentioned that the Community had already established the following main principles (cf. Chapter 6) of its action and the first measures to be adopted:

(a) Effective enforcement by Member States, in their capacity as port and coastal States, of the international rules to vessels of all flags when operating in EU waters.

(b) Promotion of a modern, coherent and harmonised development of maritime infrastructure, including waste management facilities and navigational aids to ships.

(c) Promoting actions mainly within the context of the IMO (International Maritime Organisation) to ensure that appropriate international provisions were being implemented within reasonable time limits.

(d) Adoption of directives on the minimum standards of training for certain maritime professions.

7.3   PROMOTING SHORT SEA SHIPPING: THE FIRST INDICATIONS OF A EUROPEAN PORT POLICY

The Competitiveness of the Port Industry as a Critical Parameter of the Sustainable Mobility Strategy

As already mentioned, the EU strategy for the transport sector, that was defined in 1992 and confirmed in 1998, is tightly related to the objective of achieving sustainable development. The White Paper (CEU, 1992b) specified the objectives and scope of the CTP, highlighting the need for efficient operation of the transport systems of goods and passengers and their contribution to achieving balanced regional development (since a large number of shipping areas exist in the less-developed Member States), and the achievement of environmental objectives and sustainable mobility.

According to the Commission, the achievement of environmental objectives by the CTP requires the introduction of regulations and economic measures promoting the environmentally friendly transport modes without, at the same time, causing distortions in competition between the various modes. Estimations of the average fuel consumption and emissions (Table 7.2), indicate that as regards the short-distance transport activity, the environmentally friendly modes are railways and maritime transport.

Table 7.2 Estimated Average Fuel Consumption and Emissions by Transport Mode (gr / tkm)

	Fuel Consumption	CO_2	CO	HC	Particulate	NO_X	SO_2
Road	31,33	98,30	0,48	0,23	0,08	0,98	0,03
Railway	8,91	28,33	0,20	0,10	0,03	0,47	0,04
Short sea Shipping	4,83	15,45	0,04	0,01	0,01	0,31	0,29

Notes:
CO_2: Carbon dioxide,   CO: Carbon Monoxide,   HC: Hydrocarbon,
NO_X: Nitrogen oxide, SO_2: Sulphyr dioxide

Source: CEU (1999c).

This is further confirmed by the research data published in 1999 by Friends of the Earth (quoted in: ESPO, 2001). According to these data, the external costs assigned to the transportation of a mixture of goods (i.e. vehicles, containers wood and iron) from North to South Europe and *vice versa*, are four times higher for road (49.7 million Euro/tkm) and rail (48.6 million Euro/tkm) when compared to sea transport. The latter accounts for a fraction of the others at 5.9 million Euro/tkm, despite the distance by sea being more than twice that of the other modes.

These evidences work in favour of the conclusion that the competitiveness of the maritime transport system and European ports turns out to be a critical parameter of the EU strategy.

The additional problem that had to be addressed was the unequal modal split prevailing in transport until the early 1990s and the effects of that inequality. As presented in detail in Chapter 4.2, while the transport of goods between the Member States had increased during the previous two decades, the modal spilt of that increase was clearly in favour of road haulage and against the maritime, inland waterway and railway transport. Apart from the exogenous factors that affected the relatively smaller increase in the use of the seagoing transport system (Chapter 4), to that development some endogenous factors also contributed, at least as far as short-distance transport was concerned.

The port sector was one of those endogenous factors. Ports played an important role in the transhipment of goods. The lack of basic infrastructure was not a general problem of the Community ports. It was clear, though, that to address the continuous increase in the new types of high-speed ships, as well as the new reality imposed on maritime transport by economic globalisation and European integration, new infrastructures and services were necessary (Pallis, 2002). Experience seemed to suggest that for the large Community ports this would be feasible. However, many other ports required organisational and operational changes in order to utilise as efficiently as possible the existing, and the planned establishments, when serving a part of the increasing traffic. This way they could contribute to the more balanced distribution of transport traffic.

The Policy Promoting Short Sea Shipping

Given the previous analysis it should not be surprising that a first approach towards a European Port Policy appeared within the first Community initiative concerning the development of a policy promoting short sea shipping and its connection with the combined transport networks. Short sea shipping, according to the definition adopted at the Community level, refers to maritime transport along the EU coastline, as well as between the continental ports of Europe and those situated in the European islands. It also includes the exclusive internal transport (cabotage) and the international transport within the EU or between the EU and the neighbouring countries, including the river–sea transport. In other words, it includes all seagoing transport that does not require the crossing of oceans.

The Commission's initiative, in 1995, on the challenges and opportunities for the expansion of short sea shipping (CEU, 1995e), emphasised the fact that the specific type of transport required the consumption of less energy and constituted a non-polluting option alternative to road haulage. Within that policy document, the Commission addressed several recommendations to the Member States, the regional and local authorities and the shipping industries aiming to improve the competitiveness of the sector. The Commission underlined the need to improve the quality and efficiency of short sea shipping infrastructure, including port capacity, and the need to adequately plan the development of short sea shipping in view of the forthcoming enlargement of the EU.

The Four Axes of the EU Policy Agenda

The framework of the policy promoting short sea shipping led to the formulation, during the second half of the 1990s, of proposals concerning port policy that took into consideration economic, organisational, technological and environmental parameters and were aimed at developing the port industry.

The general objectives of the approach were aimed, on the one hand, at improving the competitiveness of ports, through the creation of those conditions that would ensure their interoperability with the total of the transport modes, and, on the other hand, at promoting a regulatory framework governing employee relations that would optimise the use of port infrastructure and accelerate the establishment of competition between port users. A reference was also made to the technological developments of port activities, the adjustment of competition rules concerning ports to the new conditions, with specific reference to state aid and a port policy integrated in the framework of the TEN-T.

Those proposals that are interconnected and interdependent can be classified into four categories (Figure 7.1):

(a) Measures concerning the improvement and modernisation of port infrastructures for their inclusion in the trans-European transport network.
(b) Measures concerning the creation of a competitive framework of operation for European ports.
(c) Measures concerning the advancement of research and development (R&D) with applications to the port sector.

(d) Measures promoting an institutional debate between all stakeholders to address the problems concerning European ports.

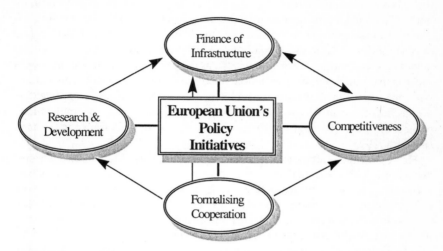

Figure 7.1: Port Policy Proposals in the Short Sea Shipping Policy Context

Modernisation of Port Infrastructure

The identification of serious shortcomings regarding certain specialised services (e.g. container terminals, roll on/roll off facilities), inadequate transhipment installations, outdated electromechanical equipment, insufficiently trained personnel, and poor inland transport infrastructure within the port area in several EU ports (especially in Ireland and the southern periphery) constituted the starting point of the first category of proposals.

Compared to the most competitive ports of North Europe, where the development of infrastructure had contributed to the application of innovations in transhipment methods, the productivity of ports in Southern Europe was lower. Based on existing studies, the Commission concluded that the productivity differential could be as high as 50%. However, even the most successful European ports needed further modernisation of their infrastructure, for different reasons though. The largest ports were aiming at integration into logistics systems. Small and medium ports were aiming to overcome their shortcomings due to less efficient and less specialised facilities and offset their weaknesses in relation to economies of scale (Seidenfus, 1987).

Devoting substantial amounts to investments in infrastructure may result in dynamic improvements in a port's productivity and efficiency of port operation. The quality of port infrastructure significantly affects the cost of the services provided (stevedoring costs, pilotage, total cost of ship time in port). The modern infrastructure systems – including the introduction of integrated management systems and electronic data interchange (EDI) linking port authorities, shippers, stevedores, ship owners, etc. – can reverse the negative picture of maritime transport as a slow and unreliable transport process that entails delays and double handling due to the lack of connections with the other transport modes. Moreover, modern port infrastructure can be a significant incentive for the increased use of ports and, by implication, reduce the negative environmental effects of the overall transport system (Ferreira, 1995).

However, the limitations of public revenue and the high public deficits during the 1980s resulted in a reduction of the relative size of European investment in port infrastructure from 5% to 3.5% of total transport infrastructure investment (ECMT, 1991). Moreover, national policies concerning investments in transport infrastructure had not recognised the importance of the potential of maritime transport networks to contribute to the fulfilment of the rapidly increasing demand for intra-EU transport activities (Chlomoudis & Pallis, 1996).

Attempting to address this situation, the supranational EU institutions increased grants of financial assistance for the improvement of port infrastructure. The European Investment Bank has been a major contributor supporting investments in transport infrastructure by providing approximately a third of the total cost of projects of common interest and of projects targeting balanced regional development. Specific port infrastructure projects were co-financed by the European Regional Development Fund. The Cohesion Fund was an additional instrument that provided for the infrastructure needs of the lagging EU regions. Complementary projects concerning port infrastructure are financed by other European programmes, which target inter-State cooperation and the financial support of the geographically isolated islands of the EU periphery.

The creation of the TEN-T, through the development and interconnection of the individual national and local transport networks according to their competitive advantages was already a central target of the EU. However, for reasons that were presented in Chapter 5, neither the draft Commission proposals concerning the development of the TEN-T, nor the amended guidelines provided for a definitive strategic or priority network of ports of community interest that ought to be established within a certain period. In the framework of the short sea shipping policy, the Commission opted to focus its attention on port infrastructure projects conforming to the following criteria:

(a) Projects facilitating trade.
(b) Projects helping to relieve congested land corridors and reducing the external costs of European transport.
(c) Projects improving the accessibility and strengthening economic and social cohesion in the EU.

Noteworthy is that in line with what had been argued during the first discussions at a European level, even though not at a Community level, on the promotion of short sea shipping (ECMT, 1982), the emphasis on the financing of port infrastructure was expected to significantly reduce not only the inefficiency but, also, the 'image' of the short sea shipping system.

All the EU initiatives, either loans or grants, were focused on support for the launching of viable projects, the identification of the missing links in the lagging regions of the EU, and the supply of financial stimuli to the national investment programmes concerning the development of infrastructure. Notably, the EU did not have sufficient financial resources that would create the necessary state of infrastructure, since the development of modern berths and terminals is highly capital intensive. The mobilisation of complementary private or public capital remains the significant requirement to accomplish the objectives of a modern and competitive port industry.

An even more important reason was the difficulties associated with the process of selecting specific ports as being 'ports of community interest'. However, even if the EU had the necessary resources, that would not be desirable since a network-related action would constitute discrimination against ports that would not be part of it. Therefore, the recommended process of identifying projects having the potential to provide smooth and efficient transition between the maritime and the land transport modes was considered more relevant than seeking to identify ports of community interest, thus causing distortions in competition. According to this logic, projects that have the potential to be co-financed included:

(a) Improvements in access to the port from the sea or inland waterway, e.g. arrangements for maritime access channels, dredging projects, navigational aids.
(b) Improvements inside the port areas, e.g. new quays.
(c) Improvements in inland transport infrastructure to sections of the trans-European transport network.

The condition that the Commission has set in order to provide funds for specific projects is their economic viability which would have to be previously assessed on the basis of a financial and social cost/benefit analysis. In the past, the lack of adequate financial resources has lead the national governments to ignore the potential economic viability of such projects. The far-reaching target of the EU policy is to reverse the specific counter-productive practice of the Member States.

Port Competition

The objective of the second category of EU actions was to ensure a high degree of competition between European ports, irrespective of geographical location. The articles of the European Treaty concerning competition, state aid, and freedom of market entry are applicable to the port industry too. Article 81 of the Treaty of Rome prohibiting restrictive agreements between undertakings, Article 82 concerning the dominant position of a firm and prohibiting the abuse of market power, and Article 86 regulating state monopolies apply not only to competition between the ports of different Member States, but also to competition between ports within a Member State and to competition within a single port.

A critical point concerning competition rules between ports is the transparency in port charges for services that directly affect the costs of maritime transport. The Commission considered that port charges ought to directly reflect the costs of the services actually rendered and the invoices ought to contain a detailed account of these services and the amounts charged. The transparency in state aid was also considered critical to competition between ports and between the port users. According to the Commission, transparency in state aid would also facilitate the abolition of monopolies that were incompatible with Articles 82 and 86 of the Treaty.

In recent years, port competition has intensified remarkably. This intensification has been the result of the increased competition for traffic to/from specific hinterland regions, for higher shares of the container transport market, and not least the development of multimodal transport. The traditional conception of the port as a 'gate' that facilitates the uninterrupted flow of transport has been gradually replaced by one conceiving ports operating as logistics centres that provide complementary services to the transport process (a transformation that was realised in the early 1990s: cf. Pesquera & De La Hoz, 1992). A direct impact of this transformation concerns the increased uncertainty faced by those ports that have not strived for the implementation of the requisite restructuring.

Given the income-generating capacity of the port industry, as well as its wider economic imperative, national governments are always mobilised and intervene to ensure/facilitate the restructuring of ports located in their territory. The most frequent form of government intervention has been the granting of direct or indirect financial assistance to ensure the adjustment of ports to contemporary challenges. Public subsidies, in the form of loans at lower than market interest rates, enable ports to launch large-scale projects under a qualitatively different economic and commercial scrutiny than would apply to private sector investments of similar magnitude. Within the EU there remains doubt whether such assistance is justifiable or not, and what, if any, form of state aid to the port industry is of 'Community interest'. In the mid-1990s, the Commission argued that it is within its jurisdiction to define and supervise the application of competition rules, to decide on which projects are of public interest, and which state aid projects support commercial activities thus causing distortions in competition.

However, the harmonisation of national policies through EU legislative acts was, and still is, quite difficult to be achieved due to different national priorities. As a result, there has been no legislative proposal to that effect during the initial stage of EU action on short sea shipping (1995). The initial EU initiatives on short sea shipping triggered a debate on the creation of a definitive Community framework. The EU alternative comprised an approach that could accommodate certain differences in the priorities of the Member States whilst ensuring that distortions in competition would be minimal and state aid measures would be transparent. The EU initiatives were concentrated on the study and clarification of the intra-industry situation in order to create Community policy measures. The Commission advocated that it had the necessary regulatory authority and legal potency to implement a reactive policy-making approach to reverse the market failures caused by the different national policies.

To implement its approach, the Commission initiated an inventory of all state aids granted by national or regional authorities to ports in the EU. The aim of that initiative was to clarify which subsidies were affecting the port services and which were concerning other services. The transparency of the financial accounts of entities creating and administering transport infrastructure was under investigation since those accounts could hide the granting of state aids. Moreover, the study of the accounts of European ports was expected to allow the European institutions to identify clearly the business–government relationships. The conclusions were expected to result in the introduction of Community guidelines concerning the transparency of port charges and state aids. Alongside, the Commission had undertaken the study of monopoly practices of certain port operators, since those were considered as being incompatible with the principle ensuring the freedom to provide services and were inhibiting the improvement of services.

Measures to improve the competitive position of the maritime transport system *vis-à-vis* the other transport modes were also under examination. In that case, a serious obstacle that needed to be overcome was the complex administrative and documentary procedures. Initiating a debate to define precisely the requirements and propose changes, wherever possible, the Commission stated that the Community priority was the harmonisation, in the intra-European context, of the regulatory, administrative and co-ordination activities in the Member States.

Other critical factors to the strengthening of competition rely on the port industry itself. For instance, changes in existing restrictive labour regulations and practices, which increase the vessels' time spent in ports and impose significant additional cargo handling costs, still remain at the discretionary authority of ports and, in some cases, national policies. Critical structural transformations having the potential to increase productivity per hour and improve ship turnabout may be achieved through changes in working hours and the provision of 'round the clock' services, the improvement of working conditions and employer–employee relations, and the deregulation of labour. The predominant view is that ports can only be competitive to the extent they satisfy the ship owners' and shippers' demand for fast, efficient and reliable services. This can only be achieved by certain industrial practices. Notably, some of these improvements are already observed in some ports and are underway in others, particularly in the context of the growing trend towards the privatisation of port terminals.

Research and Development

Research and development (R&D) programmes concerning the maritime sector is a field in which the EU institutions have worked extensively. Article 103F of the Maastricht Treaty stated that the EU objectives ought to strengthen the technological base of Community industries and to promote the research activities necessary for the implementation of Community policies concerning the improvement of the competitiveness of Community industries at international level.

Like most of the European maritime industries, ports are a high-tech industry with strong economic potential. Technological developments significantly affect the productivity and market position of ports, as well as the environmental impact of the overall transport process. The operation of sophisticated logistics systems, such as EDI, is a characteristic example of the transformation of ports to natural focal points of information concerning the transport process. The efficient application of modern electronic technology facilitates the flow of cargo, increases the degree of reliability, and promotes the safety of the transport process by introducing methods of fast notification on dangerous goods (Chlomoudis & Pallis, 1999). Apart from the application of new technological methods, research and development concerning ports is promoting the diffusion of technical knowledge necessary for the optimal utilisation of the available technological systems.

Issues concerning port facilities and the impact of ports on the hinterland comprised a part of the Community R&D framework programme attempting to enhance the competitiveness of maritime transport. The main themes of this programme were:

(a) The optimisation of berthing/unberthing procedures in terms of automation and time saving.
(b) The optimisation of loading/unloading procedures as above.
(c) The development of port equipment and of IT-based logistics systems.

Community action remains complementary to the activities of the Member States. A central EU concept has become the support of several projects aiming at the creation of a European maritime information highway called MARIS (Maritime Information System). Towards this end, three projects are underway. The first concerns the interconnection of these systems in small- and medium-sized ports, the second envisages the creation of an all-encompassing vessels reporting system, and a third deals with electronic charts. The responsibility for the implementation of these projects has been assigned to the Commission's Directorate General of Transport. At the same time, a Commission Task Force has undertaken the responsibility for the coordination of the various programmes. Representatives of the research programmes relevant to the maritime industry comprise the Task Force. The key objectives of this group are to ensure the cost-effective use of R&D funds, to coordinate the relevant national research programmes, and to make recommendations on the future EU R&D framework programme.

Formalising Cooperation

The Commission has linked the previously mentioned actions concerning the development of port policies with an attempt to institutionalise a debate between the port authorities, the port users, the providers of port services, scientists, the national and regional authorities on the problems of the port industry. A formalised dialogue on the problems arising in ports was deemed necessary for the Commission to define the objectives and the future development of the common policy through a consultation and cooperation procedure.

The Commission devoted efforts to set up periodical meetings at the local or regional level aiming to formulate proposals addressing the observed problems and to create an integrated approach to policy formulation. The already established regional working groups (i.e. North Sea, Atlantic Sea and the Mediterranean Sea working groups) and the utilisation of some of their recommendations are part of this strategy. At the same time, several meetings took place between those responsible for decision making, the industries active in maritime transport and the scientific community (for the most recent see: Peters & Wergeland, 1997). This practice not only incorporates the industry's views into the policy-making process but is in line with the subsidiarity principle as well (i.e. the coordination of the local, national and regional authorities so that policies are adopted at the lowest possible level). Nevertheless, the Community Port Working Group remains the official form of consultation between the European Commission and the representatives of the industry. The meetings take place once or twice a year to review issues of contemporary interest.

The Short Sea Shipping Concept: A Catalyst towards a EU Port Policy?

The Commission's initiative was a result of its cooperation with the maritime transport industries in the context of the Maritime Industries Forum, which evolved into a distinct part of the CTP. The Council approved (March 1996) the action programme and encouraged the Commission and the Member States to promote the necessary measures to achieve the balanced development of the maritime transport sector and its integration into the combined transport chain.[3] The Council also called the Commission to submit periodical reports regarding the progress and assessment of the measures promoting short sea shipping.

The importance of those proposals to a collective European Port Policy becomes evident in the contents of the European Parliament Resolution regarding the aforementioned Commission's initiative. Therein, the European Parliament stated that it '...regrets that, as regards action to improve the efficiency of ports, the Commission, almost as an aside and in an annex, draws up a general seaport policy going way beyond the promotion of short sea shipping, which is unacceptable in this form'.[4] A view that was not significantly different from the view that had been expressed by the representatives of the port industry, whether port authorities or port operators (Pallis, 1997).

The above concept does not, however, mean that the European Parliament opposed the prospect of adopting common policies concerning the port industry. On, the contrary, it accepted the parameters of the action programme on short sea shipping, since it endorsed the view that costs in port and port-related services were major impediments to the promotion of seagoing transport. Apart from comprehensive transparency in port tariffs, improvement of administrative procedures, elimination of harmful monopolies, the European Parliament added that '...within the *port policy* of the European Union' the shipping companies should be required to pay only for services which they actually use and which are necessary. Moreover, the European Parliament stressed the need (a) for the Member States – where necessary – to improve connections between ports and their hinterland; and (b) for private port and transport enterprises to make proposals for improvements in the information flow between ports, the operational capability of ports, and flexible access to state port services, in line with enterprises' requirements.

Regarding the progress towards a European Port Policy, the European Parliament argued that the Commission first needed to clarify the questions of organisation and structure of port administrations, the financing of public infrastructure and private superstructure, and the widely differing ways that all those were combined in each of the EU Member States. Until those matters had been clarified, the EU institutions ought to refrain from individual schemes.

In the text of its Opinion, the Committee of the Regions[5] mentioned that the European Port Policy was *ante portas* and submitted two proposals concerning the acceleration and the contents of this development. Starting from the principle that the revival of short sea shipping could significantly contribute to the development of business in small and medium-sized ports, the Committee of the Regions would like to see hard-and-fast measures put forward to ensure that the growth potential of those ports is realised. The development of transhipment ports, for instance, would make possible a revival of business in small and medium-sized ports, with investments in low-cost port infrastructure. In that context, inter-port cooperation was possible and desirable, and ought to be promoted at the European level. Funds, moreover, could be allocated to a certain number of test or pilot markets, which, by demonstrating their efficiency, and without entailing a distortion in competition, could serve as a benchmark in the promotion of short sea shipping for those ports.

With the second proposal, the CoR stated that it considered it desirable that the Commission and the Council specify clearly the detailed arrangements concerning access to European funding for port projects of shared benefit. Even though ports did not feature in the maps of the trans-European network plans, the machinery for eligibility and for the funding of projects supported by the European Union ought to include them on account of their role in general economic development and in the territorial balance of Europe, in particular for the development of the hinterland of the port areas. The Committee of the Regions expressed its view that in any event they ought to be included in the budget allocation devoted to trans-European transport networks, which would be renegotiated in 1999.

Short Sea Shipping Remains a Critical Part of the CTP

The most recent progress report on the Community policy (June 1999) contained proposals on additional actions concerning the creation of more favourable conditions for the development of short sea shipping (CEU, 1999c). Based on the available information, short sea shipping had increased considerably from 1990 to 1997 (by 17% in tonnes and by 23% in tonne-kilometres), but the performance of road had increased even more (by around 26% in tonne-kilometres). The tonne-kilometre performance of inland waterway transport grew by 10% between 1990 and 1997, and rail had a negative growth of 7% (NEA – DG VII, 1999).

The Commission proposed that ports ought to encourage short sea shipping as a part of their commercial strategy and presented plans promoting specific short sea shipping corridors with significant impact on the port sector. Those plans included actions concerning the creation or modernisation of infrastructure, superstructure and multimodal terminal services in the port of Turku (Finland), in the ports of Trelleborg and Rostock, intermodal transport services between the ports of Le Havre and Rotterdam, as well as actions linking the Netherlands and Russia, and intermodal service between Ireland and France with rail connection to Italy. Under development are several feasibility studies concerning the creation/improvement of integrated short sea shipping transport chains between ports. Examples are the connections between Antwerp–Rouen–Tillbury, Setúbal–Duisburg, Bilbao–Rotterdam, Scandinavia–Germany–Southern Europe, and the network of the Baltic Sea ports.

Three general problems were identified in the Commission 1999 Communication on short sea shipping as areas that could potentially pose obstacles to the development of short sea shipping as an alternative and complement to land transport in intermodal supply chains. One of them is the insufficiently well functioning of ports as interconnection points in seamless intermodal chains; the other two being the old-fashioned image of short sea shipping and the complexity of documentary and administrative procedures respectively.

To examine in detail those problem areas the DG for Energy and Transport initiated, in December 1999, a European-wide exercise to identify concrete bottlenecks that were hampering the development of door-to-door short sea shipping and explore potential solutions to them. The exercise was carried out in co-operation with the Short Sea Shipping Focal Points (who are representatives of national maritime administrations) and the industry. The ultimate aim is to identify bottlenecks that could be rectified.

Thirty five per cent of the 126 bottleneck reasons identified refer directly to port conditions. These can be divided into bottlenecks related to (a) port services, (b) port charges/costs, (c) port infrastructure, and (d) port hinterland connections. The first subsection contains cases of non-efficiency of cargo handling, including costs relating to it and lack of flexibility, and lack of information technologies for telematics, EDI or vessel manoeuvring. The subdivision of port charges refers to the lack of free access to port services, the lack of transparency in pricing, and the disproportionately high port costs and obligatory charges on port services that may not be needed. An area of concern is also the applied tonnage measurement in some ports. Several port users express worries that the 1969 London Convention (IMO) on tonnage measurement might not be fair to new ship types. The measurement system is the tool to calculate charges for different port services, and a system unfair to some ship types might distort competition.

Measures towards tackling concrete obstacles need to be taken at port level but also at national and EU levels. Ports ought to work according commercial criteria, thus providing efficient and non-discriminatory services to all clients. They ought to rationalise their operations so that maximum benefits could be achieved. Still, the Commission concluded its exercise by arguing that EU policy initiatives were necessary, including legislation on access to the port services market. The ultimate objective ought to lead towards the creation of a framework for open and fair selection procedures when granting authorising actions (i.e. concessions), in particular to providers of cargo-handling services and technical nautical services (pilotage, towage, and mooring) in Community ports. To the Commission, EU-level policy action considering the transparency of financing and charges is also vital (CEU-DG VII, 2000).

The common denominator regarding infrastructure and equipment problems seems to be lack of terminals and specialised equipment that result in unsuitable maritime access, as does the lack of logistics in some ports, the absence of railways and marshalling yards to receive goods in just-in-time logistics, as well as the lack or the unsuitable port hinterland connections. Once more EU-level actions, namely the TEN-T, can provide the necessary incentives to improving and constructing hinterland connections to/from ports both at political and financial levels. Actually, port-hinterland connections are considered by the Commission to justify special attention in this context.

In this vein, widening the initial action programme, the EU policy on short sea shipping now includes actions on behalf of all stakeholders: the Community, national and regional authorities, the industries and port authorities. In many cases, cooperation between the authorities and maritime industries is imperative. The study of calculating and recovering of the cost of infrastructure, according to the same principles (Chapter 4), is an object that requires the cooperation between the Commission and the national governments. The responsibility for the provision of 'package solutions' of door-to-door services that are customer-oriented and supplemented by regular and frequent routings, according to the requirements of the just-in-time system, primarily lies at the hands of the maritime transport industries. However, the responsibility for the creation of the general conditions governing the adoption of such packages is at the hands of the Member States and the Commission. The need for cooperation also extends to fields such as safety, dissemination of information on maritime transport and the services provided, continuation of the institutionalised dialogue between all the interested parties for the promotion of short sea shipping and the achievement of more harmonisation in the sector of administrative procedures in short sea shipping.

In other areas (such as cooperation between different transport modes and elements for the organisational administration of the distribution chains for the provision of integrated door-to-door services) the responsibility of the industries is larger. Finally, there are areas where the port industry alone is responsible (commercial policy, efficiency of the just-in-time services) or where the contribution of the state authorities is required (use of pilots in all cases).

The Council of Ministers Communication accepted the Commission initiatives in early 2000. The Council Resolution of 14 February,[6] emphasised the measures improving the efficiency of ports through administrative improvements, the rationalisation of administrative procedures and the assessment of the potential for financing – all these in the context of the Community action for the development of intermodal transport. It also emphasised the widening of the coordinated Community efforts towards the creation of technical opportunities and market opportunities for the development of short sea shipping.

It is worthwhile to mention that the favourable Resolution of the European Parliament (July 2000) on the Commission's report referred to the need for additional funding for ports either at a national or at a EU level. Among the measures proposed by the European Parliament is the exemption of short sea shipping ports from EU policies that increase their operational costs (Regulation concerning the waste reception facilities, pilotage charges). A further proposal of the European Parliament referred to the need to create a list of ports able to promote the development of short sea shipping using the criterion of the intermodal connections of these ports. This proposal has faced strong opposition by the port industry, which considers that the specific measure would create distortions in competition. The ports that would not be included in the list would have a comparative disadvantage in their efforts to expand their commercial activities.[7]

More recently (April 2001), the European Parliament, meeting in plenary session, adopted a report on the Draft Regulation on the granting of aid for the coordination of transport by road, rail, and inland waterway (updating Regulation 1107/70). In general, the Parliament seeks to widen the scope and acceptability of state aid and lighten the conditions under which it can be approved. Most importantly, Parliament is keen to ensure that the Regulation covers short sea shipping, including combined transport operations at sea ports. The European Parliament found it essential to state explicitly that shore-based combined transport transhipment facilities at seaports come within the Regulation's scope. The changes proposed by the Parliament are quite drastic. It remains to be seen what will be the Council's position on that question. For reasons analytically explained in the forthcoming Chapter, the issue is likely to be quite controversial in any case between the different EU institutions and stakeholders.

NOTES

1. The report was based on the study that was commissioned by the European Parliament to the companies Marconsult SpA (Italy) and Ocean Shipping Consultants Ltd (United Kingdom).
2. Unfair practices are also observed in the operation of port undertakings (e.g. abuse of dominant position, special pricing or 'fidelity discount'). As far as the specific practices are concerned, the same rules applied to the undertakings of the other economic sectors are also applicable to port undertakings, thus they do not concern the port policy.
3. Official Journal, C 99, of 02.04.1996.
4. Official Journal, C 198 of 08.07.1996, p.p. 44, paragraph 13.
5. Official Journal, C 129 of 02.05.1996.
6. Official Journal, C 56 of 29.02.2000.
7. ESPO News, Vol. 6.7 July/August 2000.

8. The Way Forward: Institutional Proposals and Stakeholders' Reactions

8.1 THE GREEN PAPER ON SEA PORTS

Reconsidering the 'non-intervention' Principle

A major step towards a European Port Policy took place in December 1997, when the Commission published its first document concerning exclusively the port industry (CEU, 1997a). In the *Green Paper on sea ports and maritime infrastructure* the Commission acknowledged the particularly negative effects of the exemption, until that time, of the port industry from the core initiatives of the CTP development, regardless of the industry's importance to the trans-European transport networks. Therefore, this document marked the launch of a wide-ranging debate on port issues and on future EU-level policies aiming to increase the efficiency of European ports. Explicit reference was made to issues concerning maritime infrastructure, the integration of seaports into the multimodal trans-European network, and the effective application of competition rules to the port sector.

Which factors contributed to conceiving the need for a new approach regarding the port sector in relation to the wider framework of combined transport, especially when it was acknowledged that European ports had already upgraded, standardised, and rationalised the provided cargo-handling services to a satisfactory level?

The main factors were the increasing dependence of European exports' competitiveness, and the reliance of the progress of European economic and social integration, on the efficiency of transport systems in general and the port industry in particular. On the one hand, the Commission underlined the turnover of the EU ports, their contribution to the effective connections of the peripheral EU regions and the islands, and the continuous increase in intra-EU mobility. On the other hand, one could not ignore the increasing importance of transport performance to the 'production–transport–distribution' chain, especially in the case of the value added goods that usually require a short time of carriage from the source to the destination.

Moreover, unquestionably important was the potential of ports to provide value added services by becoming handling, service, distribution and logistics centres for all transport modes. Finally, ports are in a position to provide new telematic and technological solutions, involving innovative administrational procedures, which depart from the Fordist[1] tradition of the past, and are becoming active commercial players in the transport chain.

Finally, the completion of the internal market and the existence and further development of inland transport networks across Europe had intensified competition among ports remarkably, while the disappearing national character of hinterlands means that pricing, port development and financing decisions of a particular port may have marked effects on an international scale. All these are taking place within a context where European ports have become nodes of the overall transport system, while investment and pricing policies of other transport modes may seriously affect the competitive position of ports.

The promotion and effective integration of short sea shipping in multimodal transport chains and networks was already a central objective of the Union's transport policy. However, despite the fact that the volume of transport in European ports had increased, the market share of intra-EU maritime traffic remained stagnant in relation to road haulage. Thus, the Commission stated that 'the time has now come to redress this situation, and to focus on the key issues relating to ports in today's competitive environment' since 'in recent years, however, trends in port organisation and financing have led to calls for a new direction in EU policy' (CEU, 1997a, pp. 2–3).

The Commission proposed several possible measures of port policy that could be compatible with the general framework of existing policies and identified other policy fields – specifically the fields of port charging and market access – to which new initiatives ought to be added. The sum of the proposals is subdivided into the following themes:

1. Ports and the Common Transport Policy.
2. Enlargement of the EU and relations with the neighbouring countries.
3. The ports as transhipment points in the combined transport chain.
4. Promotion of the development of short sea shipping.
5. Financing and charging of port and maritime infrastructure.
6. Port services and market access.
7. The significance of ports to the issues of maritime safety and the protection of the environment.
8. Research and development.

Notably, the main conclusions of the Green Paper were to a large degree in line with the conclusions of the report published by the European Parliament four years earlier (EP, 1993). The most important difference lies in the emphasis placed by the Commission on the internalisation of the costs of port infrastructure, which was absent in the report of the European Parliament.

European Ports and the Common Transport Policy

Aiming to launch initiatives to reverse the trend of ports remaining at the margins of the discussions of the EU transport policy, the Commission proposed that *sea ports, estuarine ports, and the combined transport terminals be included in the guidelines of the TEN-T*. In brief, the arguments in favour of the inclusion of ports in the TEN-T strategy can be summarised as:

(a) Increasing the efficiency of the European transport system.
(b) Encouraging growth of intra EU trade and trade with third countries.
(c) Overcoming congestion of the main land-corridors and minimising the external costs of European transport by contributing to the development of short sea shipping.
(d) Improving the accessibility of peripheral regions and strengthening the economic and social cohesion within the EU by enhancing the Union's internal maritime links, paying particular attention to island and peripheral regions.

Until then, and although since 1995 the Commission had adopted a policy indirectly concerning port infrastructure within the guidelines of the TEN-T,[2] none of the TEN-T projects in progress made reference to the port industry. Aiming to reverse this strategy, the Commission presented, in parallel to the Green Paper, a proposal amending the guidelines, including all seaports (as well as estuarine ports and terminals) into the general guidelines, and expanding the network to include the transfer points between the different transport modes. The port system was recognised as being the most probable and most important transfer point in relation to traffic and the impact on the wider area (CEU, 1997d).

With regard the specific objectives of port projects of common interest, the emphasis was on those facilitating the redirection of traffic from road to maritime transport, and encouraging short sea shipping, as well as on those strengthening socio-economic cohesion and encouraging links with remote regions, linking ports and hinterland.

That strategy was in agreement with the concept of a multimodal transport network, based on the assumption that the complete integration of ports in the

TEN-T would facilitate at the same time both the creation of a multimodal network connecting the remote regions and the encouragement of short sea shipping. The Commission proposed the adoption of objective criteria for the selection of ports that could be included in the map, in order to promote the integration of ports into the multimodal transport network chains. The criteria were turnover figures and charges as well as additional principles such as the inclusion of ports situated in all areas of the Union to the extent that they ensure important connections with the peripheral seas and the islands of the EU.

According to the Commission's proposal the seaports of the trans-European network ought to be open to all commercial shippers and be able to handle at least 1,000,000 tonnes of cargo or at least 200,000 passengers in international routings. Exempted were the ports of the Greek islands, for which the passengers in national routings are still counted in as much as the distance between ports is at least 5 kilometres. Approximately 300 European ports fulfilled those criteria.

Recognising that in order to perfect the role of ports in the transport chain the proper infrastructure connecting them with the TEN-T is of vital importance, the Commission stated, in accordance with prior proposals of the EP (1993), that it would support actions concerning the improvement of the ports' position as points of the European combined transport system. To this effort, the Commission included several additional policies: financing research, plans enhancing the administrative systems and measures promoting innovation and supporting the development of a competitive combined transport system.

The view adopted stated that the improvement of port performance would contribute to the integration of the various transport modes into an overall system. The precondition was that the interoperability and interconnection of those systems (common information system, lessening of administrative procedures, and standardisation of the loading units) would have been ensured. For this reason the Commission included in its measures the standardisation of the loading/unloading units and the integration of telecommunication systems. Returning to the relation between the quality of the port system and the EU policy promoting short sea shipping, the Commission identified as urgent priority projects concerning coastal shipping within the TEN-T as well as other financing actions for the improvement of ports (e.g. the PACT programme which was already at the planning stage aiming at offering support to combined transport projects including short sea shipping – Chapter 5) and the simplification of administrative procedures in ports.

The Commission also proposed the *extension of the part of the network that included ports to the acceding countries*, in order to integrate their transport system with those of the Union's Member States. The rationale being that the port and maritime sector was of considerable importance to the economies of a number of those countries expected to accede to the EU in the immediate future. Thus, substantial investment would be needed in transport operations and infrastructure (including ports) both prior to, and following, the accession of those countries, in order to promote their convergent development with the rest of the EU. In view of the prospect of connecting the TEN-T with the networks of Central and Eastern Europe and the Mediterranean area, the Commission proposed the establishment, in the ports of those countries, of standards comparable to those prevailing in the EU ports. Several specific EU programmes (such as PHARE, TACIS and MEDA), could offer assistance towards the achievement of that goal.

The previously presented proposals concerned the first four of the seven themes of the European Policy on sea ports: the inclusion of ports in the CTP, the enlargement of the EU and the relations with neighbouring countries, the more active EU stance concerning the ports' position as intermodal transfer points, and the promotion of the development of short sea shipping.

However, the Commission recognised that the necessary prospect of including ports in the TEN-T was not a sufficient condition for the strengthening of maritime transport. On the contrary, the latter depended on several factors affecting competition between the various transport modes. As a particular example the Commission singled-out the need for a policy concerning the charging of road transport, allowing the internalisation of the external costs this was causing, thus indirectly promoting shipping. Furthermore, another Commission initiative, published in 1995 and concerning pricing in transport (CEU, 1995b), had already contributed to the creation of such a policy, aimed towards fairer and more efficient competition among ports and transport systems and leading to more balanced distribution of traffic across Europe.

Port Infrastructure: Financing and Charging

The sum of the above proposals was linked to the development of a EU policy concerning the financing and charging of port infrastructure. The fact that the financing of ports and their infrastructure and charging policies varied, and still varies considerably, did not allow for the formulation of specific proposals. Due to the significant variation in the approaches concerning port ownership and organisation, the Commission's proposal concerned a *de facto* EU policy able to create a framework for ports, some of which were owned by the state, others by regional or local authorities, and others by private enterprises. Attempting to overcome the difficulties regarding the general form of this policy, the Commission opted for an institutionalised European debate for the creation of a uniform approach concerning port charges in the EU, and a general framework which would become a future Council Directive.

Initiating the debate, the Commission emphasised the potential to secure public financing for port infrastructure, through a charging system wherein the users would be charged according to the real costs of port installations and services. The reason behind the specific choice was the fact that the port industry was exhibiting characteristics of an 'industry in transition' and required adjustment policies analogous to those applied in other transport modes. The discussion of the specific issue in the Green Paper was necessitated by a characteristic of that transitional period: the trend to consider ports as rather commercial entities that ought to recover their costs from those directly using their infrastructure. That was a trend that contradicted the traditions of the past, when ports were entities providing services of general economic interest that ought to be provided by the public sector and be financed by the taxpayers.

Thus, the Commission reiterated the need to create an institutional framework concerning the transparency of the accounts of ports, as an essential precondition for the efficient and fair application of the rules concerning state aid. As a first step of a EU policy regarding the availability of information on the financial flows from the public sector towards the various types of ports in the Member States, the Commission proposed the creation of an inventory of all state aids granted to large ports with international traffic.

The Green Paper stressed the need to orient the European policy towards the creation of a EU framework for the determination of port charges. The implementation of a EU approach had to be progressive and dovetail with the development of a general approach to infrastructure charging and financing for all transport modes. The creation of that framework ought to take into consideration the particularities of the port industry in relation to other parts of the transport process, such as the fact that several European ports were situated in peripheral or island and less developed regions. Consequently, the EU framework ought to facilitate the reversal of irrational policies that had been observed and, at the same time, had to be quite flexible to accommodate the particular needs of several ports.

In port zones, the Commission recommended a general framework according to which it would be possible to calculate, on the basis of costs, the following distinct charges:

(a) Charges for the provision of services and equipment enabling the safe approach to the port and the use of its services by ships.
(b) Charges for the provision of specialised services.

(c) Leases, or fixed charges, for the use of space or equipment owned by the port.

With regard to the cost recovery of infrastructure investment a special reference was made to the use of three distinct approaches. Firstly, the charging of the users only on the basis of operational costs, i.e. the price would be determined by the administrative costs of infrastructure. Secondly, average cost pricing that would guarantee full cost recovery, i.e. the price would reflect the operational and external costs, as well as the construction and maintenance costs. Thirdly, marginal cost pricing, i.e. similar to the second approach without the inclusion of the costs of prior investment.

Advancing the latter option, the Green Paper supported the view that the long-term objective of a EU infrastructure pricing policy ought to be charging according to marginal social costs, which cover capital, operating, and external costs of infrastructure use. The application of that principle to the port sector would ensure that investments would be demand driven, and, in the long-term, there would be fair competition among ports.

Thus, the Commission proposed the progressive application of marginal costs internalisation, exempting the areas supported by the Cohesion Fund (Greece, Ireland, Spain, Portugal). In line with these principles, the Commission proposed a EU framework of port infrastructure financing and charging where port charges would relate to costs and reflect the cost of infrastructure investment. The latter could be estimated according to one of the following methods:

(a) A calculation according to an estimation of the cost per transport unit of the expected increase in handled volume – nonetheless, a system that does not solve the problem of defining the criteria concerning the charging of the fixed costs of users.
(b) A calculation according to the same system as the above but estimating on the basis of a specific time span.
(c) A calculation including the operation costs and ensuring the full recovery of these costs, as well as of the capital cost of the investments undertaken, within a certain period of time.

Notably, the more recent Commission initiative concerning the cost of infrastructure referred specifically to ports and considered the criterion of marginal cost as an inadequate mechanism to impose the total cost on users. For that reason, it considered that higher charges ought to be allowed, on the condition that they would not cause distortions in competition (CEU, 1998c), in essence an indirect reference to the application of the average cost pricing criterion.

Port Services: Organisation and Market Access

The priority given to the harmonised cost recovery of port infrastructure, and the emphasis on the conditions regarding state aid granting, are issues directly related to the Commission's desire to promote the creation of an EU regulatory framework concerning the systematic liberalisation of the port services market. The Commission considered this framework necessary to ensure the establishment and application of equal competition rules in a sector exhibiting considerable diversity.

According to the Commission, the factors that necessitated the creation of a legislative framework at EU level were exactly the same factors that had intensified competition between ports and within the port zones:

(a) The liberalisation of the internal market.
(b) The advancement of technology.
(c) The development of the trans-European combined transport network that provided the users with a range of options regarding transport modes and services.

Apart from the process of European integration, the reforms regarding the administration of ports introduced during the 1990s were a decisive factor that stimulated the discussion on the liberalisation and privatisation of ports. Particularly, the generalised liberalisation process, i.e. the process reducing the (regulatory, planning or supervisory) intervention of public authorities in an activity that was essentially of a private nature; a process that has taken place in several ports and has also included the administration of infrastructure.

The most rapid reforms were observed in the Mediterranean Member States and especially in Italy, Spain, and Portugal,[3] since initially in these countries the port sector was the most strictly regulated and supervised among the Member States. The main concern of these countries was to bridge the gap between efficiency and productivity through increased competition with the North Sea ports, which in fact could marginalise the Mediterranean ports as service providers. In the Mediterranean Member States, the abolition of the 'comprehensive' port model was an intermediate preparatory step towards the liberalisation of dock working and port activities.

The strong competition from the North Sea ports and especially the ports of Belgium and the Netherlands was the propulsive force behind the French reforms that not only liberalised port administration but also encouraged private investments and allowed the opening of dock activities to private enterprises. The North Sea ports, although administered more flexibly, introduced reforms tailored to increase their autonomy: the port authority of

Antwerp was legally re-established as a Public Limited Company, while the port of Rotterdam considers a similar development. In Ireland, although the option of privatisation was excluded, the implementation of measures reducing state control is underway. In the Baltic, the Finnish ports have always enjoyed a wide degree of autonomy, which in fact is analogous to that of the municipality to which they belong; municipal autonomy has been a substantial obstacle to privatisation.

All the above had as a result a specific reference to be made in the Green Paper on the various port services and the perspective of organising the provision of those services according to the requirements of a 'new port era'. Ports generally provide several services and equipment: pilotage, towing, mooring, transport of goods and passengers, warehousing, etc. They also provide ancillary services such as fire fighting, water and fuel supply, waste reception facilities. Depending on the port these services can be provided either as a comprehensive package or separately and on a mandatory or voluntary basis.

A special emphasis was placed on the efficiency of port services, since various port practices had given rise to complaints by users about alleged breaches of the EU Treaty, mainly concerning breaches of competition. The consequence of this situation was a development according to which the formulation of EU rules, governing both provision of port services and access to that market, became aligned with EU policy promoting the modernisation and better performance of the sector, given the structural developments in international competition.

Regarding cargo-related port services, cargo handling has been most profoundly affected by technological developments and intensified inter-port competition. The new market trends are characterised by capital concentration, specialisation and vertical integration. The provision of cargo-handling services has gradually shifted from the public to the private sector in order to increase efficiency and reduce public expenditure on port labour costs.

With reference to the services related to the ship, the Green Paper provided a distinction between:

- Pilotage services, a characteristic example of technical-nautical services that were monopolistically organised in most European ports.
- Towage and mooring services, which were provided either by the public or the private sector, on a voluntary or mandatory basis, on an exclusive basis or in competition with other operators.

According to the Green Paper, those port services ought to be regarded as an indispensable part of the maritime transport system. Thus, the competition rules of the EU Treaty ought to be systematically applied in that case too. According to the Maastricht Treaty (Article 295), the EU is impartial with regard to the public or private character of port services. Moreover, the EU is obliged to respect the constitutional rights of Member States to define the rules concerning the provision of port services according to their distinct geographic, administrative, historic, and technical characteristics. Still, in line with Treaty provisions, the public or private ports must compete on a level playing field where the rules and conditions comply with the four freedoms envisaged in the Treaty of the EU, i.e. the freedom of establishment, the free movement of labour, capital and services.

The Commission endorsed the prospect of an EU framework promoting the systematic liberalisation of port services in ports with international traffic, which would result in higher inter- and intra-port competition and would promote the application of appropriate safety measures. That framework ought to be based on the following four principles:

(a) *Free access to the market of port services through transparent and non-discriminatory procedures.* Especially in the case that entails authorisation for the provision of services on a monopoly basis, exclusive rights should only be granted for a limited period of time that would allow normal recovery of investments.
(b) *Obligations of public services*, wherever necessary, to be fairly applied between the various operators of port services.
(c) *Harmonisation of professional qualifications at a Community level*, to encourage the mobility of labour and free market access.
(d) *Harmonisation of the charging systems*, to ensure that the final prices reflect the internalisation of all external costs of transport infrastructure and services provided.

The above EU framework is compatible with the proposal of the European Commission concerning the differentiated pricing policies by any enterprise active in sectors characterised by markets that are either partially competitive or fully competitive.

Safety Issues Associated with Ports

The Green Paper also emphasised the significance of ports to maritime safety and the harmonised application of international legislature to all ships using EU ports, as well as the protection of the environment through the enhanced quality of installations and the promotion of new technologies. The issue, although focused mainly on the vessels safety, had direct implications for ports, thus, the Commission expressed the intension to cooperate with port authorities for the proper implementation or enforcement of the legislation, and to ensure a high level of port services such as pilotage, mooring and towage, that are intrinsically related to the safety of ships.

The Commission also argued for the continuation of its efforts to ensure the efficient and harmonised application of international legislation by all ships using EU ports, as well as the harmonised application within the EU of various provisions of the International Maritime Organisation (IMO) and of the International Labour Organisation (ILO) concerning the ship/port interface. Examples are cargo handling and the protection of workers involved in cargo operations. Furthermore, in order to improve the integration of environmental considerations in port planning, and to ensure environmentally friendly solutions in the port sector and at sea, the Commission stated that it would continue to promote the development of integrated coastal planning and management, including strategic environmental assessment, and foster new technology to make port operations as efficient as possible and to ensure a better use of existing facilities.

Supporting Research and Development

As regards EU actions supporting the promotion of port-related research and development, the Commission stressed the need to ensure the compatibility and integration of the various information systems through analyses of the administrative information and organisational framework of ports, as well as through the support of specific projects. The latter include cargo tracking and tracing systems, Automatic Equipment Identification systems and Electronic Chart Display and Information Systems. Those initiatives were expected to address also environmental issues, such as the application of international rules in ports, efficient dredging, new technologies, and the relations between ports and the surrounding urban environment.

8.2   INSTITUTIONAL REACTIONS TO THE GREEN PAPER

European Parliament

The European Parliament perceived the Commission's document as *a basis for a wide Community discussion* on ports. However, in the adopted Resolution on the Green Paper, it expressed its disagreement with the Commission's view on the application of the subsidiarity principle to the policy concerning sea ports due to the considerable diversities in their geographical location, the nature of ownership, the institutional and organisational structures, the administrative methods and their significance to the EU and the Member States. According to the European Parliament, the EU ought to progressively develop and implement an effectively limited, but efficient European Port Policy, specifically planned to ensure fair competition and strengthen the international position of Europe.[4]

By that Resolution, the European Parliament called the Commission to investigate the conditions of competition between the European ports, between the port regions and between port enterprises, and to submit draft proposals on comprehensive and specific Directives regarding the control of subsidies granted to ports.

As far as state aid to port infrastructure is concerned, the European Parliament considered the issue as the principal factor causing distortions in competition. Nonetheless, the EP prompted the Commission to ensure the state financing of specific port and maritime infrastructures. The rationale behind that request was that the problem of imbalance between the European ports was reflecting the problem of regional imbalance in the EU, since the degree of modernisation, and consequently of economic performance, differed extensively between the northern and the Mediterranean ports. The European Parliament proposed the categorisation of public financing initiatives into financing of (i) public port infrastructure with unrestricted access to all users, (ii) port infrastructure to be used by specific users, and (iii) port superstructure, and applying the following criteria per category:

(a) *The projects of financing public port infrastructure to which all users have access* do not constitute state aid as defined in Article 92 of the Treaty, thus they are exempted from the provisions concerning public notification, control and prohibition.

(b) *The projects of financing port infrastructure to be used by specific users* are not considered as state aid if they are financed at cost level; in every other case they are subject to the EU legislation on stated aid that requires public notification, control and prohibition.

(c) The *projects of financing port superstructure* are always subject to EU legislation on state aid. The public financing of these projects is always prohibited except from the case of public administered ports or port operations and the cases stated in Article 92(2) and 92(3) of the EU Treaty – to the extent that there is no distortion in competition between and within ports.

The European Parliament endorsed the inclusion of ports in the TEN-T proposing, in relation to the Commission guidelines, the introduction of a traffic criterion of 1.5 million tonnes annually, as a necessary condition for the inclusion of a port in the TEN-T, and the exemption of superstructures from EU assistance – excluding the relevant initiatives of the Cohesion Fund. The first criterion was stricter than the Commission's (traffic more than one million tonnes or 200,000 passengers annually), and in agreement with the European Parliament's view that the, under formation, European Port Policy ought to be limited to the largest European ports, which were vital to the international trade of the EU.

On the other hand, the European Parliament rejected the idea of a EU framework on the charging of port infrastructure and the determination of port and/or terminal charges at EU level. It also rejected the idea of introducing EU legislation on the administrative structure and the access to the port services market – considering that the existing framework was adequate to ensure the necessary transparency, the obligations of public services and high safety standards.

The European Parliament's view was based on the assessment of the implications of the fact that during the last decades (especially during the 1990s) the European port system had undergone significant and satisfactory modernisation at the institutional level, in infrastructure, in superstructure and in its regulatory framework, in an attempt to respond to long-term changes in maritime transport technologies and the transport system in general.   This generalised phenomenon was mainly the result of the international and local policy of individual ports, which were fiercely competing to attract the new traffic flows. That fact was unavoidably leading to excess port capacity, even if temporal. In other words, it was leading to port capacity that could not be employed in the medium or long term. The European Parliament argued that the elimination of those implications through the internalisation of external infrastructure costs would result in excessive increases in the final cost or problems concerning the balance between the ports that had completed the modernisation process and those that were still lagging.

Acknowledging the significance of promoting a Common policy regarding the port sector, the European Parliament further specified its views and proposals in a report published a few months later (European Parliament, 1999).

Economic and Social Committee

The Economic and Social Committee expressed a positive Opinion on the proposals stated in the Green Paper. Its opinion stressed, at the same time, the need for a more systematic EU approach towards the description of the various port activities and the analysis of measures that were necessary for those activities.[5]

The Ecosoc considered that the EU port policy ought to be based on the assumption that ports were commercial enterprises, operating in a market economy and applying 'the user pays' principle. Thus, expressing a different view from the EP, it argued that the creation of a framework defining the pricing criteria regarding the provision of specific port facilities ought to be an object of the EU policy initiatives. It also considered necessary, due to the complexities associated with the definition of state aid, the creation of a EU framework defining the concepts of *state aid* and *infrastructure* and clarifying the meaning of *open access* to port services. On the other hand, the Ecosoc remained cautious with regard the capacity of a Council Directive on a framework concerning the charging of infrastructure to resolve problems associated with unfair competition or abuse of dominant position. Therefore it stressed the need for the 'strict application' of the relevant Articles 81 and 82.

On the issue of liberalisation of port services markets, Ecosoc strongly supported the Commission's proposal for the development of a regulatory framework at EU level, in order to enhance efficiency and ensure a level playing field between and within EU ports. The Ecosoc approved this framework on three conditions: it ought to be aligned with the safety standards regarding ports, it ought to be applied to ports with international traffic, and it ought to be taking into consideration the particularities and diversities of those ports.

8.3   INTEREST GROUP MOBILISATION

Policy Actors and the Progress towards an EU Port Policy

Apart from the EU institutions and policy makers responsible for port planning at the national level, several interest groups representing the port sector have expressed their views on the progress towards a European Port Policy. Principally, these views are expressed through the European interest groups, which were created in the early 1990s. When the discussions on issues concerning the port sector in the framework of the CTP intensified, both the port authorities and the administrators of private European ports attempted to cooperate more closely and achieve representation at EU level. Nowadays, these stakeholders are the most active policy actors in the discussions on the formulation of the final decisions regarding the port sector. Port authorities also participate in the Community Port Working Group, which was created by a Commission initiative in 1974. The representatives of the European port regions are also expressing their views collectively at EU level.

Participating in the European Sea Port Organisation (ESPO), created in 1993, are port authorities representing 98% of the EU seaports and more than 500 ports throughout Europe. It comprises representatives of the 13 Member States having access to the sea and, as observers, representatives of ports from applicant countries to accede to the EU. These ports represent a wide spectrum of size, development, ownership and management philosophy. However, they have opted for a uniform representation at the European level in order to ensure more efficient influence on the EU decision-making process. The ESPO participates in the Maritime Industries Forum (MIF), cooperates closely with the European Commission, especially with the Directorates General of Transport, Environment, and Competition, while it also contributes to discussions between the thematic Committees of the European Parliament on issues concerning the port sector.

The ESPO argues that sea ports need to provide services and efficient transport of passengers and goods in conditions of competition. Moreover, it has expressed its arguments on the necessity of a safe seas policy according to 'the polluter pays' principle. In this context, the activity of the ESPO is aiming to achieve a EU policy on a safe, efficient and environmentally sustainable European port sector, which operates in conditions of unrestricted and fair competition and, at the same time, is a significant element in the transport chain.

The Community Port Working Group was set in 1974 in order to bring closer the ports and the EU institutions. For almost two decades, it was the only systematic forum for the discussion of issues on European port policy. Due to the creation of new conditions in the early 1990s (namely indications of a revision of the 'non-intervention' principle, more intense discussions on issues concerning the port sector at a European level, introduction of the 'horizontal' approach), the representatives of ports considered it necessary to create the ESPO due to the need for a comprehensive response and direct interest articulation to the policy proposals under discussion. The Community Port Working Group, operating parallel to the ESPO, remains the institutional forum where twice a year port authorities and the Commission meet. Two meetings take place each year: one between the Commission and the Community Port Working Group, and one between the Commission and the Community Port Working Sub-Group on Statistics.

The Community Port Working Sub-Group on Statistics comprises of members of the ESPO, representatives of the Commission (Directorate General Transport, Eurostat), and other policy actors such as the European Community Shipowners Association (ECSA). This sub-group was set to help in the preparation of a Directive concerning maritime statistics, thus addressing the lack in the relevant field (Chapter 6). Today it ensures the participation of ports in the statistical processing of the relevant data. The main success of the sub-group is the creation of a fast and efficient system of exchanging statistical data in which 32 European ports participate, providing information available only to the participating ports and the Commission. It also supervises the implementation and development of the Directive on maritime statistics and cooperates with the International Maritime Statistics Forum (IMSF).

In early 1994, the Federation of Private Port Operators (FEPORT) established its offices in Brussels. Nearly 700 individual private port operators that account for almost 90% of total cargo handled by private ports decided to uniformly express their views on issues relating to European policies affecting their activities. FEPORT supports the promotion of port services privatisation and has expressed its objections concerning the creation of a common port policy regulating all port activities. However, this interest group believes that the EU should play an important role in several issues, such as EU actions improving the competitiveness of maritime transport, inclusion of ports in the multimodal transport networks, and ensuring safe transport processes. A precondition for the achievement of these objectives is that EU policy is formulated only after a dialogue with the port industry has been taken place.

The main views of the representatives of port industries, in relation to the progress towards a European Port Policy, have been traditionally influenced by the diverse characteristics of the European ports and the need to apply the principle of subsidiarity. The implementation of a 'comprehensive' all-embracing European Port Policy faces objections due to the diverse strategic goals of the European ports. Because of this divergence, the representatives of the port industry encourage mostly those initiatives that are less likely to directly affect their commercial position, such as issues related to research and development and EU policy initiatives concerning maritime safety and reduction of sea pollution.

On the other hand, the Commission has been accused of its 'false assumption' that improving port operations and procedures, in other words the effectiveness of ports, would resolve all negative aspects of maritime transport. Without denying the prospects of further progress, the port industry stressed that structural improvements achieved in European ports (such as reductions in dock workers, use of modern technology) were attributable to a natural response of ports to the market forces. At the same time, the representatives of the port industry focused on the responsibilities of the rest of the maritime sector, i.e. the shipping industry, in relation to the modernisation of maritime transport, such as the problems associated with operating ships that cannot be integrated into the logistics chains.

To the extent that the EU competition policy remains under development, it is difficult to infer conclusions about the port industry's perceptions concerning the total of the EU institutions' initiatives towards a European Port Policy. On the one hand, the representatives of port industries are positively inclined towards the Commission's efforts to address issues of competition. On the other hand, various preferences exist in relation to port competition rules. In modern, capital-intensive ports, there is a natural tendency towards concentration. This tendency constitutes a phenomenon that perplexes the issues concerning monopolies and 'dominant' position: ports exploiting a monopoly position are unlikely to agree with any changes.

The homogeneous position of ports with regard the legitimate forms of state aid is also complex, particularly since national port policies differ significantly. To give an example, there are divergent views as regards which decisions concerning infrastructure development are satisfying planning needs and fall in the category of state aid, and which constitute application of national environmental policies in transport. True, there has been a compromise that distinguishes between: (a) port access infrastructure and security infrastructure that should be within the responsibility of the public sector, (b) port infrastructure that is constructed by the public sector but its cost is recovered by the users, and (c) port superstructure, whose responsibility is in the hands of the port operator. However, this common view is not unanimously accepted. In Member States such as the United Kingdom, port users pay for the use of the access infrastructure to ports, i.e. they pay maintenance charges for dredging. The respective privatised port authorities wish that the relevant expenses were covered by the public sector, however they do not accept that the contribution of the public sector to infrastructure projects should be recovered according to 'the user pays' principle.

Nonetheless, EU support is unanimously accepted in the case of regional aid or in the framework of the Cohesion Fund. Foremost, the emphasis is on the significance of creating common policies ensuring fair competition between the various transport modes, especially with regard measures internalising the cost of all transport services.

Comparing these views to the respective views of the port industry in the early 1980s (Baird, 1982) it can be inferred that the port industry was then reluctant to agree with the creation of a 'comprehensive' EU port policy. However several of its representatives agreed with the EU thoughts that a 'step-by-step' approach towards a common port policy might lead to positive outcomes. The contemporary views of the industry (see: ESPO and FEPORT annual reports) prove that this assessment is still valid. This fact is confirmed by the views expressed as a response to the Green Paper on ports.

Of course, the previously mentioned representatives of port industries are not the only policy actors in the context of the progress of the Common Maritime Transport Policy. As has been mentioned, the framework of the

Maritime Industries Forum has provided a mechanism mobilising all the maritime industries. Organised interests, such as the ones represented by the European Community Shipowners Association (ECSA) or the European Shippers Council (ESC), are active and express their views on specific port issues at least through the MIF. However, their views mainly remain at a level of general principles in relation to the directions of port policy.

A different alliance of interest representation was formed in 1994 after an initiative of several members of the European Parliament. It is the Alliance of Maritime Regional Interests in Europe (AMRIE), which provides a basis for cooperation between regional or local authorities with the other stakeholders (public or private) for the future of the EU maritime regions. The objective of the AMRIE is to create the conditions that will enable the maritime regions of the EU to voice their opinion on issues affecting the level of employment or quality of life of their citizens, to stimulate the EU interest in maritime activities and to highlight the significance of the maritime sector to the European economy.

Reactions to the Green Paper

Via the federations articulating its interests at the European level, the port industry published position papers and other documents commenting on the Green Paper. All stakeholders accepted the necessity of the Commission's initiative to publish a document that would launch a discussion on the issues concerning ports and maritime infrastructure. However, they were, more or less, critical of the contents of the proposals expressed by the Commission in that document.

The position papers of the European Sea Port Organisation (ESPO, 1998), the Federation of Private Port Operators (FEPORT, 1998) and the Alliance of Maritime Regional Interests in Europe (AMRIE, 1998) expressed support, but also criticisms to the policy initiative in question. All three interest groups agreed with the Commission's views on the efficiency of ports and fair and unrestricted competition as well as the significance of ports to the logistics chain. The ESPO applauded the acknowledgement of the ports' significance to the European transport system; however, it expressed its criticism on the contents of the Green Paper. The FEPORT expressed a general opinion on EU policy regarding ports, underlining the approach on issues concerning its members. The AMRIE put forward its opinion along with specific proposals to the Commission on the handling of issues mentioned in the Green Paper. At the same time, reference was made to ambiguities and omissions. For example, the FEPORT stressed that the terms *port* and *port infrastructure* were not clearly defined, a fact that was impeding the progress of any port policy. The AMRIE made the same remark, adding that reference ought to have been made to the prospects of European spatial planning development.

An indication of the significance of the Commission's initiative to the port authorities was the fact that several of them published their views parallel to the ESPO, even though their views did not differ substantially from those expressed by the ESPO (of which those port authorities were active members). An example was the North Sea Port Chambers of Commerce whose members include some of the most important European ports.[6] In a position document, the Chambers of Commerce, in agreement with the views of the ESPO, considered it necessary to stress the Commission's duty to define the terms of competition. Moreover, it argued that the issue of port infrastructure charging ought to constitute the second phase of the European port policy – expressing at the same time the objections of its members to the creation of a uniform charging system. Finally, it pointed to the significance of private sector action in the determination of working conditions. With regard to issues concerning safety and protection of the environment, the Chambers of Commerce called the Commission to undertake a more active approach exceeding its role of simply supervising the application of regulations.

European ports and the Common Transport Policy

The criticism of the ESPO, mainly based on the diversity of European ports regarding ownership and the state of technological development, can be summarised in the view that the improvement of port performance can be achieved through the promotion of free and unrestricted competition between ports, rather than through the pan-European coordination of port development. According to that perception, even the selection of a specific number of ports to be included in the TEN-T was considered as a negative development, since it would be incompatible with the principle of independent decision-making by commercial enterprises.

The ESPO supported the proposals concerning the interconnection of the EU transport networks with the respective networks of the neighbouring countries, as well as those initiatives concerning the advancement of combined transport, including the promotion of short sea shipping. Moreover, it supported the simplification of administrative controls and procedures, stressing, among others, the importance of EDI to several adjustment requirements.

In contrast, the FEPORT and the AMRIE were more positively inclined towards the prospect of including ports in the TEN-T, in the context of free port competition, a condition they assumed that already existed. The expressed disagreement concerned the selection process and conditions of ports to be included in this concept. The FEPORT considered positive the selection mechanism, proposed by the Commission, i.e. significant annual traffic of cargo or passengers and the co-financing by the Cohesion and Structural Funds for specific projects in eligible regions. Nonetheless, it proposed the adoption of stricter criteria, so that the resulting limited number of ports included in TEN-T projects would mean that port competition remained unaffected. The AMRIE reserved the right to examine the criteria adopted, striving for the identification of those ports promoting short sea shipping and combined transport, and the possibility of introducing additional criteria for the identification of such ports. Aiming to accelerate the promotion of short sea shipping over a limited period, the AMRIE suggested that priority ought to be given to improving the efficiency of small and medium-sized ports – an opinion that was favourably greeted by all EU maritime regions and was also expressed in the document published by the CoR. According to the AMRIE, the EU financial support to investments in port infrastructure ought to be directed towards the implementation of EDI systems in the port sector and to projects that would contribute to the development of combined and intermodal transport.

The representatives of port operators and authorities also accepted the EU intention to develop a policy connecting the TEN-T concept with the ports of Eastern and Central Europe and the Mediterranean countries that do not belong to the EU. However, they argued that the funds to be used ought not to be drawn from the already limited budget of the TEN-T but from other EU programs aiming to promote the development of those countries. The objective of that proposal was to ensure that, on the one hand, the specific financing would not affect competition between the recipient ports and EU ports whilst, and on the other hand, it would facilitate the modernisation of those ports in parallel to the application of basic safety standards and environmental provisions.

Stronger were the reactions of the private companies operating European ports to the Commission's references to ports as the 'weakest link' in the intermodal transport chain. FEPORT challenged the accusation, on the basis that massive investments had already been undertaken, or were underway, in several European ports, upgrading terminals and improving the speed, efficiency, and quality, of port services supplied. Nonetheless, it agreed that the responsibility of such adjustments ought to be shared between terminal administrators, customs authorities, public authorities, and trade unions, as actions of any of these stakeholders could cause delays and higher costs.

Financing and charging for ports and maritime infrastructure

The fact that port charging policies defined and exercised at national levels vary considerably, and depend on the degree of involvement of the private sector to the provision of port services, has heavily influenced the remarks of the representatives of the port industry on the development of a common EU policy regarding the financing and charging of port infrastructure. The contemporary dominant trend considers ports as commercial entities, and in limited cases as providers of public goods. Consequently, like any other enterprise, European ports must recover the cost of infrastructure from the port users.

According to ESPO, the correct Green Paper observation on the increasing degree of private sector involvement essentially imposes the absence of any EU policy regarding the charging of port infrastructure. The ESPO's opinion on the charging policy of infrastructure was that port users ought to bear the cost of the services and installations they use; however, the application of that principle ought to be compatible with the competition policy of the EU. Therefore, to the extent that such a policy was not considered or implemented concurrently in all transport modes, the emphasis of the Green Paper on creating a framework regarding port infrastructure charging, that would also entail the internalisation of external costs, would undoubtedly reduce the competitiveness of the sector *vis-à-vis* the other transport modes.

The transparency of the financial flows from public authorities to ports, and the existing guidelines on state aid, combined with the critical case-by-case assessment of the public practices followed, were considered as adequate conditions preventing distortions in competition and enhancing market functions. The ESPO also proposed the implementation of a port policy distinguishing between infrastructure in the 'internal' port zone and the 'external' port zone. All infrastructures facilitating the access to the port ought to be the responsibility of ports. On the other hand, the infrastructures outside the port area ought to be the responsibility of the local public authorities.

With regard to the same issue, the FEPORT agreed with the Commission on the need for a new policy direction on infrastructure charging, so that ports and port operators would compete on fair conditions. That policy could also provide the most effective remedy to avoiding the risk of creating wasteful overcapacity in the European port system. However, a significant precondition of that development was expressed: designing that policy required the clarification of the relations between the rules on state aid and the proposed charging framework. Moreover, a significant objection was raised concerning the role of the Commission. According to the FEPORT, the role of the Commission was to secure the functioning of the market, rather than regulating overcapacity. Whether overcapacity associated with container traffic was justifiable, or not, remained an issue to be judged by the 'market reality'.

Considering important that the proposals under discussion would eventually result in concrete measures concerning the port sector, the FEPORT proposed a framework distinguishing between general port infrastructure, terminal-related infrastructure, and port superstructure, stressing the need to take into consideration certain sensitive issues such as regional differences in port development. The proposed approach advocated the application of the marginal cost principle to infrastructure charging only if this would be applied to all transport modes. Investment and maintenance costs of terminal-related infrastructure and superstructure would have to be paid by the user, either directly or indirectly. The proposal concerned general port infrastructure costs. On the other hand, the external costs ought not to be included in the cost recovery pricing schemes of any kind of port and maritime transport investment, unless the same applied to all other modes of transport and all sectors of the economy.

The AMRIE agreed with the need to make an inventory of pubic finance given to main ports with international traffic to ensure transparency and adequacy of state aid guidelines. However, it considered that the Commission ought not to proceed towards the creation of an EU port infrastructure-charging framework. The main reason behind that opinion was the fact that the AMRIE did not agree with the application of the 'user pays' and 'marginal cost' principles.

First, such a policy solution would augment the observed imbalance between European ports, notably because it would favour those that had already completed all their investment projects, using both public and private funds. Following the adoption of this policy solution, those ports which would want to respond to the adjustment pressures, would have had to add the cost of further investments in their charges, in essence be penalised for essential infrastructure upgrades. Second, there were objections in relation to the Commission's claim that the application of the marginal cost principle would ensure that new investments would be demand driven. According to the AMRIE, new capacities are often justified for flexibility reasons, or because of new traffic needs. Thus, it argued that ports ought to be free to use the price mechanism to increase the utilisation of existing capacity, or create new capacities, if circumstances appeared to dictate them.

The AMRIE also noted that the user-pays principle could apply only to commercial investments and not to investments in public goods or investments responding to 'public service' obligations. Maritime access to ports, including locks and dredging, and coastal aids to navigation when vessels are outside the port were all issues associated with safety and general public interest. Therefore, they ought to be paid by Member States as responsible for the maritime authorities.

If the principles of 'user-pays' and 'marginal cost' were to be retained, the AMRIE would welcome the intention of the Commission to put forward a policy initiative on a general EU approach to infrastructure charging and financing for all modes of transport. Otherwise, sea transport would be in a disadvantageous position, compared to other transport modes. The latter would be in contradiction with the aim to promote maritime transport. In any case, the application of these principles, if decided, ought to provide for temporary exemptions.

Port services: organisation and market access

In relation to port services, the ESPO was advocating the application of the free competition principles. The most proper way to achieve this aim, according to the ESPO, was the case-by-case study of the conditions favouring the liberalisation of port services, rather than adopting EU regulations and/or directives. The rationale being that it would be extremely difficult for a single regulatory framework to address all possible circumstances. Two points that the ESPO considered of particular significance were the prohibition of monopoly conditions through the application of Article 86 of the Treaty of Rome and the application of a 'choice principle', i.e. the potential of the user to select the port services provided and charged.

Supporting the attempts to liberalise port services, the FEPORT proposed a dynamic EU approach towards the cargo-handling sector. That was due to the fact that, although not a generalised problem, several European ports were exhibiting monopolistic conditions and restrictions regarding the provision of port activities. However, it expressed the view that the Commission ought to refrain from applying some kind of minimum standards concerning training and qualifications.

The AMRIE also supported the development of a EU regulatory framework aiming at a more systematic liberalisation of the port service market in the main ports with international traffic. It also agreed with the Green Paper provision that common rules for access to the port services market would ensure that this access would be attained in an objective, transparent, and non-discriminatory, manner, while cargo handling would be the responsibility of private companies and the market.

Maritime safety and the environment

Reacting to the Green Paper, the representatives of the port authorities emphasised the contribution of their efforts to the existence of a self-regulating process regarding environmental protection, and the fact that the cooperation of port authorities at the EU level had already promoted such a process. Indeed, through the ESPO, they had already proceeded to the creation of an Environmental Code of Practice (ESPO, 1995b), which they intended to implement. Stressing the danger of overproduction of regulations, they argued that ports with relatively small turnover were likely to face several problems associated with the implementation costs of the relevant environmental legislation. Consequently, environmental legislation ought to always take into account the need to ensure that port competition was not distorted. The ESPO recently (ESPO, 2001) launched a Review of its Code of Environmental Practice based at the progress since the publication of the Code. It further sets out a series of innovative recommendations for future action, including a system of environmental assessment (named 'self diagnosis methodology') by which ports could carry out an audit of their environmental strengths and weaknesses.

Respectively, the FEPORT and the AMRIE applauded the Commission's attempt to raise the standards of ships and increase safety at sea. However, both interest groups opposed the implementation of a EU policy of mandatory application of IMO recommendations, maintaining that the EU ports would be in a disadvantageous position *vis-à-vis* other European (but non-EU) ports, which were not obliged to apply the specific recommendations. Hence, it would be preferable, in their opinion, to achieve safety through the application of international rules.

Research and Development

As one might expect, the ESPO, the FEPORT, and the AMRIE, applauded the EU action on the promotion of R&D programmes aiming to improve the efficiency of ports and make maritime transport a more attractive option. They also agreed with the Commission's view that the relevant EU actions would contribute to the assessment of various policy scenarios and considered that action of great significance to the decision-making process regarding port issues. Finally, they stressed that a closer link between research tasks and market needs would be mutually desirable.

8.4 THE SECOND EP REPORT IN THE 1990s: OLD PROBLEMS, NEW PARAMETERS

The period 1995–1998 was marked by the publication of the views of EU institutions and interest groups. All the policy actors involved in this process anticipated the formulation of final proposals and the finalisation of EU policies, at least on issues raised by the Green Paper (1997). Reflecting on these developments the European Parliament prepared and published in 1999 a new report on the European Sea Port Policy.

The starting point of the Report was the rapid and significant structural changes of the port industry observed during the 1990s. Moreover, the European Parliament considered it necessary to intervene in the discussion of the two crucial issues that remained controversial after the publication of the Green Paper: (a) the financing and modernisation of port infrastructures, and (b) the framework governing the liberalised port services.

Nevertheless, the new document of the European Parliament was not just an update of the 1993 EP Report, solely due to the significant modernisation and radical changes in the European port system at the institutional level, its infrastructures, superstructures and the rules regulating port activities. Rather than that, and through an analysis of (a) the state of the European port industry, (b) the thoughts on the impact of infrastructure to the competitiveness of the port industry, and (c) the developments in port services market, the European Parliament concluded in the formulation of proposals on the role and the contents of future EU initiatives concerning the sector in question.

Port Infrastructure, Capacity, Competition

The first issue addressed by the European Parliament referred to the needs of upgrading of port infrastructure and the potential policy approaches to secure the necessary financing. The European Parliament examined the effects of port overcapacity in the container sector, which was observed in several European ports, and its implications for the development of port competition.

Adjustment to contemporary developments: the importance of an EU framework

Two main reasons justified the emphasis on port capacity, and the possible policy level to address the situation (Community, national or local). These were the new conditions created by the radical technological innovations, on the side of the production and provision of port services, as well as on the side of demand, and the effects of these changes to the port industry respectively. The previous report of the European Parliament did also refer to the technological developments in maritime transport. However, in the most recent document the analysis was focused on the transition from the use of ISO_1 to ISO_2 containers and the steady increase in the tonnage of vessels, which was partly the result of this transition.[7]

The application of the 'second generation' container handling system was accelerating the design and construction of new generation seagoing vessels, capable of accurate cargo handling through the use of computerised cargo management systems. The need to reduce costs in a highly competitive shipping market, and the alignment of ships' cargo capacities with the larger size of containers, were key reasons explaining the increase in the tonnage of ships.

The first implication for the port industry resulted from the fact that the increase in tonnage was contributing to the growth of short sea shipping. In particular, it was augmenting transhipment and feeder traffic, since large vessels generally have higher running costs thus making it advisable to reduce the number of ports of call. Hence, the economic necessity to concentrate the unloading of a large container ship in a single port, from which the containers are then moved, through feeder traffic, to other seaports or hinterland destinations.

The second implication relates to the fact that, since transhipment was becoming all the more important to the modern transport process, ports were increasingly assuming the role of hinges between the various modes of transport. Thus, they could attract maritime traffic by offering appropriate intermodal structures, especially if, by virtue of their geographical position and access to navigable inland waterways, they could establish a connection point between high seas traffic and short sea and river transport.

The third implication for the port sector was attributable to the new competitive relation between the maritime transport system and the other modes of transport, particularly the road networks. Given the various degrees of ease of adjustment, the widespread use of new generation containers seemed to favour road freight transport, rather than the European ports. A significant difficulty of port adjustment concerned the bringing of the existing equipment, and especially the cranes, into line with the new standards. For example, the construction of telescopic wideners for cranes would cost an average 20% of the initial investment cost. Apart from the technical characteristics of port superstructure, the adjustment of ports also depended on the state of terminal organisation.

As was exactly the case for seagoing vessels, it was imperative to use advanced computer systems to administer the whole process, together with the likely necessity of physical reconstruction of port terminals. The increasing tonnage of shipping was causing particular problems to ports situated in river estuaries, which ought to increase the depth of the access channels (estuary or canals – such as the projects undertaken by the ports of Antwerp and Hamburg) or create a satellite port on the coast (i.e. as did Rotterdam in the case of Maasvlakte). Those problems were mainly observed in the North Sea region, where estuarine ports were concentrated. In conclusion, when European ports did not have the necessary equipment to handle second-generation containers, the road networks were benefiting. The adjustment of the latter has always been faster and entailed lower costs.

Acknowledging the aforementioned reality the European Parliament stated that '...the gradual spread of large containers, 45 and 49 feet in length, a trend from which European ports are virtually excluded, is creating objective problems with the global competitiveness of the entire European transport system' (European Parliament, 1999, p. 46). Most important was probably that, because of the previously mentioned implications, even if an individual port did proceed to the necessary investments in upgrading its infrastructure and superstructures, it still would not be able to resolve those problems on its own. The resolution of such problems could only be achieved through long-term decisions in the context of the transport policy, along with the necessary infrastructure upgrading of the other modes of transport. To the European Parliament, the EU contribution towards this end was not only necessary, but also imperative.

Infrastructure development and port competitiveness

The above developments affected the advancement of port infrastructure and its significance to port competition. The adjustment of infrastructure and superstructure is now a decisive factor affecting the competitiveness of a port. It enables the reception of ships that would otherwise choose a different port, either for technical reasons, such as the physical ability to moor at suitably large wharves equipped with the superstructures to allow the handling of the containers they carry, or for economic reasons, such as the reduction in costs due to the full exploitation of the ships' technical capacity. Thus, new conditions arise demanding responses to issues concerning the ways that new infrastructure is financed. The Green Paper on seaports (1997) referred to the significance of resolving the problem of adequate financing of port infrastructure in conditions of equal competition.

Several European ports had adopted a policy of massive infrastructure and superstructure investment with a view to bringing them into line with technological changes and increasing their competitiveness, or maintaining that competitiveness in the face of identical strategies pursued by other ports. Indeed, a quantitative overall assessment of infrastructural investments by ports cannot draw upon any trustworthy database. This is because of the varied classification of the investments (ECIS, 1996), due partly to the institutional reforms in the sector, which has split the source of public investment and increased the private contribution.

With that proviso in mind, it can be said that during the 1990s investments in port infrastructure by the Member States accounted for a consistent proportion of overall investment in transport infrastructure (European

Parliament, 1999), though this was going through a period of decline within a framework of general restrictions on public spending caused by the policy of financial austerity imposed by the implementation of monetary union.

Generally, it seems that in the final years of the 20th century overall investment in port infrastructure increased on the basis of multi-annual programmes mainly directed at the North Sea and Mediterranean ports. These investments, both public and private, did not however include superstructure investments. The effort to achieve technological modernisation and capacity increase and upgrade concentrated on infrastructure projects. Further, in some cases the levels of overall investment in infrastructure were in decline during the 1990s, a fact that was attributable to the port expansion projects that preceded the institutional reforms.

Overcapacity: two schools of thought

In certain European ports there has appeared a significant imbalance in the container sector, to a certain extent as a consequence of the above-presented developments. The maximum volume that certain European ports can handle given the existing infrastructure and plant, i.e. their *port capacity*, appears to be quite high compared to the actual volume of existing traffic. According to the European Parliament (1999), for the two most dynamic port regions in the EU in 1997, the overcapacity in the container sector was estimated at 35% for the Mediterranean ports and 52% for those of the North Sea. The figures for 1992 were 42% and 46% respectively.

The disagreements on competition and financing of port infrastructure issues, within the context of discussions on the Green Paper, were attributable to the fact that certain sea ports were concerned with the prospect of additional public policies that would level-out their intensive prior infrastructure modernisation strategy *vis-à-vis* other ports. Additional public policies, whether undertaken at the EU level or not, could potentially level-out infrastructure projects financed by port authorities as well. The key to understanding these disagreements is the existence of two schools of thought on the causes of overcapacity. The different interpretation of the causes of the problem corresponds to different opinions on potential policy responses.

According to the first school of thought, *the oversizing of infrastructure causes the existing overcapacity of ports*. Those endorsing this view advocate that the competitive role of investment triggered a spiral of investment decisions, which is the cause of excess port capacity. Their critics deplore the consumption of national resources by the ports to the detriment of other modes of transport.

The advocates of this school have cited the example of the investment plans of the North Sea ports, which increased their container-handling capacity by 50% by the year 2000 when, during the planning period of these investments, the same ports were using only 67% of their capacity.[8] During the last years, these ports also adopted a strategy of massive investments in container-handling superstructure. According to the plans of the port authorities, they will continue the same strategy for the next ten years. These strategies were considered necessary in order to bring ports into line with technological changes, although in many cases their role was limited to controlling further reductions in port traffic.

Among other things, overcapacity resulted in the collapse of port dues (e.g. the price wars between the major terminals of the British ports and between the North Sea ports), which was making it more difficult and slower to recover the investment and repay the loans taken out. Furthermore, since overcapacity is particularly heavy in the container sector, it is the bulk cargo sector that will eventually have to bear a major share of the investment cost. Finally, a fall in employment has been observed, although this deterioration may be regarded as a transitory effect caused by the readjustment of the employment market towards less protected forms.

Furthermore, a particular impact could be felt by the 'secondary' ports, which do not adopt the same strategies of investment and technological adjustment as the major ports, they are still dedicated to the traffic in bulk cargo and the provision of services to their own hinterland. Thus, precisely because they do not have to bear massive financial burdens, they may be able to provide better investment opportunities for private capital.

The second school of thought argues that *the underutilisation of port capacity causes overcapacity*. Specifically, the capacity of a port is mainly that of its terminals, with the latter not being dependent exclusively on the infrastructure. Other factors comprise superstructures, mechanical equipment, and the operational efficiency achieved and the criteria for handling containers in relation to their destinations, which may reduce the capacity of the terminal (Marconsult, 1998). Apparently, this view takes a different standpoint: that of the role of surplus capacity in competition between groups of ports, i.e. port regions, which is however the sensitive point of the Community competition policy in the sector. Nevertheless, it can be argued that the non-utilisation of some of the capacity may be attributable to its less than optimum use, rather than to oversizing of the infrastructure. Therefore, an improvement of the port management system might increase the utilisation rate, thus contributing to creating conditions of equal competition.

Indeed, it is a matter of principle to explore thoroughly the relation between port capacity and potential bottlenecks in the context of an efficient port terminal system. In this case, those factors that limit production capacity can be eliminated where overcoming them does not involve any particular difficulties or high investment costs. Moving on, then, to the subsequent elimination of the possible bottlenecks, it is possible to eliminate the effects of the major infrastructures: wharves and storage yards. At the container terminals, the wharves today are usually not a factor that limits production, given the high productivity of the wharf cranes and the resulting very short periods for which ships remain at moorings. Conversely, the storage yards may be a factor that imposes serious limits on production: it is not a matter of chance that the availability of space on land is the bottleneck against which the terminals are really fighting as they develop their traffic.

EU strategy and overcapacity: the view of the European Parliament

Taking into account these conceptualisations, the European Parliament (1999) adopted the position that the existing infrastructure might determine the level of excess capacity. This results in a situation where unnecessary port capacity is financed by state aid, without the latter being included in the calculation of port dues and tariffs.[9] Therefore, the European Parliaments advocates that excess capacity is a phenomenon distorting the competition between European ports.[10]

In this vein, the European Parliament proposed an EU strategy for the elimination of competitive distortions centred on reducing excess capacities. By limiting new investments and controlling the full passing on of infrastructure costs through port charging, that strategy could help to avoid dumping phenomena. The remedies in that case could be transparency in the setting of dues and tariffs, EU control over state aid, and the resizing of the infrastructure to bring it into line with actual demand, thus achieving the elimination of excess capacity.

Although closer to the first school of thought, the European Parliament acknowledged as correct the view (Heaver, 1995) that, due to the existence of bottlenecks, it should always be taken into consideration that a port, even after liberalisation, enjoys a monopolistic power which, as often happens, can result in inefficient performance. However, the EP maintained, that it was evident that the negative impact of investment activity was stronger. As far as the effects of bottlenecks were concerned, it could be possible to avoid, or reduce them, by better management without any interference with investment.

The proposal of the European Parliament constituted a medium-term effect brought about by a strategy for acquiring a greater market share in the long term. At the same time it was taking into account that, from an industrial standpoint, a port is a highly capital intensive business whose equipment, apart from the need to adapt to changing technology, has a long service life and, therefore, a low annual rate of depreciation. In other words, the port authority can accept a negative result (due to sub-optimal use of capacity) in the short term in order to acquire a larger market share in the long term. That hypothesis, according to the EP, was confirmed by the fact that phenomena of surplus capacity existed even in privately run ports. Thus, the long-term objective of the European Port Policy towards a demand-driven infrastructure ought to be defined as a function of the timeframe of demand, which ought to serve as a reference for investment policies.

Public financing of port infrastructure: the 'accessibility' criterion

A question that arose was the following: which would be the most appropriate way to implement the above-mentioned strategy? In relation to the EU framework concerning state aid, the European Parliament suggested, in agreement with the Commission's views expressed in the Green Paper, that between the various criteria proposed for the classification of the infrastructure facilities, the most appropriate for the examination of the impact of public financing on competition, was the *accessibility criterion*.

Three types of accessibility criteria exist. The most common classification takes under consideration *territorial* criteria. On the basis of territoriality, infrastructure belongs to the port area and can be distinguished between maritime access and defence infrastructure (for example canals, lighthouses, and outer harbour walls) and port infrastructure in the strict sense and superstructures. A second criterion is the so-called *functional* criterion. Adopting this criterion the classification of infrastructures may be distinguished between the sea defences, special infrastructures and superstructures. The third criterion is based on *accessibility* to the user, distinguishing between works that are:

(a) Accessible to all users on a non-discriminatory basis.
(b) Accessible to all or some users on a discriminatory basis, this group including those for the exclusive use of one user, including the superstructures.

The selection by the European Parliament of the third criterion was based on the fact that its two categories can easily be extended to include the categories of the other criteria as well. Sea access works and defence works clearly form part of the first category, while the superstructure, the specialised infrastructure according to the functional criterion and most of the port infrastructure fall within the second. The EP considered that given its non-discriminatory use, the problem of public financing did not arise for infrastructure of the first type, though it did for the second. In order to avoid distortions in port competition, the use of infrastructures of the latter type ought to be paid for on the basis of the user-pays principle.

Conversely, the European Parliament essentially rejected an EU policy for public financing distinguishing between infrastructures which increase the port capacity and infrastructures which upgrade or replace existing infrastructures as a consequence of technological changes in maritime transport, and for environmental and safety purposes. According to those advocating a policy grounded on this distinction, in the latter case the beneficiary of the public finance would not be the user but the public as a whole, thus public financing should not be taken into account when calculating the tariff. The doubts expressed by the European Parliament related to the incompatibility of that proposal with other EU policies and principles. The principle of sustainable development, which is integrated into all EU policies, is irreconcilable with the public financing of infrastructure intended for purposes of environmental protection, which, on the basis of the polluter-pays principle, ought to be internalised in the costs borne by the user/polluter.

Port infrastructure pricing and internalisation of external costs

Regarding the development of an EU framework defining the tariffs for using port infrastructure, the EP argued that the elimination of distortions in port competition could be achieved if those tariffs were made transparent, regardless of the formal criteria for the calculation of the pricing policy. It rejected, in other words, the criterion of marginal cost adopted by the Commission in the Green Paper on seaports. To the European Parliament, each of the three criteria, which have been mentioned in the discussion of the subject, would favour or penalise specific ports.

The operating cost criterion would result in the most moderate tariffs but would not allow the internalisation of infrastructure costs. Besides, it would not be a disincentive for new investment and hence would not restrict the increase in the capacity of ports. On the other hand, that criterion would favour the ports with greater internal efficiency, by reducing their surplus capacity. The average cost criterion would result in the highest tariffs and would induce the total internalisation of the infrastructure costs. However, that version would favour the ports that had invested less in the preceding years, since the historical cost of their infrastructure would be lower, and was intended to reduce its impact over time.

Finally, the marginal cost criterion would result in tariffs whose level would fall between those of the two previous criteria, and probably closer to the lower level. The European Parliament advocated that the 'marginal cost' charging method would discourage new investments, as their cost would be the only type of cost to be internalised. By favouring those ports that had undertaken the greatest investment efforts in the preceding years, this method would work against those which initiated their modernisation and expansion at a later stage. Therefore, it could result in the technological obsolescence of the European port system in the medium and long term.

Liberalisation, Privatisation and Port Development

The second set of issues addressed by the European Parliament was based on the positive assessment of the recent developments regarding the liberalisation and privatisation of European ports – two aspects of a general trend favouring reduced public intervention in the port sector, where every privatisation process required a prior liberalisation process. The EP proposals regarding the EU position on this issue can be summarised by three basic concepts: 'European port model', 'the port as an enterprise', and 'development of an EU policy framework ensuring port competition'.

Towards a European Port Model?

According to the European Parliament, the liberalisation reforms that had been introduced by Member States had enabled several port authorities to adopt entrepreneurial strategies, i.e. to define business objectives and to administer their resources with full autonomy. The advantages of that development included the greater administrative flexibility for terminal operators, and the better adaptation of the supplied services to the needs of the port customers. Liberalisation was expected to allow the port system to be more adaptable to changes in the transport sector, not only in maritime transport but also in intermodal transport, to the advantage of the economy as a whole. An additional positive effect referred to the elimination of public ties and controls, though it was considered difficult for those to be removed entirely if they were not accompanied by privatisation.

Thus, the European Parliament favoured the process of privatisation arguing that the main advantage would be the removing of any preferential treatment to public owned ports and, by implication, the elimination of distortions in competition between ports. A second advantage would be the involvement of private capital in the construction, maintenance, and administration of port infrastructure. The European Parliament considered a positive development the involvement of the private sector, since it would ensure that the scale of investment would be proportionate to its profitability, thus imposing a brake on excess capacity. However, that would not necessarily be true if technological modernisation, especially of superstructures, represented a factor affecting competition or even actual survival in the marketplace. Moreover, the European Parliament recognised that privatisation could have the disadvantage of overshadowing the performance of those unpaid public functions that the port authorities were undertaking, in particular those connected with safety issues and the protection environment. It also stressed the need to prevent the prospect of replacing a public monopoly with a private one. Consequently, the European Parliament concluded that preference ought to be given to a *port model in which the port authority would remain the administrator of the infrastructure but it would not be involved in carrying out the (private) port operations.*

The picture that resulted is one of general liberalisation of the port system throughout the EU, following a progression based on quite similar criteria in most Member States: greater autonomy of the port authorities, and a gradual reduction of public sector control of port working, with the significant exception of pilots. The phenomenon of privatisation, too, has followed similar criteria in most of the Member States: cargo-handling activities are now administered almost everywhere by private companies. The level of privatisation of port activities relating to ships is lower, but still significant. The privatisation of the superstructures and infrastructures has paralleled that of the port activities: where the physical components of the port have been privatised, this has generally followed the privatisation of the activities for which those components exist. However, some port professions have succeeded in retaining forms of corporate protection.

Although it remains premature to talk about the existence of a European port model there are indications of an advanced level of harmonisation of port systems in the various Member States – with the notable exception of the United Kingdom, which opted for complete privatisation in 1989 – based on a system of reducing public control to the minimum essential to safeguard those public interests that rule out an exclusively market-based approach, such as safety and environmental protection.

According to the European Parliament, in this 'model', the port authority, which enjoys a large degree of autonomy, is responsible for managing the infrastructure and, though with sharp differences from country to country, for building it, and also for the promotion of the port. Private companies take over the port activities and the associated superstructures and infrastructure, the latter to a lesser degree. In other words, the port authority is involved in the port's external competition, while the private sector is involved in internal competition. The two areas of competition are mutually interdependent since the authority's investment, charging and promotional strategies determine the factors that affect the other area of competition, and the level of charges imposed for the port activities has an effect on the success of the promotion of the port.

The Port as an Enterprise: The role of the European Port Policy

The need to adjust port services to technological changes, the conception of the port as a facilitating platform integrated into an overall transport system, the sharp decline in the connection of ports with their immediate hinterland, the keen inter-port competition and the positive overview of the outcomes of the port services liberalisation, have lead the European Parliament to the conclusion that ports should be regarded as (commercial) 'enterprises'. The highly competitive environment within which ports operate demands that port undertakings and port authorities take full responsibility in decisions relating to the provision of services to port users. Their decisions must be flexible, and geared to the specific requirements of the traffic entering a particular port.

This conclusion determines the European Parliament's view on the role of the EU port policy, as well as the port industry itself. The model of relations between the EU, the Member States, and the ports, should therefore be the model established in any sector of production between the first two actors and the enterprises. Ports are responsible for their economic and financial success in their market operations. The Member States, within the framework of their respective industrial and development policies, and possibly making use of EU funds, intervene with financial aid and services. The supranational institutions of the EU monitor compliance with the rules on competition, with particular regard to state aid.

Thus, given the position of the EU, the European Parliament concluded by stressing '...the need for a European port policy, which is in any case also necessary from the standpoint of integrating the ports into the transport system' (EP, 1999, p. 62). In this way, it would be possible to overcome the conflicts of interest between the ports in the various regions of the EU regarding the criteria of infrastructure costs internalisation, while the private administration of ports would ensure coverage of the infrastructure costs within a timeframe serving as a basis for a business strategy that would provide an adequate return on invested capital.

Regarding the institutional aspects of privatisation, the European Parliament was critical of the Commission's view that the necessary changes could be effected by means of a more coordinated approach at the pan-European level, since it was substantially similar to the traditional 'gradual' approaches of the national Member States policies. Considering as a focal point the inability of the EU, as well as of every other, public policy to address the institutional aspects of the privatisation of European ports, the European Parliament was stressing an alternative approach adopted by UNCTAD that was dealing with the question of privatisation from the eminently practical standpoint of the arrangements and was taking the option for granted (including credit, guarantees, and joint funding by public structural funds and specialised banking and other financial institutions).

8.5   COUNCIL AGREEMENT ON THE INCLUSION OF PORTS IN THE TEN-T

A Landmark of the Process towards an EU Port Policy

On 5 June 2000, the Council formally adopted a common position concerning the inclusion of ports in the TEN-T. That constituted a distinctive decision on the progress towards a common European policy on ports. Specifically, the Council agreed to define the criteria for inclusion of maritime and inland ports in the Trans-European Transport Networks, thus amending the relevant Decision 1692/96.[11] That agreement, seen in the context of the preceded analysis, was undoubtedly a development that marked the significant steps towards the creation of the Community approach on the European port system.

In the initial proposal for the amendment of Decision 1692/96 on the Community guidelines for the development of the TEN-T (CEU, 1997d), and extending the Green Paper to ports, the Commission had supported the need to strengthen the position of sea ports, inland ports and intermodal terminals, in the framework of the TEN-T. The aim was to improve the coordination of infrastructure development of the overall European transport system.

To this end, it was proposing the inclusion of 300 seaports, 35 inland ports and 210 intermodal terminals in the 'outline plan' for the trans-European network and in the list of projects declared to be eligible for Community co-financing. Priority was given to the funding of port projects designed to promote short sea shipping and intermodal transport. The Commission was also proposing to amend the title of Essen project No.8 'Motorway Lisbon–Valladolid' to 'Multimodal link Portugal–Spain with the rest of Europe'.

The favourable Opinion of the Ecosoc[12] was followed by the Opinion of the Committee of the Regions.[13] The Committee endorsed the Commission's proposal, but stressed that Community involvement in that area ought to comply with the subsidiarity principle and be based on close consultation with the regional and local authorities. It also reiterated its preference for an integrated overall approach to transport policy, and advocated taking into consideration spatial planning aspects and the associated real costs. It also wanted account to be taken not just of goods transport, and recommended the regular updating of Annex III to the decision, which lists the 14 priority network projects.

However, while endorsing the Commission's proposal, the European Parliament[14] raised certain objections regarding the criteria concerning the selection of ports to be included in the TEN-T. The objections were in accordance with the two EP Reports, on a European port policy concerning only the 'main' EU ports, according to the volume of transport traffic they serve. More specifically the European Parliament wanted to include in the scope of the future decision inland ports with a total annual traffic volume of at least 500,000 tonnes of freight and seaports with a total annual traffic volume of at least 1.5 million tonnes of freight (compared with the figure of 1 million tonnes proposed by the Commission). The amended Commission proposal did not accept this proposal. Conversely, the amended proposal included amendments referring to the finalisation of the criteria for the support of intermodal terminals, which the Commission and the EP wanted to include in the TEN-T.

The proposed decision, as set out in the common position, would include seaports and inland ports in the trans-European transport network in order to recognise the importance of port infrastructures as interconnection points and ensure the more efficient use of the network in both operational and environmental terms.

In practice, the Council's decision would give 250 to 300 seaports the possibility of benefiting from Community co-funding under the TEN-T scheme. Maritime ports are eligible according to three categories:

(a) Sea ports with a minimum annual volume of traffic equal or above 1 million tonnes of freight or 200,000 passengers.
(b) Ports with a minimum annual volume of traffic equal or above 500,000 tonnes of freight or 100,000 passengers.
(c) All the ports located on the islands that are not connected to the continent by fixed links.

Contrary to the Commission's proposal, the Council considered that intermodal terminals would not be included in the new definition of the trans-European network.

In accordance to the Community co-decision procedure, applicable to the decision-making process concerning the TEN-T related policy, the final criteria regarding which ports will be eventually included in the EU plans will be finalised after an agreement between the Council and the European Parliament. This fact demands the mutual understanding of the different approaches that will determine the future developments of the EU policy. However, it does not refute the significance and symbolic importance of the common position adopted by the Council of Transport Ministers in June 2000.

Different Approaches and Dilemmas Remain

The contribution of the Amsterdam Treaty (1997), which extended the co-decision procedure between the Council and the European Parliament to all legislative proposals on the TEN-T, becomes apparent in the amendments that the EP included in its Resolution (October 2000) concerning the common position adopted by the Council. Given its enhanced role in the finalisation of the decision, the European Parliament issued several amendments aiming towards an unambiguous distinction between superstructure and infrastructure, in order to determine which projects will be financed in the selected ports.

As regards superstructure projects, the European Parliament advocated that investment in installations for commercial activities within the port zone should not be eligible for Community financing under the TEN-T. However, in certain peripheral EU regions similar investment could be financed, *par exemption*, by the Cohesion Fund or the Structural Funds, provided that the specific financial support would not result in distortions of competition between and within the EU ports.

Regarding infrastructure projects within the port zones, the European Parliament insisted in the restriction of providing financing only to inland ports with a total annual traffic volume of at least 500,000 tonnes of freight and seaports with a total annual traffic volume of at least 1.5 million tonnes of freight. The Council had rejected these criteria arguing that the restriction on the number of eligible ports would not allow the optimal distribution of the available Community resources. The European Parliament reiterated the need to include intermodal terminals in the TEN-T, a proposal that was also supported by the Commission, but had been rejected by the Council.

The Commission's approach differed from that of the EP in relation to the 'size criteria', since it was aiming to include in the EU policy a larger number of ports. It agreed, however, with the other amendments that were stated in the second EP reading. An amended proposal concerning the revision of the Community guidelines on the TEN-T is at the preparatory stage. It is remarkable that the Commission chose to issue this proposal in parallel to a new document on the strategy of the CTP since it considered that the two initiatives, to a large extent, ought to raise similar issues and thus were interconnected. Although significant changes are not expected in the direction of the CTP, which has been determined up to 2010, this development is important to the port sector since these initiatives are aiming to integrate the European ports in the maps of the TEN-T.

Apart from the 'size criteria', significant differences have also remained between the Council and the European Parliament / Commission regarding whether the specific decision ought to include the intermodal terminals

8

8

8

8

8

8

8

8

8

situated in EU ports. The reasons behind the differences are connected to the general difficulty of deciding on the integration of multimodal links in the TEN-T. This difficulty is attributable to techno-economic and political factors. All Member States acknowledge the significance of such a decision; consequently, the European Parliament and the Commission want to promote EU action in this sector. However, a basic conclusion is that networks of multimodal links cannot be supported throughout the EU. In certain areas multimodal transport with the participation of maritime links can be developed, while in others this is practically impossible. Similar examples also hold in the case of the other modes of transport. The available Community resources are limited, thus crucial choices have to be made, which will determine the future development of certain areas.

Given that issues concerning intermodal terminals are discussed on an individual-mode basis or even on an individual-project basis, the above conclusions result in difficulties to achieving a political agreement and long-term commitments. The difficulty of the Council of Ministers is even greater, not only due to the pressures from the Commission and the European Parliament, but also because of the fact that multimodal transport issues entail elements of national planning. Given the flexibility associated with the establishment of combined transport links, neighbouring Member States may support the creation of such links simply for internal political reasons or because each member state would want to establish the conditions that would enable the necessary links with non-member neighbouring countries. Therefore, estimations concerning intermodal terminals, in the context of the final determination of the TEN-T plans on ports, are rather risky, especially to the extent that such a consideration is not part of an integrated strategy for all transport modes and their possible combinations.

NOTES

1. For the importance of the overcoming of the application of the Fordist model concerning the organisation of port production and management: Chlomoudis & Pallis (1998).
2. Decision 1692/96 23.7.1996 – see Chapter 5
3. Although geographically located in the Atlantic, Portugal, prior to the introduction of reforms, had a port system similar to those of the Mediterranean countries.
4. European Parliament (1998). European Parliament Resolution on the European Commission's Green Paper *on sea ports and maritime infrastructure*, 13.1.1999.
5. Official Journal C 407, of 28.12.1998.
6. North Sea Port Chambers of Commerce – Transport Committee (1998). Opinion *on the Green Paper on Sea Ports and Maritime Infrastructure*. Members of which are the ports of: Amsterdam, Antwerp, Hamburg, Bremen, London, Newcastle, Rotterdam and other smaller ports.
7. ISO_1 containers are the ones having dimensions of 20 and 40 feet in length, the width and height in both cases being 8 feet. ISO_2 containers are larger, the length being 24.5 and 49 feet, with a width and height of 8.5 feet. There is also a 'high cube' version that is the same

length but of 9.5 feet in height, as well as the 'super high cube' in sizes of 45, 48 and 53 feet, primarily used in North America. Moreover, the use of containers smaller than the ISO_1 standard has been recently observed to the extent that their generalised use cannot be excluded.

8. Some characteristic examples in several North Sea ports include: (a) The decision of the port of Antwerp to construct the first container terminal in 1986 persuaded the ports of Le Havre, Zeebrugge, and Rotterdam to follow suit; (b) the decision by Rotterdam to respond to Antwerp's initiative with an improved technology prompted Antwerp to open a second container terminal and triggered further programmes by the other North Sea ports; and (c) the second Antwerp terminal compelled Rotterdam to launch Project 2000-8, comprising eight new terminals, resulting in further development programmes at Antwerp and the other North Sea ports.

9. However, it would not appear that any dumping phenomena can be realistically attributed to the over-sizing of the infrastructure, but rather to a deliberate policy on the part of port undertakings. Moreover, economic research confirms that the costs relating to infrastructure have such a slight direct impact on the costs of renting that infrastructure that they produce no distorting effects on the final tariff of the activity that makes use of it (Suykens, 1986).

10. In theory, distortions could also exist between the various operators within one port, but it is taken for granted by the European Parliament that the conditions of infrastructure use are equal for all operators.

11. EU Bulletin 6-2000, point 1.3.106.

12. Official Journal, C 214 of 10.7.1998.

13. Official Journal, C 373 of 2.12.1998.

14. Official Journal, C 175 of 21.6.1999.

9. Towards a European Port Policy: The Next Day

9.1 TOWARDS A LONG-TERM EU STRATEGY

Transport constitutes a systemic economic sector where interdependent industries develop their activities. European ports comprise a distinctive part of this system and a significant means of achieving sustainable mobility. The initiatives on the development of the Common European Transport Policy (CTP) are gradually incorporating policies to improve the competitiveness of the European port industry. The systematic and intensifying efforts regarding the formation of a policy network concerning various sectors (environment, transport, mobility) encompass the elements of creation and development of a *European Port Policy*.

As international trade and maritime transport are exhibiting dynamic progress, the economic conditions and the development prospects of the port industry appear to be positive. The demand for port services is primarily a derived demand, i.e. there is a close correlation between economic growth and total volume of maritime traffic. The importance of ports is becoming more critical since maritime transport constitutes an alternative, environmentally friendly, and energy-saving transport mode. Furthermore, due to the geographical characteristics of the EU, the increase of maritime trade is likely to enhance its socio-economic cohesion.

In conclusion, either as an autonomous economic sector or as a part of a wider transport system, European ports constitute a significant part of the European economy. An efficient, reliable, and competitive transport system is of paramount economic, environmental, and strategic importance to the European economy and the operation of the Single European Market.

Ports, a mixture of industry and services, that serve particular productive activities, are undergoing a process of structural change. The port product becomes compound and part of the interlinked functions of a node (the port), which is incorporated, in a further chain, the logistics chain. These significant changes have as a result altered the nature, the position, and the size of a port's hinterland. European ports have evolved into a sector of services and infrastructure that serves national, intra-EU, and international transport activities. At the same time, due to competitive pressures, even in the case of ports that have a central port authority, the presence of private companies has been intensified.

Nonetheless, the European port system still exhibits significant variability even within the borders of a single Member State. Variabilities in size, geographical position, management, operations and employment have significant impact not only on efficiency but, also, on the conditions of operation, organisation and administration of the EU ports. Taking into consideration the historical factors underlying port diversity, along with the lack of any conclusive relation between the adopted operational frameworks and the commercial results achieved, there is wide consensus among policy actors – whether public authorities or stakeholders – that the homogeneous organisation of the industry at a pan-European level lacks any logical base.

After a long period characterised by the absence of any interest in the creation of a European Port Policy, the EU commenced a systematic effort culminating in the development of a policy of *ad hoc* answers to the most important problems concerning ports. This became particularly obvious after 1991, when the objective of sustainable mobility was incorporated into the CTP, and was to be enhanced by the adoption of the policy regarding the development of the TEN-T. The policy results of the new strategy regarding the port sector became visible from the horizontal approach towards the maritime transport system (1991), the promotion of short sea shipping (1995), the reorientation of the shipping strategy (1996), the Green Paper on ports (1997) and the reports submitted to the European Parliament towards a European Port Policy (1993 and 1999). An attempt to formulate integrated proposals and strategy regarding the European port industry is under way. The competitiveness of European ports and the measures taken at a supranational level are not concerning only the EU institutions but, also, the port industry, the port users, and the policy makers of national policies.

Part of these proposals includes a series of other policies regarding, directly or indirectly, European ports. Prominent examples are the decisions on combined transport and the interventions on the relation of transport, sustainable mobility, and socio-economic cohesion of the EU. Quite recent is the ratification, by the Council of Transport Ministers, of the political decision regarding the incorporation of seaports and of inland-waterways ports into the TEN-T (June 2000) and the endorsement of this decision by the EP within the respective conciliation procedure (February 2001).

In the historic course of European integration and within the evolutionary framework of the Common Transport Policy (CTP), the progress towards a Port Policy can be divided into three periods, each exhibiting certain unique features. The first period lasted from 1957 to 1973 and was characterised by the exclusion of the transport sector from the Common Transport Policy. The second period, which was characterised by a policy of non-intervention in the port sector, lasted from 1974 to 1990. European ports were not a part of the issues concerning the CTP.

The third period, beginning in 1991 and lasting to the present day, is characterised by the resumption of initiatives and the formulation of proposals within a steady course towards a European Port Policy. This constitutes a development parallel to the new starting point of the CTP and to a wide spectrum of measures, actions, and initiatives, the aim of which is the creation of a liberalised market in the transport sector in the perspective of sustainable mobility. The Treaty on European Union has expanded the objectives of the CTP, while the provisions on the TEN-T, the issue of economic and social cohesion, and the issue of sustainable mobility provide a new base for the development of the transport sector.

The last decade of the 20th century was characterised by the acceleration of the process culminating to a European Port Policy. The Green Paper on seaports and maritime infrastructure (1997) constitutes a focal point of this evolution. This fact should not come as a surprise. The Commission's initiative constituted the first attempt towards an integrated port policy, and consequently it initiated a heated and important debate between the port industry and the EU institutions. At the same time, as was demonstrated by the analysis of other initiatives and the views of other policy actors, the proposition that ports are playing a significant part in the operation of multimodal, door-to-door transport was gaining consensus. The latter is of paramount importance to intra-EU trade and to the trade between the EU and third countries. The signs of progress towards a long-term European strategy are confirmed by:

(a) The reconsideration of the 'non-intervention' policy principle by the Commission in the context of the Green Paper on sea ports and maritime infrastructure;
(b) The new proposals of the European Parliament (1999); and
(c) The visible mobilisation of all those related to the port sector, and those affected by it, towards the formation of specific proposals regarding the role and contents of the European Port Policy.

During the same period, there was a change of gear in the attempts to formulate an integrated EU policy regarding the transport sector. The completion of the Single European Market and the economic growth of the European economic space resulted in additional requirements in relation to the increasing mobility of goods and persons. The Treaties of Maastricht, Amsterdam, and Nice reconfirmed the objectives of creating a European transport system able to contribute to the perspective of sustainable development and to the strengthening of the social cohesion of the EU. Towards the materialisation of these objectives, various EU policies are being developed regarding: (a) transport infrastructure, such as its cost of creation or upgrading and charging; (b) the development of trans-European transport networks; and (c) the development of the conditions for the operation of multimodal transport. Those policies concerned, for the first time, all parts of the European transport network. Parallel to that, decision makers at the EU level acknowledged the increasingly important role of maritime transport in the facilitation of the sustainability of the inland transport system. Due to increasing demand for transport and environmental concerns, maritime transport and ports are expected to serve a larger volume of traffic than they have in the recent past.

The EU endeavours to formulate common policies aimed at the achievement of the balanced and sustainable development of its territory but, also, improvement in the accessibility and the development of the lagging EU regions. It constitutes progress complementary to the process of transport liberalisation, in accordance with the subsidiary role of the EU framework in the promotion of social and territorial cohesion. In this perspective the interventions of the EU regarding combined transport of goods and in the trans-European corridors are incorporated. These policies have an impact on the organisational and operational characteristics of ports. According to the principle of subsidiarity, the CTP was oriented towards actions that the individual Member States where in no position to implement and, because of the scale or their implications, it was deemed preferable that the responsibility be undertaken by the EU.

While there still does not exist, nor is it considered desirable, a complete policy to regulate in detail all the issues concerning the port industry, a series of proposals, indicate and make noticeable the progress of the last decade towards a European Port Policy. The points of the port policy on which interest was focused in the recent past and accordingly which are adopted or finalised as new initiatives, at present and in the immediate future, can be divided into three categories:

(a) The inclusion of ports in the TEN-T and in the CTP in general.
(b) The systematic approach of regulations regarding access to the port services sector.
(c) The financing of port services.

In 2001, the Commission has completed and presented a proposals package regarding ports, known as the 'port package' (CEU, 2001a; CEU, 2001d). The port package consists of the results of the Commission's research into public financing and charging practices in EU ports, proposals

for the transparency of port financial accounts, unrestricted access to port
services, and the update of the Green Paper on ports and maritime
infrastructure.

The specific proposals, having as the objective the improvement of the
quality of port services, since ports are recognised as a vital element of
European transport, are already exposed to further debate without however
being included in the issues debated at the Councils of Transport Ministers
for the year 2001.

Meanwhile, the Commission has expressed its intention to develop further
EU action in the sector of intermodal transport in two ways: first by
proposing the revision of Directives 96/48 and 92/106, and second by a
Regulation on the promotion of the interconnection and the combined use of
different transport modes. The PACT Programme is replaced by MARCO
POLO, which has an increased budget and favours projects involving short
sea shipping.

The White Paper on a European Transport Policy for 2010

A renewed assessment on the future of the Common Transport Policy, which
was published (after several postponements) by the Commission in the form
of a White Paper in September 2001 (CEU, 2001b), and a revision of the
TEN-T guidelines, currently under preparation, will accompany these policy
actions.

The White Paper on a European Transport Policy for 2010 will have
certain implications for the port sector. Whereas the port package focuses
essentially on competition within and, to a lesser extent, between ports, the
White Paper is likely to address the crucial aspect of competition between
transport modes. This will bring the highly controversial issue of
infrastructure charging again to the forefront, an issue which has been widely
debated before, but which so far has never come out of its theoretical context.
The Commission in any case seems to have the intention of addressing port
and maritime tariffs as well, although maritime transport can be regarded as
one of the most environmentally friendly modes of transport.

Another aim of the White Paper is the development of concrete measures
to support the environmentally friendly modes of transport. Again, this
debate is not new. The Commission, however, has indicated that it intends to
go beyond 'moral' support (besides the White Paper is entitled 'time to
decide') by envisaging the creation of funds to stimulate, for instance, the
start-up of new short sea lines. Such operational aid measures are already
available for other modes (notably rail). This will no doubt trigger a
discussion between the principle position that no operational aid should be

available for any transport mode and the pragmatic viewpoint that what is available for other modes should also be available for maritime transport.

This endeavour is part of the Commission's call to transform sustainable development as their core objective of the review of any common policy. In line with the Göteborg European Council (June 2001), the progress in the Cardiff process for environmental integration into Transport (and other sectoral) policies should continue to deepen and give input to the implementation of the Sustainable Development Strategy. This work should rapidly be brought to an implementation phase. These strategies should be reviewed regularly, based on indicators that must be a fundamental part of the strategies. To this end, the Commission focuses on four areas of the Common Transport Policy, each having the potential to contribute more positively to the sustainable development strategy (CEU, 2001d):

(a) Limiting climate change and increasing the use of clean energy.
(b) Addressing threats to public health.
(c) Managing natural resources more responsibly (in that framework, the EU legislation on environmental liability will be put in place by 2003 and indicators on biodiversity and resource use will be established).
(d) Improving the transport system and land use.

In this vein, in the attempt to address the issues of pollution and congestion caused by transport, key measures at the EU level should include a framework for transport charges and prioritising investments, notably in short sea shipping. Moreover, the Commission intends to report to each Spring European Council on the progress in implementing the Sustainable Development Strategy.

The preceding developments resulted in a renewed assessment having the potential to be included in the agenda of the Council of Transport Ministers in 2002, thus confirming the importance of ports to the efficiency of the European transport system.

9.2 PORTS AND THE TEN-T: A FINAL DECISION

Regarding the participation of ports in the TEN-T, the broad EU framework concerning the establishment of an integrated, intermodal transport system was defined in 1996 by a Decision agreed between the Council of Ministers and the European Parliament. Despite the provision of guidelines on specific projects and conditions and despite the consensus on the necessity for inclusion of European ports in the TEN-T, agreement could not be reached on which ports ought to be included in the TEN-T outline plans (maps). The main reason was the inability to agree on the criteria regarding the volume and/or the type of traffic that ports included in the TEN-T ought to serve.

Based on the debate between the EU institutions and the representatives of the port industry, the Commission re-assessed the situation and undertook the commitment to specify more clearly in the guidelines the criteria regarding the inclusion of ports in the TEN-T. As a result, the Commission proposed, using objective criteria, the identification of 300 ports for inclusion in the TEN-T. The adoption of a common position in the Council of Ministers reconfirmed the political will of the EU to foster the inclusion/relation of ports and TEN-T. A still unresolved issue is the finalisation of the specific criteria mentioned above. The finalisation of the criteria will be the outcome of convergence of the different opinions expressed by the European Parliament, the Council of Ministers, and the Commission.

In January 2001, the Council and the European Parliament agreed, in principle, on the contents of a complementary amendment of Decision 1692/96. An agreement that is closer to the spirit of the 'restrictive' approach of the EP rather than the 'generous' view of the Common Position of the Council of Ministers. The points of agreement permit the financing of a port only if it fulfils one of the following criteria:

(a) International ports (Category A), whose annual traffic exceeds 1.5 million tonnes or 200,000 passengers that have established intermodal links with the TEN-T.
(b) Community ports (Category B), whose annual traffic exceeds 500,000 tonnes or varies between 10,000 and 199,000 passengers that have established intermodal links with the TEN-T.
(c) Local ports (Category C) that do not fulfil the criteria A and B but are located in islands or remote inland areas and are considered necessary for the provision of steady connections with specific areas.

At present, the institutions are seeking to finalise the agreement and a satisfactory resolution is likely to be published and come into force in the form of a Decision. This finalisation, after more than three years of negotiations, will enable the financing of ports by the TEN-T programme, especially of ports that facilitate the development of the TEN-T and the conduct of combined transport.

The Commission also intends to revise the priorities of the trans-European networks in two phases. As Decision 1692/96 establishing the guidelines for the TEN-T specifies, these guidelines should be regularly reviewed. The White Paper on transport recently adopted by the Commission reports that the guidelines should be adapted owing to the delays in completing certain network projects, saturation of some major routes, the gradual opening up of the transport market and the predicted growth in traffic. In making these changes, the Commission intends to update the maps of the outline plans (i.e. including a limited number of new priority projects) and to incorporate the most recent EU legislation on the environment. These proposals are a natural follow-up to the call from the Gothenburg European Council for greater priority for rail, inland waterways, short-sea shipping, intermodal transport, and the corresponding connections.

The aim of the first step is to reduce and modify the priorities of the trans-European network so as to optimise its capacity by concentrating investment on the creation of a rail network, giving priority to freight, including port connections; the development of a high-speed network for passengers, integrating rail and air; and intelligent transport systems, in particular through plans to deploy traffic management systems along congested routes. A second step, estimated to take place in 2004, focuses on coastal motorways and the integration of candidate countries in the networks, in order to prepare the trans-European network for 2020–2025 in an enlarged EU.

The EU contribution is expected to be extended to 20 per cent of funding, since experience has shown that in some cases, especially where cross-border projects are concerned, the current maximum level of support of 10% is not enough to encourage public or private investment that is needed. Still, despite the increase of this EU financial contribution, the Commission estimates that investment totalling Euro 400 billion will be needed to build the TEN-T. In view of the limited amount of EU funding available, via the TEN budget (estimated funding Euro 4.2 billion), the Cohesion Fund (Euro 9 billion), the Structural Funds (approximately Euro 4–6 billion), and other EU support (i.e. EIB annual loans of approximately Euro 4 billion), most of the required financing will have to be provided by the Member States. Nonetheless, this funding accelerates the completion of the TEN-T which, following the preceded policy developments, includes 273 international seaports and 210 inland ports.

9.3 IMPROVING THE QUALITY OF PORT SERVICES: THE PORT PACKAGE

Market Access to Port Services

The discussions of the EU initiatives, along with the recent developments in the European port sector, make apparent that port services are, or at least are considered as, 'commercial goods'. Consequently, concepts such as quality, efficiency, and price–performance ratio, have become key elements of European port competitiveness. The contemporary reality indicates a further development: the conventional methods of service production and rendering of infrastructure in ports have been successfully challenged. This development, while being positive, is far from uniform. In addition, on many occasions it has not been accompanied by clear and reliable procedural rules setting out the rights and obligations of national and port authorities in the framework of the new operational reality.

In the newly established conditions, the participating policy actors desire all port markets to enjoy the same level of liberalisation and degree of competition that prevail in the Single European Market. Thus, efforts are intensified with the objective that all port services of a commercial nature are produced under competitive conditions as defined by the Treaty of the European Union: the freedom of establishment, the free movement of workers, goods, and services – also known as the 'four freedoms'.

European Port Policy developments should not however ignore the particular characteristics of ports. Ports aim to serve different markets and are subject to specific development restrictions. The resulting diversity requires a differentiated approach towards the governing regulatory framework. Inevitably, since there are no 'identical' ports, a number of decisions regarding the level of market access to port services are influenced by the individual characteristics of a specific port on a case-by-case basis.

The debate between the port industry, national authorities and EU institutions has exposed widespread support for a regulatory framework at the EU level, aimed at the establishment of systematic rules regarding access to services in European ports with international traffic. There is also a consensus to take into due consideration maritime safety, environmental requirements, and public service obligations, while respecting the inherent heterogeneity of the industry. This framework should accompany and guide national measures, which continue in the attempt to eliminate existing restrictions in the port services market. On grounds of the subsidiarity principle, this process adequately respects local, regional, and national port specificities.

Following consultation, a proposal has been put forward by the Commission on a regulatory framework regarding access to the port services market (CEU, 2001a), to be discussed within the EU decision-making mechanisms. Price and quality of services are the key elements in the selection of a port. Therefore, the Commission maintains that EU rules are necessary, in order to ensure a level playing field, especially when there is continuous displacement of the production of port services from the public to the private sector, without the systematic application of the four freedoms and competition rules in the port sector. While all ports adhere to the rules defined by national authorities, the diversity and complexity of these rules along with the high degree of uncertainty characterising the procedural issues continue to attract the interest (and complaints) of port users and port services producers. Consequently, the Commission is proposing a series of rules applicable to all EU ports, to ensure that competition between and among ports takes place on equal terms.

Grounded on the heterogeneity of European ports, this is a proposal for the adoption of a Directive to be applied parallel to port planning at the national level. It is also recognised that the EU framework on port services should not be applicable to ports of all sizes. Otherwise, its application by the Member States would, in most cases, result in additional workloads for the authorities that, in the case of small ports, will be disproportionately large in relation to the expected outcome. This is because the relatively small volume of traffic and number of passengers do not usually require many producers of port services.

Under these conditions, the Commission advocates that it is necessary to establish a EU-wide legal framework that ensures, on the one hand, access to the port services market according to the provisions of the EU Treaty. On the other hand, the said framework will need to allow Member States and the relevant authorities to make complementary specific rules, taking in due consideration the geographic and other characteristics of ports along with the local, regional or national specificities. This framework should be shaped in accordance to the conclusions of the European Council of Lisbon (March 2000) where the Commission, the Council and the Member States were called to '...accelerate the liberalisation in sectors such as ... Transport'.

The proposal that the Commission put forward, concerned every port, or system of ports, of a Member State open to general commercial maritime traffic whose average annual traffic during the last three years was not less than three million tonnes of cargo or 500,000 passengers. The adoption of the proposed Directive will establish common rules for:

1. The implementation of the principle of freedom of entry and provision of port services. A far-reaching objective of the Commission in the context of the Single European Market is the existence of at least two port producers for every port service of the three following categories. Firstly, techno-navigational services regarding: (a) pilotage, (b) towage, and (c) mooring. Secondly, cargo-handling services which include: (a) stevedoring, stowage, transhipment, and other intra-terminal transport, (b) storage, depot, and warehousing, depending on cargo categories, and (c) cargo consolidation. Thirdly, passenger services including embarkation and disembarkation.
2. Member States' right to require prior authorisation for the provision of port services and to define the duration of the relevant permit. This right is granted in order to ensure proper management of a port with its

inherent constraints as well as to ensure a satisfactory level of professional qualifications. Member States may operate a system of prior authorisation for providers of port services.

3.   Member States' right to limit the number of service providers. The number of authorisations can only be limited for reasons of constraints relating to available space or capacity and/or maritime safety. Member States must carry out a transparent, objective and non-discriminatory selection process of the service providers.

4.   Procedures to be followed in the process, including transparency and non-discrimination of service providers. These rules concern exclusively the professional qualifications of the provider, its financial condition, adequate insurance coverage, the safety of maritime transport, the safety concerning port facilities, equipment, and personnel, as well as the protection of the environment. In the case where a public service must be provided this ought to concern the safety, tidiness, continuity, quality, and the price, of the specific service.

5.   The implementation of the right to self-handle if port users believe that such action provides better use of their resources and gains in efficiency of their own services. This right refers to the possibility that a port user self-handles one or more categories of port services when no contract has been signed with a third party for the provision of the said services. Self-handling, according to the port package proposal should be subject to an authorisation for which the criteria must not be stricter than those applying to providers of the same or a comparable port service.

6.   The rights and obligations of port managing bodies in their dual functions of authority and service provider. Where the managing body of the port provides, or wishes to provide, port services in competition with other service providers, it must be treated like a competitor provider. This requires that the managing body must not be involved in the selection procedure of service providers, must not discriminate, in its function as managing body of the port, between service providers in which it holds an interest and must, in particular, separate its port service accounts from its other activities.

Member States should implement the above rules according to the principle of good governance. In other words, they will have to ensure full transparency of all procedures in relation to the provision of port services, as well as the availability of appeal procedures, including a judicial review.

The challenge for the European Port Policy lies in the combination of policies regarding safety, the environment and public requirements, within an institutional framework that will ensure the compliance of all port practices with the competition rules of the EU Treaty and the necessary transparency in the relations of public authorities, port service providers and the users of these services.

Port Competition, Transparency, and Public Finance

The formulation of an EU framework regarding the public financing and charging methods of port services constitutes a third field of activity that lies at the centre of EU interest for more than a decade. Whilst in the past it was thought that the port product was a public good that ought to be financed by the public budget, the modern trend considers it as a commercial product whose cost should be borne by its user and at the same time it should yield profit to its provider. The existence of competition among the EU ports requires a common European approach to the conditions regarding their public financing and their charging practices. A requirement that turns out to be indispensable, since the completion of the Single Market has intensified competition between ports while at the same time great diversities characterise the relevant national practices.

The Commission, in order to formulate this approach, initiated research into public financing and charging practices in the most important ports in the EU. The lack of satisfactory data on the existing practices constitutes to this day the main restrictive factor in relation to the formulation, or even the rejection, of any common policy in this field. The conclusions of the research initiative, even if limited to the research of specific, and not all, European ports, reflect static rather than dynamic data of the port industry.

According to the data gathered by the Commission (CEU, 2001d) the formulation of an EU framework appears to be necessary for a number of reasons. First, despite the growing role of private involvement in port developments, 90% of the EU maritime trade is estimated to be handled in ports where investments and other policy and managerial decisions (e.g. charging) are, to various extents, dependent or influenced by public bodies. Second, the transparency of public financial flows is unsatisfactory. The financial accounts of ports cannot provide aggregate information on the flow of public funds. Charging and cost recovery systems exhibit considerable variation among the ports of Member States. Third, the port services sector is developing and access possibilities to the market are clearly increasing. The EU must create the rules according to which these possibilities are provided and used.

Fourth, the public financing of port services, according to the Commission's research in 52 European ports situated in thirteen Member States, is estimated to be in the region of Euro 3–5 billion per year. This amount represents some 5–10% of total public financing of the transport infrastructure in Europe and the estimations of the Commission lead to the conclusion that the real magnitude of public investment in ports is two or three times higher. Undoubtedly this financing still exhibits significant variation, in relation to magnitude and direction, according to the geographical region of Europe. In certain cases, this financial contribution focuses on infrastructure modernisation (i.e. in the Mediterranean), while elsewhere it focuses on new infrastructure construction (i.e. in the Baltic).

Specifically, in the North Sea region, handling via major ports some 50% of the European port traffic, public financing, in absolute terms, and in relation to traffic per tonne is the highest in comparison to other EU regions. Public investments, particularly in port infrastructure and maintenance, are showing one of the highest growth rates in comparison to other EU maritime regions.

Data on public financing show a different picture for the *Baltic* region. Here clearly the emergence of new markets is reflected in the boom for typical 'start-up' investments in ports such as land purchase, basic maritime access and infrastructure links. The same can be said for public support in more commercially oriented investments like superstructure and services, whereas, for obvious reasons, spending on maintenance is less prominent. Considering the relatively small share of overall EU port traffic, public funds play an important role in creating an operational port sector in this region.

The share of total public spending in Atlantic ports is, in absolute terms and over time, one of the lowest in the EU. Indeed, overall public investments in these ports seem to indicate a trend, which is contrary to a steady growth in traffic. However, a clear orientation towards commercialisation and increase in port efficiency is indicated in the dynamic evolution of public support, albeit in low absolute levels, for investments in superstructure, services, and maintenance.

Similar to the North Sea region, the Mediterranean is experiencing high growth rates of public investment in port infrastructure, indicating considerable increases in capacity and/or efficiency within existing ports. On the other hand, decreasing (though still substantial) public financing for typical 'start-up' investments seem to support the conclusion that the number of ports in this region is adequate.

Given the problems associated with excess capacity in certain ports and the different interpretations for the reasons behind it, as well as the interpretation of the conditions that shape port competition, the formulation of common practices seems necessary.

The transparency of accounts remains an unresolved issue for the development of the European Port Policy. Considering that ports accounts are currently monitored by different accounting systems (e.g. accounts of a private-sector nature, public accounting or 'budget' approach, and 'bundled' accounts incorporated in the financial affairs of the wider public body as a whole), the creation of conditions of adequate information is the next step of the EU policy actions. Especially since the necessity for relevant action has been expressed by various port authorities, and the goal of the European Port Policy is to distinguish: (a) which public funds are directly available to ports, (b) which public funds are indirectly available to ports, and (c) to which activities are these funds devoted.

9.4   REACTIONS TO THE PORT PACKAGE

Interest Groups Reactions

Reacting through the ESPO mechanisms, European port authorities have adopted a collective stance *vis-à-vis* the Commission proposals, based on the belief that a European port policy should both address competition within and between European ports in order to maintain the strong competitive position of the European port sector on a worldwide level.[1]

As regards competition within ports, the ESPO advocates that a specific framework for the port sector, taking into account its specificities and diversity, could have added value. Therefore, it supports the basic principles of the Commission's Directive proposal on market access to port services, which forms the most substantial element of the 'port package'. The organisation nevertheless expressed substantial concerns about the practical implementation of the measures proposed by the Commission. These concerns include the potential risks since the current proposal could discourage investments in ports; undermine the vital strategic function of the port authority; introduce a 'one size fits all' policy for all port users; not contribute to the creation of a 'level playing field'; or lead to additional bureaucracy.

Given the serious character of these concerns and the complexity of the debate, the ESPO maintains that the Directive proposal needs substantial amendments. Without *a priori* excluding any type of port service from the scope of the proposal, the ESPO is of the opinion that a more in-depth analysis is necessary to respond to the concerns related to different port management philosophies.

With regards to the issue of competition between ports, the ESPO argues that the development of a common charging policy based on sound and pragmatic market-related principles is the ultimate tool to create a level playing field among ports in terms of public financing. Nevertheless, it shares the view of the Commission that it would be counterproductive and unfair to apply such a policy only to the port sector. The ESPO therefore looks forward to the development of a common charging policy for all modes of transport in the context of CTP. In the short term, the application of Directives 80/723 and 2000/52 on transparency of financial flows between Member States and public undertakings and on financial transparency between certain undertakings, should be extended to all ports. Together with a clear guidance on the application of Treaty rules with regard to State aid, port authorities advocate that this would be a first major step towards the establishment of fair competition between ports.

Two further developments are noteworthy, as far as the reaction of European port authorities is concerned. The first of them is that before an official reaction, the ESPO decided to publish an initial evaluation. The first of three reasons for this development, according to the organisation's chairman,[2] is that the European Parliament had been in a hurry to adopt a position at first reading on the port package. Competition with Council, to which many refer, may be one of the explanatory factors of this intention. Another reason was the 'leaks' in the press that had led to speculations about the ESPO's position on the 'package', which were often misleading. Therefore, they demanded an initial, but official, reaction from the ESPO to put these in the right context again. The latter reason is inextricably linked with the fact that several European ports had expressed the intention to broadcast their individual views on the Commission's proposals. The absence of a European perspective would add to confusion and would confirm the image of a sector which is too diverse to come to any common views, an image which would in the end only weaken the overall lobbying power of the sector.

Overall, as the Commissioner for Energy and Transport, has said, the fact that the ESPO has found a compromise between the positions of ports basically managed and financed by public authorities, private ports, and all other ports whose system of organisation and ownership lies somewhere between the two extremes '...is a small miracle in itself...'.[3]

Representing European shipowners, the ECSA welcomed the proposed Directive as '... a first and necessary step in the effort to raise the efficiency of the European transport chain and to optimise the use of maritime transport'.[4] The European shipping industry is pleased that the basic principles submitted jointly by the ECSA and the European Shippers Council in 1998 in line with the philosophy and as a follow up to the Green Paper on ports, addressing the liberalisation of ports and port services have to a large extent been taken into account, in particular: open markets, free and fair competition between and within ports, no imposed services, fair and transparent pricing and the abolition of outmoded labour practices.

To European shipowners, the regulatory framework governing market access to European ports has to be amended as there are still cases of unsubstantiated compulsory use of services, of excessive tariffs based on a monopolistic position, of charges that cannot be substantiated, of non-transparent tariffs, and of rigid and harmful labour prescriptions. In this vein, the ECSA statement strongly opposed any 'weakening down of the basic principles' as counterproductive to the ongoing process of increasing the efficiency and competitiveness of maritime transport in the overall supply chain. The ECSA advocated that the scope of the proposed Directive should be widened since all ports should be covered by the Directive and consequently there should be no thresholds. Foremost, it would also be illogical for a port to be within the scope of the TEN-T and outside the scope of the proposed Directive. If any ports are excluded from the application of the Directive, the Commission should supply a list of those excluded ports.

The ECSA also advocates that it is of key importance that port services such as pilotage and towage provided on rivers, canals, fairways and the archipelago giving access to ports, as well as landside port services (i.e. port/handling agencies, water/electricity supply to vessels and waste reception facilities) are a full part of the proposed Directive.

Notably, the MIF *ad hoc* group on nodal points, also attempted to analyse the proposed measures and develop an MIF strategy of member associations with regard to the 'port package' and to follow up on the port-related short sea bottlenecks identified by the Commission, aiming to develop a number of recommendations on the more general issues.

As regards labour, the International Transport Workers Federation has reacted strongly, and decided to proceed to actions at the European level, ranging from demonstrations to industrial action, depending on national legislation and/or national or local circumstances and tradition. The purpose of the action, according to a letter of the Committee of the Transport Workers in the EU, addressed to both the FEPORT and the ESPO, is twofold. First, '...to demonstrate that port workers unions in the EU condemn and reject the text of the Directive proposal and denounce the fact that there was no serious consultation process' and, second, '...to express condemnation of the absence of any form of social dialogue within the European port industry'.

Institutional Reactions

Meanwhile, controversies, and the submission of a high number of amendments, have lead to the postponement of the European Parliament vote on the port package proposals. In his draft report, the European Parliament's Rapporteur proposed the amendment of the Commission's Directive proposal on market access to port services in two ways. First, to limit the scope of the 'market access' provisions of the Directive to technical-nautical services. At the same time, the draft report demanded a Commission report for each Member State on the state of application of the basic Treaty rules to seaports in general. Second, to add a chapter on 'fair competitive conditions' to the current proposal which will introduce, both the application to all TEN ports of the provisions of the Transparency Directives and basic criteria for the application of state aid rules to port investments.

Several MEPs agreed with the amended proposal that excluded pilotage from the 'market access' directive. They disagreed however on whether self-handling and the right for service providers to employ staff of their own choice should be reorganised as 'basic right' and, hence, should be observed and enforced in the port sector together with the basic rights laid down in the Treaty. On the other hand, the shadow Rapporteur from the Green fraction supported the withdrawal and the rewriting of the entire proposal on the grounds that attention should be paid to the cooperation between ports in order to avoid wasteful overcapacity. A third view was that financial transparency and an impact assessment of the proposed Directive act as prerequisites before the said directive could enter into force. On the other hand, several MEPs also advocated that there is no reason to change the scope of the directive as drastically as the Rapporteur had proposed and that cargo handling should stay within the scope of the proposed directive. Apparently, the debate reflected several of the divergent views expressed by the stakeholders' positions.

After several compromises, a vote took place in the European Parliament's Committee on Regional Policy, Transport and Tourism (October 2001). The EP Committee wanted to give Member States the possibility of limiting market access if necessary to guarantee not only maritime safety (as specified in the proposal) but also economic efficiency. It also deleted the provision in the proposal stipulating that, where there were constraints on available space or capacity, the port authority would authorise at least two service providers. Another amendment sought to broaden the scope of the directive to include waterways providing access to a port, although this should be at the discretion of the Member State. The scope of the annex relating to cargo handling should be extended to include loading and unloading. The committee also said that, as pilotage was an obligatory public service, it should continue to be supervised by the Member States and hence excluded from the scope of the directive.

With regard to selection procedures, the committee pointed out that not only tendering but also other equivalent award procedures could be used. Member States should also have the right to include their own specific rules in the specifications for the tendering of a service contract. Where a new provider was chosen, it should compensate its predecessors at the current market rate for the value of the immovable assets that it inherited. Other points raised by the report included the need to ensure that Member States whose social legislation offered workers greater protection could continue to apply those provisions. Compliance with employment legislation should be included among the criteria to be fulfilled by applicant service providers. The committee also said that deciding on limitations and the selection of port service providers in cases where the managing body of a port was itself a competing service provider could best be solved on a case-by-case basis by national anti-trust organisations. Lastly, it wanted Member States to be allowed to restrict self-handling to port users whose vessels fly the flag of a Member State.

At first sight, the outcome could be seen as a sign of support for the main thrust of the Commission's proposal, as the intention of the Rapporteur, to exclude cargo-handling services, was rejected, albeit with a narrow majority. The outcome of the vote was far from clear and many contradictions occurred before the European Parliament voted in the plenary session. This is confirmed by the successive briefings to MEPs by a coalition of port users, including the Euro-federations representing shipowners (ECSA), shippers (ECS), freight forwarders (CLECAT), and backed by the influential European Employers organisation (UNICE). The petition asks MEPs to fully maintain the scope of the Directive proposal, including nautical services, cargo handling, and passenger services.

Finally, the plenary session of the European Parliament rejected the proposal of the Green fraction to send the proposal back to the Commission and voted (November 2001) in favour of an amended legislative proposal and an accompanying legislative resolution amendment.[5] At the first EP reading of the Commission's proposal, a narrow majority voted against the exclusion of cargo handling from the scope of the directive and a substantial majority voted in favour of excluding pilotage. The EP furthermore voted in favour of the following amendments that would make the proposal more 'flexible':

- Elimination of the requirement to have minimum two (2) service providers.
- More flexible role of the separate competence authority (supervisory role).
- Equally strict authorisation criteria for self-handling.
- Extended authorisation criteria for the port authority to refuse potential service providers without this being a limitation (e.g. policy of the port).

In addition to the recommendations by the committee responsible, the Parliament has introduced an amendment which states that in cases where the service provider will make no or insignificant investments in order to carry out the provisions of services, the maximum duration of its authorisation shall be eight years as opposed to the Commission's five years. Parliament also emphasised the point that care must be taken not to discriminate against publicly owned seaports or seaport systems and port undertakings, therefore Parliament introduces a new article formulating the principles for state aid applying specifically to seaports.

On the other hand, amendments to exclude private ports and to have longer maximum duration for significant investments and a simplified transitional regime however did not survive the vote.

The prospects of formulating EU rules governing the public financing of ports, in line with the 'special regimes' practice applied in accordance with Article 73 of the Treaty in other transport sectors (i.e. shipping, airlines), seems improbable. According to the opinion that was developed and dominated the debate that took place subsequent to the publication of the Green Paper (1997), there is no need for specific policy action but for the implementation of the recent Transparency Directive on the transparency of financial relations between Member States and public undertakings as well as on financial transparency within certain undertakings.[6] The careful legal phrasing and implementation process of this Directive will formulate long-term conditions of access to the port services market. The specific Directive advocates the separation of accounts for every kind of economic activity. It also gives the Commission the power to investigate whether 'over-compensation' is offered for the undertaking of activities of general interest, or whether some commercial activities are subsidised. The point of view that similar Directives are necessary only when an economic sector receives substantial subsidies (something that is not the case in the port sector) is gaining support.

Several policy actors that support the creation of a EU port policy framework favour such a development, in order to ensure the prohibition of any public financing of ports. However, the Commission argues that the general rules of the Treaty, which prohibit public financing when it is likely to result in distortions in competition, are effective, therefore, they should also be applied in the case of the European port industry. The formulation of specific EU Directives regarding ports will not be an object of debate at least in the near future. The relevant EU policy on European ports appears to be clarified because of the legislature produced by the ECJ in the process of judging cases concerning ports.

As demonstrated by this study, many interested parties have supported (for a 'German perspective': Hinz, 1996) that there is a need to differentiate between port infrastructure open to all users, port infrastructure for specific users, and superstructure. The formulation of this differentiation does not seem adequate to replace the criterion posed by Article 87(1) of the Treaty of the European Union on the possibility of *par exemption* public financing of economic activities, i.e. the criterion of 'selectivity'. Among others, the differentiation between 'general' and 'user specific' infrastructure poses substantial difficulties to endeavours for a widespread categorisation of the total port infrastructure.

Concerning port charging practices, the Commission advocates a mutual approach according to which port charges ought to be based on the cost of port operations and infrastructure. These charges would take account of the capital costs, the operational expenses, the environmental cost, and the costs arising from congestion. The European Parliament Committee on Transport and Tourism proposes the total revision of port charging in order to take into account the size of the ships, fuel consumption and the services provided. A revision that ought to be in line with the position that 'the user pays the cost of transport infrastructure' through a methodology that quantifies the internal and external costs taking into account, at the same time, the particularity of transport modes.

However, apart from taking into account the practices of port pricing in Europe, and design a preferred strategy, EU policy developments should seriously consider the substantial difficulties and costs associated with the requirement to collect, process and effectively interpret complex, high-quality cost information as a precondition to achieve efficient pricing. At the moment, as Verbeke *et al.* (2001) have rightly point out, the EU policy documents on efficient pricing in the port sector are relatively 'weak' insofar as these requirements are concerned, whilst they remain 'strong' to the (academic) requirement to implement marginal cost pricing as an effective strategy. On the other hand, as the same scholars observe, the EU initiatives attempting to foster some type of coherent EU-wide port pricing system have rightly taken into account the substantial dependencies of present financing and pricing routines on both (sub)national institutional settings external to ports (i.e. judicial, cultural, organisational, and managerial heritage) and (sub)national political decision making which may use ports as a lever to achieve broader policy goals (i.e. growth pole effects, employment, distributive equity).

Despite the expressed views, final EU decisions regarding the charging of port services are not expected before 2004. Given that the relevant decisions on other transport modes are at the pilot stage (1998–2000: introduction of a system of charging in rail infrastructure and airports; 2001–04: system of per kilometre charging for road and rail infrastructure), one might expect that the finalisation of charging systems of these modes in the framework of the CTP will be expanded to include maritime transport and ports.

In the meantime, further evaluation and recommendations of other parties concerned by the port package proposals will be published, and the Commission will put forward an amended proposal for a 'market access' directive endorsing some, or all, of the suggested amendments. Nonetheless, 'life after the port package' is already marked by a debate critical to the development of stakeholders' recommendations for the EU political process regarding the regulatory framework and the future of the European policy.

9.5 EPILOGUE

Important steps took place during the 1990s towards the formulation of a EU framework on European ports. The proposals contained in the recent port package, and the other 'port-related' EU policies that remain under development in the early 2000s, have triggered a profound debate involving all relevant maritime industry players and European policy makers in order to achieve concrete results on the formulation of EU policy decisions on a series of other, equally important, issues.

Overall, the recent EU policy actions have highlighted the importance of the port system to the prospects of sustainable development of Europe, and have promoted initiatives regarding the operation of an efficient port system in conditions of free competition. The EU has at its disposal two methods of achieving its objectives: the formulation of Regulations and the financing of specific port projects. The other parameters of the operation of European ports, based on the principle of subsidiarity, remain a responsibility of the Member States, which may decide on the operational and managerial models and of the port services providers themselves. Besides, sound European port policy is not just a question of new legislation and policy documents it is often also a matter of proportional application of existing legislation, which can often be of a more general nature.

As demonstrated by the longitudinal analysis of this course it is essentially a dynamic process. Not only the policies that are developed but, also, the parameters of the debate are changing rapidly according to the (frequently structural) changes in the port industry. In any case, the search for a long-term strategy and progress towards a European Port Policy should acknowledge, comprehend, and respect the diversity of European ports – a diversity that remains clearly observable at the beginning of a new millennium.

NOTES

1.   ESPO News, Volume 7.6, June 2001.
2.   See: Whitehead D. (2001), *Editorial*, ESPO News, Volume 7.6, May 2001.
3.   Loyola de Palacio (2001). Opening statement, *Public Seminar 'European Sea Port Policy, Challenges and Solutions'*, October 11 2001, Belgium: Port of Antwerp.

4. ECSA, (2001). Comments of the European Community Shipowners' Associations on the Proposed Directive on Market Access to Port Services, Brussels: ECSA.
5. The amended legislative proposal was adopted with 292 votes in favour, 223 against and 32 abstentions. The accompanying legislative resolution was adopted with 284 in favour, 230 against and 31 abstentions.
6. Directive 2000/52, of 29.07.2000.

Bibliography

Abbati, D.E. (1986), *Transport and European Integration,* Luxembourg: Official Publications of the EC.

Alliance of Maritime Regions in Europe (AMRIE) (1998), *Comments on the Green Paper on Sea Ports and Maritime Infrastructure*, Brussels: AMRIE.

Anastasopoulos, G.N. (1994), *Horizontal Production (or Transport in Greece and Europe)* (in Greek), Athens: Euro-Community Publications.

Baird, A. (1982), 'Transport decision makers speak: The seaport development in the European Communities Research Project', *Maritime Policy and Management*, **9** (2), 83–102.

Baird, A. (1995), 'Privatisation of Trust Ports in the United Kingdom: Review and analysis of the first sales', *Transport Policy*, **2** (2), 135–143.

Baird, A. (1996), 'Unitisation and decrease of Urban European ports', *Maritime Policy and Management*, **23** (2), 145–156.

Baird, A. (2001), 'Trends in Port Privatisation in the World's top–100 Container Ports', in Proceedings of the 9th World Conference on Transport Research, Seoul, July 2001.

Bayliss, B.T. (1979), 'Transport Policies in the European Communities' *Journal of Transport Economics and Politics*, **13** (1), 28–43.

Bayliss, B.T. and Millington, A.I. (1995), 'Deregulation and Logistics Systems in a Single European Market', *Journal of Transport Policy and Economics*, **29** (3), 305–316.

Benacchio, M. Cariou, P. and Haralambides, H. (2001), 'Dedicated Containers Terminals: Costs and Benefits from a port perspective', in Proceedings of the 9th World Conference on Transport Research, Seoul, July 2001.

Bredima-Savopoulou, A. (1990), *The Common Shipping Policy of the EC*, Amsterdam: Elsevier.

Bromhead, P.A. (1979), 'Transport Policy', in Coffey, D. (ed.), *Economic Policies of the Common Market*, London: Macmillan, pp. 122–145.

Buck Consultants International (BCI) (1996), *Seaports and their Hinterland*, Nijmegen: Buck Consultants International.

Burke, R. (1978), 'Introductory Address', in *Transcripts of the Seatrade Conference 'Towards a Shipping Policy for the EEC'*, Brussels, September 1978, Colchester: Seatrade, pp. 9–36.

Butt Philip, A. and Porter, M.H.A. (1995), *Business, Border Controls and the Single European Market: Free Movement of Goods in Europe?* London: Royal Institute of International Affairs.

Button, K.J. (1984), *Road Haulage Licensing, and EEC Transport Policy*, Aldershot: Gower.

Button, K.J. (1993), *Transport Economics* (2nd edn), Aldershot, UK and Brookfield, US: Edward Elgar.

Button, K.J. (1998), *Transport Networks in Europe*, Cheltenham, UK and Northampton, MA, US: Edward Elgar.

Cafruny, A.W. (1991), 'Toward a Maritime Policy', in Hurwitz, L. and Lequesne, C. (eds), *The State of the European Communities, Vol. 1, Policies, Institutions and Debates in the Transition Years*, Colorado: Lynne Rienner, pp. 285–299.

Commission of the European Union (CEU) (1961), Memorandum on the general lines of a Common Transport Policy. Com (61)50 final. 10 April 1961.

CEU (1970), Note on port options on a Community basis. Doc 16/VII/71 24 March 1970.

CEU (1977), Report into the current situation in the major Community seaports drawn up by the port working group. Doc CB-22-77-863.

CEU (1985), Memorandum on the progress towards a Common Maritime Policy. Com (85)90, final. 14 March 1985.

CEU (1989), A future for the Community shipping industry: measures to improve the operating conditions of Community shipping. Com (89)266, final. 3 August 1989.

CEU (1990), Towards the development of trans-European networks: a Community action framework. Com (90)585, final. 10 December 1990.

CEU (1991a), New challenges for Maritime Industries. Com (91)335, final. 20 September 1991.

CEU (1991b), Internal document. Sec (91)2274. 29 November 1991.

CEU (1992a), Green Paper on the impact of transport on environment: a Community strategy for sustainable mobility. Com (92)46, final. 20 February 1992.

CEU (1992b), Communication and legislative proposals concerning the creation of a European combined transport network. Com (92)230, final. 11 June 1992.

CEU (1992c), Transport Infrastructure and legislative proposals on the creation of a trans-European network: the creation of a road trans-

European network; and the creation of a European inland waterway network. Com (92)231, final. 13 June 1992.

CEU (1992d), European maritime industries: further steps for the improvement of their competitiveness. Com (92)490, final. 18 November 1992.

CEU (1992e), The future development of the Common Transport Policy. A global approach to the construction of a Community framework for sustainable mobility. Com (92)494, final. 10 April 1992.

CEU (1993a), A common policy for safe seas. Com (93)66, final. 24 February 1993.

CEU (1993b), Towards the implementation of a comprehensive approach for the maritime industries: the first tangible results. Com (93)526, final. 4 November 1993.

CEU 1994, Proposal for a European Parliament and Council Decision on Community guidelines for the development of the trans-European transport network. Com(94)106, final, Brussels, 7 April 1994.

CEU (1994), Proposal for a Council Directive on statistical returns in respect of carriage of goods and passengers by sea. Com (94)275, final. 4 September 1994.

CEU (1995a), The trans-European transport network: Transforming a Patchwork into a network. Luxembourg Office for Official Publications.

CEU (1995b), Amended proposal on Community guidelines for trans-European transport networks. Com (95)48, final. 22 February 1995.

CEU (1995c), The development of short sea shipping in Europe: prospects and challenges. Com (95)317, final. 5 July 1995.

CEU (1995d), The Common Transport Policy – Action programme 1995–2000. Com (95)302, final. 12 July 1995.

CEU (1995e), Towards fair and efficient pricing in transport policy-options for internalising the external cost of transport in the European Union – Green Paper. Com (95)691, final. 20 December 1995.

CEU (1996a), Maritime strategy. Com(96)81, final. 13 March 1996.

CEU (1996b), Shaping Europe's maritime future – A contribution to the competitiveness of Europe's maritime future. Com (96)84, final. 13 March 1996.

CEU (1996c), Action programme on combined action. Com (96)335, final. 24 July 1996.

CEU (1996d), Proposal for a Council Decision on the development of sustainable mobility. Com (96)654, final. 13 December 1996.

CEU (1997a), Connecting the Union's transport infrastructure network to its neighbours: towards a co-operative pan-European transport network policy. Com (97)172, final. 23 April 1997.

CEU (1997b), Trans-European rail freight freeways. Com (97)242, final. 29 May 1997.

CEU (1997c), Intermodality and the intermodal carriage of goods within the European Union. Com (97)243, final. 29 May 1997.

CEU (1997d), Commission Report on the implementation of Directive 92/106. Com (97)372, final. 18 July 1997.

CEU (1997e), Public–private sector partnerships in trans-European transport projects. Com (97)453, final. 22 October 1997.

CEU (1997f), Green Paper on seaports and maritime infrastructure. Com (97)678, final. 10 December 1997.

CEU (1997g), Proposal for a Council Decision amending Decision 692/96 regarding seaports, inland ports and multimodal transport terminals, and project No 8 of Appendix III. Com (97)681, final.10 December 1997.

CEU (1998a), Trans-European transport network: report on progress and implementation of the 14 Essen projects. Com (98)356, final. 3 June 1998.

CEU (1998b), Communication from the Commission to the Council and the European Parliament – Towards a trans-European positioning and navigation network: including a European strategy for Global Navigation Satellite Systems (GNSS). Com (98)29, final. 21 January 1998.

CEU (1998c), Proposal for a Council Directive amending Council Directive 92/106/EEC on the establishment of common rules for certain types of combined transport of goods between Member States. Com (98)414, final.10 July 1998.

CEU (1998d), Fair payment for infrastructure use: a phased approach to a common transport infrastructure charging framework in the EU – White Paper. Com (98)466, final. 22. July 1998.

CEU (1998e), Trans-European transport networks: report on the implementation of the guidelines and priorities for the future. Com (98)614, final. 28 October 1998.

CEU (1998f), The common transport policy – Sustainable mobility: perspectives for the future. Com (98)716, final. 1 December 1998.

CEU (1998g), Cohesion and transport. Com (98)806, final. 14 January 1999.

CEU (1998h), Trans-European transport network, report on the implementation of the guidelines – Basic data on the networks. Sec (98)1993.

CEU (1999a), Amended proposal for a Council Directive on port reception facilities for ship generated waste and cargo residues. Com (99)149, final. 20 April 1999.

CEU (1999b), Amended proposal for a Council Decision amending Decision 692/96 regarding seaports, inland ports and multimodal transport terminals, and project No 8 of Appendix III. Com (99)277, final. 17 June 1999.

CEU (1999c), The development of short-sea shipping in Europe: a dynamic alternative in a sustainable transport chain. Com (99)317, final. 29 June 1999.

CEU (1999d), Report on the implementation of the action framework on intermodality and the intermodal carriage of goods in the European Union. Com (99)519, final. 27 October 1999.

CEU (2000a), Proposal for a Directive of the European Parliament and of the Council amending Council Directive 9457/EC on common rules and standards for ship inspection and survey organisations and for the relevant activities of maritime administrations. Com (2000) 142, final. 21 March 2000.

CEU (2000b), Amended proposal for a Council Directive on port reception facilities for ship generated waste and cargo residues. Com (2000)236, final. 19 April 2000.

CEU (2000c), Report from the Commission to the Council on the rules governing the public private sector partnerships. Com (2000)429, final. 4 July 2000.

CEU (2000d), Report from the Commission for the Biarritz European Council on the Community's strategy for safety at sea. Com (2000)603, final. 27 September 2000.

CEU (2001a), Reinforcing quality services in sea ports: a key for European transport. Com (2001)35, final. 13 February 2001.

CEU (2001b), Report of the European Commission on public financing and charging practices in the Community sea port sector (on the basis of information provided by the member states). Sec (2001)234 final. 14 February 2001.

CEU-DG VII (2001) Note on exercise to identify bottlenecks in short sea shipping and their potential solutions. Brussels, 17 October 2000.

CEU-DG VII. Transport in Figures. Periodical publication – Various issues.

CEU. Panorama of the EU Industry. Annual publication – Various issues.

CEU. General Report on the Activities of the European Communities. Annual Publication – Various issues.

Chlomoudis C.I. (2001), *Port Organisation and Management* (in Greek), Piraeus: J.&J. Hellas.

Chlomoudis, C.I. and Pallis, A.A. (1996), 'Investment policies in ports' infrastructure in the perspective of the European short sea shipping networks: the case of Greece', in Peeters, C. and Wergeland, T. (eds) (1997), *European Shortsea Shipping*, Delft: Delft University Press, pp. 315–335.

Chlomoudis, C.I. and Pallis, A.A. (1997), 'Investments in Transport Infrastructure in Greece: Have the EU Initiatives promoted their Balanced and Rational Distribution?', *World Transport Policy and Practice*, **3** (4), 23–29.

Chlomoudis, C.I. and Pallis, A.A. (1998), 'Ports, Flexible Specialisation, and Employment Patterns', Paper presented at the 8th World Conference on Transport Research, Antwerp University, July 1998.

Chlomoudis, C.I. and Pallis, A.A. (1999), 'Adjusting Port Management and Organisation to New Technologies', in Proceedings of the Conference on Decision Science and Info Systems: Integrating Technology and Human Decisions, Athens, Greece, July 1999.

Chlomoudis, C.I. and Pallis, A.A. (2000), 'Services in Commercial Ports: On the need to overcome in practice the "Public Utility – Private Good" Dilemma', in Proceedings of the International Association of Maritime Economists Conference, Naples, September 2000.

Chlomoudis, C.I. and Pallis A.A. (2002), 'Trends In Investments in Port Infrastructure in the Mediterranean Countries: Convergence or Divergence To EU Policies?', *Spoudai*, **52** (1–2), 65–82.

Chlomoudis, C. I., Karalis, A.V. and Pallis, A.A. (2001), 'Do ports enter into new Worlds of Production? Organisational Adjustments to offer the new port product', in Proceedings of the 9th World Conference on Transport Research, Seoul 2001.

Chlomoudis, C.I., Lambridis, C. and Pallis, A.A. (1999), 'Does the Practice Respond to the Rhetoric? On the Contribution of the Contemporary EU Investment Policies in Transport Infrastructure to a Sustainable Future', in Proceedings of the 1999 European Transport Conference, Cambridge, UK, September 1999.

Comité des Constructeurs Français d'Automobiles (CCFE), (1989) *Proposal for a European fast train network*. Paris: CCFE.

Containerisation International (2000), *Containerisation International Yearbook 1999*. London: Containerisation International.

de Lagen P.W. (2001), 'A Framework for analysing seaport clusters', in Proceedings of the 9th World Conference on Transport Research, Seoul, July 2001.

de Palacio L. (2001), 'Opening statement', Public Seminar 'European Sea Port Policy, Challenges and Solutions, 11October 2001, Belgium: Port of Antwerp.

de Weale, A. (1993), 'Epilogue', in Polak, J. and Heertje, A. (eds), *European Transport Economics,* Oxford: Blackwell, pp. 286–292.

Despicht, N. (1969), *The Transport Policy of the European Communities*, London: Chatham House.

European Court of Justice (ECJ) (1973), Case 167/73. Commission v. France (1974)ECR 359.

ECJ (1983), Case 13/83. European Parliament v. Council of Ministers (1985)ECR 1513.

European Conference of Ministers of Transport (ECMT) (1982), Short Sea Shipping in the Economy of Inland Transport in Europe, Report of the 60th Round Table on Transport Economics, Paris: OECD.

ECMT (1990), Private and Public Investment. Report on the 81st Round Table on Transport Economics, Paris: OECD.

ECMT (1991), *Investment Trends in Transport Infrastructure in ECMT Countries in the 1980s*, Paris: OECD.

ECSA, (2001). 'Comments of the European Community Shipowners' Associations on the Proposed Directive on Market Access to Port Services', Brussels: ECSA.

European Parliament (EP) (1993). 'European policy for seaports', Transport Series E1.

EP, (1999). 'European sea port policy', Transport Series 106.

Erasmus University (1991), 'Factors Influencing Modal Choice: Final Report', Rotterdam: Erasmus University.

Erdmenger, J. (1983), *The European Community Transport Policy: Towards a Common Transport Policy*, Aldershot: Gower.

Erdmenger, J. (1996), 'Seaports in the trans-European transport network', in Bekemans, W. L. and Bekwith, S. (eds), *Ports for Europe: Europe's Maritime Future in a Changing Environment*, Brussels: European Interuniversity Press, pp 131–156.

European Sea Port Organisation (ESPO) (1995a), *A Statement on European Sea Port Policy*, Brussels: ESPO.

ESPO (1995b), *Environmental Practice Code*, Brussels: ESPO.

ESPO (1998), *Final Report on the Green Paper on Sea Ports and Maritime Infrastructure*, Brussels: ESPO.

ESPO (1999), *ESPO and its Policies*, Brussels: ESPO.

ESPO (various issues), *Annual Report*, annual publication, Brussels: ESPO.

ESPO (various issues), *ESPO News*, monthly publication, Brussels: ESPO.

European Centre of Infrastructure Studies (ECIS) (1996), *Report 1996*, Brussels: ECIS.

European Logistics Association (2000), *Transport Optimisation,* Brussels: European Logistics Association.

European Round Table of Industrialists (ERTI) (1981), *Missing Networks: A European Challenge,* Brussels: ERTI.

Eurostat (various issues), *External Trade by Mode of Transport*, Annual publication.

Eurostat (various issues), *Basic Statistics*, Annual publication.

Fearnleys (2000), *Fearnleys Review 1999*, Oslo: Fearnleys.

Federation of Private Port Operators (FEPORT) (1998), *FEPORT Paper on the Green Paper on Sea Ports and Maritime Infrastructure*, Brussels: FEPORT.

Ferreira, C.H. (1995), 'The development of Short Sea Shipping in Europe: Prospects and Challenges', Paper presented at the Short Sea Europe 1995 Conference, Towards 2000 – Meeting the Customers' Needs, 10–11 October 1995, Amsterdam, Netherlands.

Finney, N. and Young, F. (1995), 'Environmental zoning restrictions on port activities and development', *Maritime Policy and Management*, **22** (4), 319–329.

Giannopoulos, G.E. and Koukouloudi, E. (2000), 'Telematics for Port-to-Port Communication to increase maritime safety and efficiency', in *Proceeding of the 2ⁿᵈ International Conference*, 2001, Chios, Greece.

Gwilliam, K.M. (1979), 'Transport Infrastructure, Investment and Regional Development', in Bowers, J.K. (1979) (ed.), *Inflation Development and Integration*, Leeds: Leeds University Press, pp. 244–262.

Gwilliam, K.M. (1980), 'Realism and the Common Transport Policy of the EEC', in van der Kamp, J.B. and Polak, J.B (eds), *European Transport Economics,* Oxford: Blackwell, pp. 38–59.

Gwilliam, K.M. (1990), 'The Common Transport Policy', in El-Agraa, A.M. (ed.), *The Economics of the European Community* (3rd edn), London: Harvester Wheatsheaf, pp. 230–242.

Haralambides, H. and Veenstra, A., (1997), 'World wide experiences of Port Reform', in Meersman, H. and Van de Voorde, E. (eds), *Transforming the port industry*, Leuven: Amersfoort, pp. 107–143.

Hayuth, Y. (1996), 'Container traffic in Ocean Shipping policy', in W Bekemans, L. and Bekwith S. (eds), *Ports for Europe: Europe's Maritime Future in a Changing Environment,* Brussels: European Interuniversity Press.

Healey, N.M. (1995) (ed.), *The Economics of The New Europe: From Community to Union*, London: Routledge.

Heaver, T.D. (1993), 'The many facets of Maritime Economics in association', *Maritime Policy and Management*, **20** (2), 121–132.

Heaver, T.D. (1995), 'The implications of increased competition among ports for port policy', *Maritime Policy and Management*, **22** (2), 125–133.

Heaver, T.D. Meersman, H. Van de Voorde, E., (2001), 'Co-operation and Competition in International Container transport Strategies for ports', *Maritime Policy and Management*, **28** (3), 293–306.

Hinz, C. (1996), 'Prospects for a European ports Policy: A German View', *Maritime Policy and Management*, **23** (4), 337–340.

Institute of Shipping and Logistics (ISL) (1990), *Port Management Textbook, vol. 1*, Bremen: ISL.

International Road Federation (IRF) (1990), *Road Transport Network for Europe*, Geneva: IRF.

ISL (various issues), *Shipping Statistics and Market Review,* monthly publication, Bremen: ISL.

ISL (various issues), *Shipping Statistics Yearbook*, Bremen: ISL.

Jansson, J.O. (1993), 'Government and Transport Infrastructure – Investments', in Polak, J. and Heertje, A. (eds), *European Transport Economics,* Oxford: Blackwell, pp. 221–243.

Johnson, D. and Turner, C. (1997), *Trans-European Networks. The Political Economy of Integrating Europe's Future,* Basingstoke: Macmillan.

Johnston, G. (1995), 'UK port policy – the impact of privatisation', *National Transport Conference of the Chartered institute of Transport in Ireland*, Dublin, November 1999.

Kanellopoulos, P.I. (1999), *EU Law* (in Greek), Athens: A. Sakkoulas.

Kessides, C. (1993), 'The contributions of Infrastructure to Economic Development', World Bank Discussion Papers, No 213, Washington DC: World Bank.

Kingdon, J.W. (1984), *Agendas Alternatives and Public Policies*. New York: Harper Collins

Kinnock, N. (1998), 'Linking Europe through transport infrastructure', Address to the Conference: Bridging Gaps in Financing Infrastructure, Amsterdam, 31 March 1998.

Lak, S. (1998), 'Ports focal points for Regulation', in Haralambides, H. (ed.), *Quality Shipping*, The Netherlands: Erasmus University Publications, pp. 49–52.

Lindberg, L.N. and Scheingold, S. (1970), *Europe's Would-be Polity*, New York: Practice Hall.

Machpul, F. (1977), *A History of Thought on Economic Integration*, London: Macmillan.

Marconsult, (1998), 'The Green Paper on sea ports and maritime infrastructure – critical observations', Unpublished document commissioned by the Italian ports association.

Mayer, M.D. (1999), 'Demand Management as an element of transportation policy: using carrots and sticks to influence travel behaviour', *Transportation Research Part A*, **33** (7/8), 575–599.

McKinnon A. (2001), 'Integrated Logistics Strategies', in Brewer, A.M. *et al.* (eds), *Handbook of Logistics and Supply Chain Management*, Amsterdam: Elsevier, pp. 157–170.

MDS Transmodal (1983), *European Container Freight Market: Containers by Sea* (1st edn), Chester: MDS.

MDS Transmodal (1998), *European Container Freight Market: Containers by Sea* (4th edn), Chester: MDS.

Meady, J. (1955), *The Theory of International Economic Policy*, London: Oxford University Press.

Meersman, H. and Van de Voorde, E. (eds) (1997), *Transforming the Port Industry*, Leuven: Amersfoort,

MIF (1993), Results of the Plenary Session of the MIF, Athens, 27&28/6/1993.

Molle, W. (2001), *The Economics of European Integration: Theory, Practice, Policy* (4th edn), Aldershot: Ashgate.

NEA – DG VII (1999), 'Transport demand for certain freight flows', Study Commissioned by the DG VII of the European Commission, The Netherlands: NEA,

Nielsen, J.U.M., Heinrich, H. and Hansen, J.D. (1992), *Economic Analysis of the EC* (2nd edn), Berkshire: McGraw-Hill.

North Sea Port Chambers of Commerce – Transport Committee (1998), *Opinion on the Green Paper on Sea Ports and Maritime Infrastructure*, The Netherlands: NSPCC.

Notteboom, T.E. and Winkelmans, W. (2001), 'Structural changes in logistics: how will port authorities face the challenge?', *Maritime Policy and Management*, **28** (1), 71–89.

Pallis, A.A. (1997), 'Towards a Common Ports Policy? EU-Proposals and the Industry's Perceptions', *Maritime Policy and Management*, **24** (4), 365–380.

Pallis, A.A. (2002), *The Common EU Maritime Transport Policy: Policy Europeanisation in the 1990s*, Aldershot: Ashgate.

Peeters, C. and Wergeland, T. (eds) (1997), *European Shortsea Shipping: Proceedings from the 3rd European Research Roundtable on Shortsea Shipping*, The Netherlands: Delft University Press.

Pelkmans, J. (1984), *Market Integration in the European Community*, The Hague: Martinus Nijhoff.

Pesquera, M.A. and De La Hoz, L. (1992), 'EDI Key for shortsea shipping development: the Arcantel platform', in Winjnolst, Ir.N. Peeters, C., Liebman, P. (eds) (1993), *European Shortsea Shipping, Proceedings from the First European Research Roundtable Conference on Shortsea Shipping,* London: Lloyd's of London Press, pp. 193–210.

Peters, H.J. (1989), *Seatrade Logistics and Transport*, World Bank Policy Research Series, No 6, Washington DC: World Bank.

Power, V. (1992), *The EC Shipping Law*, London: Lloyd's of London Press.

Rietveld, P. and Nijkamp, P. (1993), '*Transport and regional development'*, in Polak, J.B. and Heertje, A. (eds) (1993), *European Transport Economics*. Oxford: Blackwell, pp. 130–151.

Ross, J.F.L. (1994), 'High-Speed Rail: Catalyst for European Integration?', *Journal of Common Market Studies*, **32** (2), 191–214.

Ross, J.F.L. (1998), *Linking Europe Transport Policies and Politics in the European Union*, London: Praeger.

Saundry, R. and Turnbull, P. (1997), 'Private profit public loss', *Maritime Policy and Management*, **24** (2), 319–334.

Seidenfus, H.St. (1987), 'European ports in the context of the World economy and the European economy: Changes in sea transport', *International Journal of Transport Economy*, **14** (2), 133–138.

Sishelschmidt, H. (2000), 'The EU programme trans-European networks – a critical assessment', *Transport Policy*, **6** (2), 169–181.

Slack, B., Comtois, C. and Sletmo, G. (1996), 'Shipping lines as agents of change in the port industry', *Maritime Policy and Management*, **23** (3), 289–300.

Stead, D. (2001), 'Transport intensity in Europe – indicators and trends', *Transport Policy*, **8** (1), 29–46.

Suykens, F. (1986), 'Ports should be efficient (even when this means that some of them are subsidised)', *Maritime Policy and Management*, **13** (2), 105–126.

Suykens, F. and Van de Voorde, E. (1998), 'A quarter of a century of port management in Europe: Objectives and tools', *Maritime Policy and Management*, **25** (3), 251–262.

Swann, D. (1999), *The Economics of the Common Market: Integration in the European Union'* (8th edn), London: Penguin.

Teilet, B. (1996), 'Intermodal traffic in International sea trade', in Bekemans, W. L. and Bekwith S. (eds), *Ports for Europe: Europe's Maritime Future in a Changing Environment*, Brussels: European Interuniversity Press.

Thomas, B. (1994), 'The privatisation of the United Kingdom seaports', *Maritime Policy and Management,* **21**(2), 135–148.

Tsoukalis, L. (1993), *The New European Economy* (2nd edn), London: Oxford University Press.

Turró, M. (1999), *Going Trans-European: Planning and Financing Transport Networks for Europe*, The Netherlands: Pergamon.

UNCTAD (1993), Sustainable development for ports, Report UNCTAD (SDD/Port), 1, 27/8. Geneva: UNCTAD.

UNCTAD (1995), Comparative analysis of deregulation, commercialisation and privatisation of ports, Report by the UNCTAD Secretariat.

US Department of Transport, (1998), A report to Congress on the status of the public port of the United States 1996–1997, Washington DC: US Department of Transport.

Valleri, M. (2000), 'Transport integration in the Balkan area: the role of ports', in Proceedings of the International Association of Maritime Economists Conference, Naples, September 2000.

Van de Voorde E., Meersman, H. and Steenssens, C. (1998), 'Safer and More Ecological Shipping: The Impact on Port Competition', in Haralambides, H. (ed.), *Quality Shipping*, The Netherlands: Erasmus University Publications, pp. 217–226.

Van der Kamp, J.B. and Polak, J.B. (eds) (1980), *Changes in the field of Transport Studies: Essays on the Progress of Theory in relation to Policy making*, Hague: Martinus Nijhoff.

Vanhove, N. and Klaasen, L.H. (1987), *Regional Policy: A European Approach* (2nd edn), Aldershot: Gower.

Verbeke, A. Haralambides, H. Musso, E. and Benacchio, M. (2001), 'Seaport pricing in Europe: desirability and scope of a new EU policy', in Proceedings of the 9th World Conference on Transport Research, Seoul, July 2001.

Verhoeven, P. (2001). The EU Directive on Port Reception Facilities for ship generated waste and cargo residues from a port authorities' perspective. ESPO / IAPH Workshop on Port Reception Facilities for ship generated waste and cargo residues, Rotterdam, 14 June 2001.

Vickerman, R.W. (1992), *The Single European Market*, London: Harvester Wheatsheaf.

Vickerman, R.W. (1994), 'Transport Infrastructure and Region Building in the European Community', *Journal of Common Market Studies*, **32** (1), 1–24.

Viner, J. (1950), *The Customs Union Issue*, New York: Carnage Endowment for International Peace.

Whitelegg, J. (1988), *Transport Policy in the EEC*, London: Routledge.

Whitelegg, J. (1993), *Transport for a Sustainable Future: The Case for Europe*, London: Belhaven.

Winjnolst, N. Peeters, C. and Liebman, P. (eds) (1993), *European Shortsea Shipping, Proceedings from the First European Research Roundtable Conference on Shortsea shipping*, London: Lloyd's of London Press.

World Bank, (1994), *World Bank Report 1994: Infrastructure and Development*, Washington DC: World Bank.

World Commission on Environment and Development (1987), *Our Common Future* (The Bruntland Report), Oxford: Oxford University Press.

Index